Urban Constellations

MATTHEW GANDY [ED.]

INTRODUCTION

Matthew Gandy

Urban Constellations brings together five years of work and ideas associated with the UCL Urban Laboratory, which was set up in 2005 as a unique collaboration between four different faculties for urban teaching and research. This collection reflects an array of disciplines at UCL that have engaged with the Urban Laboratory, ranging from architecture and engineering to anthropology and film studies. It also reflects the international profile of the Urban Laboratory in terms of its networks of expertise and its attraction of exceptional graduate students, some of whose work is included in this collection. This is not the first time such an initiative has emerged at UCL—in 1958 the sociologist Ruth Glass and her colleagues set up The Centre for Urban Studies— and this volume builds on these earlier interdisciplinary dialogues. "London can never be taken for granted," wrote Glass in 1964, "the city is too vast, too complex, too contrary and too moody to become entirely familiar."[1] These sentiments might apply to any city at any time: the tenor of this collection is contemplative and reflective; there are no bullet-point lists of what should be done, no definitive answers, but rather an opening up of discussion and the identification of critical themes.

The book is divided into five sections. Part one, entitled "Urban lexicons," reflects on a range of key ideas that have been the focal point of recent discussions about the future of cities and urbanisation. In part two, "Crises and perturbations," we turn to processes and developments that are shaping contemporary cities such as the effects of financial instability, the housing crisis, and the emergence of new social formations. In part three, "Excursions," we show some examples of work by young artists and photographers, who have been exploring different facets of contemporary urbanisation and urban life. In part four, "Places and spaces," the emphasis shifts to a range of specific locales to explore concrete examples of urban change, such as the impact of specific projects, the political ecology of urban nature, and the presence of collective memory in urban culture. Finally, in part five, "Projections," we link urban discourse to the visual arts and consider various vantage points from which artists, film makers, photographers, and others have sought to critically engage with processes of urban change.

The title chosen for the collection—Urban Constellations—relates to Walter Benjamin's use of the term "constellation" as a way to combine ostensibly disparate elements into a historically and intellectually intelligible schema. This implicit lineage to Benjamin's work underpins a close attention to the details and textures of everyday life in the modern city. It informs an understanding of the term "constellation" as a metaphor for context, historical specificity, and multi-dimensionality; it works against sameness, stasis, and reductionism. In Benjamin's hands, a materialist historiography "explodes the homogeneity of the epoch."[2]

The emphasis on small essays draws on Siegfried Kracauer's use of "urban vignettes" to explore specific facets of city life where even small observations are woven into a sophisticated cultural and political critique. This is not a book aimed at a narrowly specialist readership, nor is it some kind of text book containing attenuated distillations of more interesting things that lie elsewhere. Many of Kracauer's original observations on Weimar Berlin and other cities were written for newspapers rather than scholarly journals though this does not reduce their perspicacity or sophistication in any way.[3] This essay collection is aimed beyond the academy to a larger cultural arena of thinking, writing, and acting; a space in which all can play a role in the intellectual project of reimagining urban possibilities.

The authors have responded very differently to the challenge of writing small essays, ranging from the use of imaginary scenarios to more experimental forms of writing. Some essays are more personal or autobiographical in tone whilst others adopt a more distanced position in relation to their subject matter. Different writing strategies and methodological approaches are also matched by a diversity of locales extending from long-standing foci of urban research such as Berlin, Chicago, and London, to less extensively studied cities such as Chennai, Jakarta, and Lagos. The essays illuminate an interconnected skein of developments that blur both disciplinary boundaries and schematic distinctions between global North and South.

The idea of the "urban" encompasses far more than the "city" as a bounded or discrete entity, since the cultural, political, technological, and ecological impacts of urbanisation extend to the most remote regions. Yet we cannot dispense entirely with this distinction between cities and urbanisation because cities have served as catalysts for successive waves of modernity and many "city-states" also perform specific roles as nodes for connectivity and exchange.

But where should we look? What types of urban spaces should form the focus of our attention? Some of the most interesting developments can be observed at the urban fringe or in marginal zones that unsettle existing categories, concepts, or analytical approaches. In other cases, our starting point might be a single building or one cultural artefact. Questions of scale are not only relational but also strategic: we cannot include everything in our analysis—to do so would not only be impossible but also perceptually overwhelming. Much of the city must remain forever opaque: simply unnoticed or lost as fragments of memory.

Our understanding of urbanisation, or capitalist urbanisation to be more precise, is inseparable from the disruptive, pervasive, and transformative impact of capital itself, which is present either explicitly through flows, instruments and transfers, or implicitly through traces of past investment or the ideological parameters of urban culture. "Money," as Georg Simmel observes, "with all its colourlessness and indifference, becomes the common denominator of all values; irreparably it hollows out the core of things, their individuality, their specific value, and their incomparability."[4] In this context, we can see that much urban politics and culture is precisely a struggle against the levelling effects of money and capital: the articulation of social difference, the recasting of the public realm, the defence of autonomous spaces, the creation of possibilities for creative thought itself. Yet forms of cultural and political heterogeneity can in themselves mask the spectral ubiquity of capital: in what circumstances do forms of cultural and political activity undo rather than reinscribe existing relations of power? And in what sense do forms of cultural or political upheaval periodically facilitate little more than a reorganisation of the existing order?

And what of ourselves as flesh and blood, as living inhabitants of urban space? We are part of urban nature yet also apart from it: urban nature is in a state of flux ranging from its metabolic reconstruction (power, water, and other engineered elements of urban life) to various modes of spontaneous co-existence such as bugs, dogs, and weeds. If we consider nature as an active constituent of urban life, which is itself in a state of behavioural or evolutionary change, then the presence of zoonoses or other pathogens in urban space contains an unpredictable dynamic of its own.

The materiality of urban space—the ubiquity and versatility of concrete, the advent of steel-frame buildings and ever more complex technological entanglements—also produces new kinds of vulnerabilities to disruption. At the same time, our increasingly sophisticated methods of collecting, storing, and analysing data engender a certain technological euphoria about the capacity for controlling or modifying space that becomes another element in the techno-managerial evisceration of the political realm.

Readers may detect a certain lament in some of these essays for the lost promise of modernity, whether located in the peripheral housing estates of Copenhagen or the roads and bridges of Lagos. The prospects for design, planning or other forms of expert intervention have been thrown into question. Emerging spaces of improvisation have been accompanied by a radical dilution of the putative "metropolitan centre" to produce a more polyvalent form of global urbanism: the epicentre for modernity no longer passes through a teleological sequence from nineteenth-century Paris to its late-modern apotheosis of Los Angeles. In the place of archetypes or grand-theoretical synecdoches, we encounter a much more variegated urban terrain that links space and theory in new ways. But to what extent are these different modes of theorisation spanning neo-Marxian and other approaches philosophically commensurate? In what ways can they help us to disentangle urban developments or provide fresh insights into the history of the present? The creeping regularisation of space reflects an emerging elision between geo-political anxieties and neo-conservative moralities. As thinking human subjects we must contend with the flickering landscapes of alienated consumption and wonder what might have been different.

Endnotes

1 Ruth Glass, "Aspects of change," in *Centre for Urban Studies, London: Aspects of Change* (London: MacGibbon and Kee, 1964), xiii.
2 Walter Benjamin, "On the theory of knowledge, theory of progress," in *The Arcades Project*, trans. Howard Eiland and Kevin McLaughlin (London and Cambridge, MA: Belknap / Harvard University Press, 1999 [1927–40]) [N9a,6], 474.
3 Siegried Kracauer, *Straßen in Berlin und anderswo* (Berlin: Das Arsenal, 1987 [1964]).
4 Georg Simmel, "Metropolis and mental life," in *The Sociology of Georg Simmel*, trans. Kurt H. Wolff (New York: The Free Press, 1950 [1903]), 414.

Acknowledgements

There are many people who have made this project possible: the core team at the UCL Urban Laboratory—Pushpa Arabindoo, Andrew Harris and Füsun Turetken—along with many other UCL colleagues including Johan Andersson, Ben Campkin, Richard Dennis, Craig Patterson, David Price, Ian Scott, Stephen Smith, Margaret Lloyd, and Suse Keay. The editorial, design, and marketing team at jovis—Philipp Sperrle, Susanne Rösler, Anja Müller, and Jutta Bornholdt-Cassetti—have also been outstanding at every stage. Thanks also to Inez Templeton for her careful copy editing of the text. Above all, Maren Harnack, whose work appears in this collection, has been an enormous source of advice and encouragement. She has been a loyal friend and astute critic throughout the project.

1

URBAN
LEXICONS

PLANETARY URBANISATION

Neil Brenner
Christian Schmid

During the last several decades, the field of urban studies has been animated by an extraordinary outpouring of new ideas regarding the role of cities, urbanism, and urbanisation processes in ongoing global transformations.[1] Yet, despite these advances, the field continues to be grounded upon a mapping of human settlement space that was more plausible in the late nineteenth and early twentieth centuries than it is today.

The early twentieth century was a period in which large-scale industrial city-regions and suburbanising zones were being rapidly consolidated around the world in close conjunction with major demographic and socio-economic shifts in the erstwhile "countryside." Consequently, across diverse national contexts and linguistic traditions, the field of twentieth-century urban studies defined its theoretical categories and research object through a series of explicit or implied geographical contrasts. Even as debates raged regarding how best to define the specificity of urban life, the latter was universally demarcated in opposition to a purportedly "non-urban" zone, generally classified as "rural." As paradigms for theory and research evolved, labels changed for each term of this supposed urban-rural continuum, and so too did scholars' understandings of how best to conceptualise its basic elements and the nature of their articulation. For instance, the Anglo-American concept of the "suburb" and the French concept of *la banlieue* were introduced and popularised to demarcate further socio-spatial differentiations that were occurring inside a rapidly urbanising field.[2] Nonetheless, the bulk of twentieth-century urban studies rested on the assumption that cities—or, later, "conurbations," "city-regions," "urban regions," "metropolitan regions," and "global city-regions"—represented a particular *type* of territory that was qualitatively specific, and thus different from the putatively "non-urban" spaces that lay beyond their boundaries.

The demarcations separating urban, suburban, and rural zones were recognised to shift historically, but the spaces themselves were assumed to remain discreet, distinct, and universal. While paradigmatic disagreements have raged regarding the precise nature of the city and the urban, the entire field has long presupposed the existence of a relatively stable, putatively "non-urban" realm as a "constitutive outside" for its epistemological and empirical operations. In short, across divergent theoretical and political perspectives—from the Chicago School's interventions in the 1920s, and the rise of the neo-Marxist "new urban sociology" and "radical geography" in the 1970s, to the debates on world cities and global cities in the 1980s and 1990s—the major traditions of twentieth-century urban studies embraced shared, largely uninterrogated geographical assumptions that were rooted in the late nineteenth and early twentieth centuries' geohistorical conditions in which this field of study was first established.

During the last thirty years, however, the form of urbanisation has been radically reconfigured, a process that has seriously called into question the inherited cartographies that have long underpinned urban theory and research. Aside from the dramatic spatial and demographic expansion of major mega-city regions, the last thirty years have also witnessed several far-reaching worldwide socio-spatial transformations.[3] These include:

- *The creation of new scales of urbanisation.* Extensively urbanised interdependencies are being consolidated within extremely large, rapidly expanding, polynucleated metropolitan regions around the world to create sprawling "urban galaxies" that stretch beyond any single metropolitan region and often traverse multiple national boundaries. Such mega-scaled urban constellations have been conceptualised in diverse ways, and the representation of their contours and boundaries remains a focus of considerable research and debate.[4] Their most prominent exemplars include, among others, the original Gottmannian megalopolis of "BosWash" (Boston-Washington DC) and the "blue banana" encompassing the major urbanised regions in western Europe, but also emergent formations such as "San San" (San Francisco-San Diego) in California, the Pearl River Delta in south China, the Lagos-centred littoral conurbation in West Africa, as well as several incipient mega-urban regions in Latin America and South Asia.

- *The blurring and rearticulation of urban territories.* Urbanisation processes are being regionalised and reterritorialised. Increasingly, former "central functions," such as shopping facilities, company headquarters, research institutions, prestigious cultural venues, as well as spectacular architectural forms, dense settlement patterns, and infrastructural

BETWEEN MARX AND DELEUZE: DISCOURSES OF CAPITALISM'S URBAN FUTURE

Jennifer Robinson

"At this point in history, this has to be a global struggle, predominantly with finance capital, for that is the scale at which urbanisation processes now work." [1]

"In order to understand domination we have to turn away form an exclusive concern with social relations and weave them into a fabric that includes non-human actants." [2]

Anglo-American analyses of cities in the current era of globalisation are caught between the approaches signposted here by two of the more influential thinkers of space in our generation. David Harvey sees global capitalism as the ultimate determinant of urban futures, and identifies effective resistance at a global scale as the response that is needed to continue to secure life in the city, and the right to the city. Bruno Latour, not himself an urbanist, has inspired a trend in urban studies that builds on his observation that there can be no pre-given category of "the social," and that it is necessary to explore how it is that particular social situations—and cities—are made up through all sorts of associations of actors and actants, people, and things. This chimes very well with longstanding ideas of cities, such as Henri Lefebvre's notion of cities as sites of "assemblage" and Louis Wirth's sense of "heterogeneity" as a key feature of urban life. [3] This approach is framed by interpretations of the writings of the philosopher Gilles Deleuze, who Michel Foucault once declared would quite likely define the horizons of the next century of (Western) thought, and who likewise seeks to focus attention on how entities come into being. Drawing on this approach, urbanists seek to consider the relative openness of the possibilities created as the accumulation of different kinds of things in cities gives rise to new kinds of social and spatial entities.[4]

Both Marxian and Deleuzian interventions are grappling with new forms of global urbanism, as emerging powers put distinctive urban forms into circulation and as innovative financial instruments and transnational organisations tie cities together in a labyrinth of risk, debt, and speculation.[5] The dispossessions resulting from capital's explorations of new urban frontiers of accumulation are stark—as David Harvey, Mike Davis, and others enjoin us to notice—perhaps especially in relation to the privatisation of the provision of life-giving urban services and the splintering of urban space in the interests of profitability, which leaves the poorest in mortal danger from the settlements they must inhabit.[6] In wealthier urban contexts, the repackaging of debt and income streams amortise urban lives long into the future. This all seems to somewhat deaden the hopefulness that Deleuzian conceptual speculations associate with the global dispersal of governmental technologies.

However, Aihwa Ong's Deleuzian-inspired "low-flying" methodology for tracing the paths of governmental technologies calls attention to an important arena of global city-making the circulations of urban policy across the world of cities[7]—which is where (some of the) future possibilities for capitalist urbanisation are being made. Does this offer an opportunity to press through the current theoretical impasse between Marxian and Deleuzian approaches to cities—perhaps even in the interests of the global resistance Harvey anticipates? A few examples of the discourses shaping capitalism's urban future can help us here.

Recent reports by global business consultants on the urban future in China and India (by McKinsey Global Institute) and Africa (by Monitor) assemble policy conventions, available data, opinions, and evidence on forms, styles, and actors in city governance; and generate some telling statistical predictions about coming investments in urbanisation in these three areas of the globe, set to be the sites of the most rapid rates of urbanisation, and the highest levels of urban dwelling.[8] There are some telling differences across the documents: where Indian governments receive stern injunctions to proceed with decentralisation and privatisation of often less than effective institutions for local service delivery, the Chinese governmental structure receives little commentary or advice, perhaps in the interests of all-important influence with the key investment drivers there, mostly governmental actors. Monitor's assemblage of the facts of future infrastructural development in Africa—opportunities for capitalist investment—are rather pale compared to the astonishing scale of the predicted Chinese urban future. And they make little attempt to advocate reform of African urban government *tout court*. Instead, after a polite genuflection to philanthropy, they propose that in the interests of economic growth, policy, and investment should focus on well-serviced, safe, and globally competitive parts of cities in Africa. In line with Michael Porter's cluster model of urban competitiveness, they carve out a niche for themselves on this crowded highway of global urban policy by picturing an Africa in which capital can find small footholds to "hop" (as James Ferguson so evocatively put it[9]) safely from one investment opportunity to another.

The orchestration of urban policy ideas, analytical concepts, and corporate ambition in these documents draws attention to the ways in which governmental technologies are put to work in particular "sites"—the policy circulation highway, the audience with governments, the unsolicited consultancy report—and by particular agents. The difference these places and actors make to how cities' futures are being imagined and made is well illustrated by placing another kind of circulating urban policy statement alongside these extended corporate adverts. UNCHS (Habitat) has prepared two "State of African Cities" reports, in 2008 and 2010, which to some extent run along the same tracks as the McKinsey and Monitor reports—we see headline data on astonishing trends, showing that African cities are going to play host to extraordinary growth in their populations, that cities are where poverty is going to be concentrated, and where governmental resources are already stretched too thin to impact on the challenges of urban life.[10] These two reports certainly draw on commonly circulating ideas that shape consultant-driven ambitions, like the potential for transnational global city-regions to host new kinds of dynamic economic growth. But the authors also call for "people-centred cities" and note, *contra* Monitor, that "the promotion of the social, economic and political failure of this increasingly important human habitat is simply not a viable option."[11] Their audience is arguably not the property capitalists who are busy speculating on which bits of Africa are going to attract the investors hovering in search of profitable ventures (or, as Filip de Boeck indicates in relation to Kinshasa, those speculating on inaction[12]). Rather, they seek to engage the local and national governments who they hope will find the skills, resources, and motivation to make cities more liveable, more focussed on enabling, rather than shortening, life.

It is the quote above from Latour that can perhaps help to tie both the opposed Marxian and Deleuzian theoretical discourses and these different kinds of city reporting together. For we might ask of the "actor network" proponents why it is useful to trace links and connections amongst things, people, ideas, and practices across and between cities? At times, it seems as if the aim is to propagate a politics of hopefulness as opposed to the noir urbanisms of some writers on the global urban future.[13] Certainly, it is vital to look for openings to newness and innovation—an urbanist who has lived through and/or thought through significant political transformations might find her writing inflected with hope, perhaps even long after the grounds for that have disappeared. But even in such times of hope, of transformation, or of collective struggle, cities in the context of global capitalism are shaped through highly uneven and deeply unequal power relations.

We should assume then that the power relations within which cities are made, and which cities also help create, are amongst the things we most need to attend to as we explore the diverse circulations and assemblages of policies, practices, and technologies of urban governance—in either Deleuzian or Marxian modalities. The conditions of emergence of sedimented power relations, the exclusion of the poor, the elaboration of the ambitions of global capitalism (as shorthand transnational firms, sprawling international institutions, liquid value streams, fixed assets like land and buildings extracted for global mobility, the financialisation of land and life) all need to be kept in view. Instead of introducing power and inequality as an afterthought, somehow exterior to the emergent actor-networks and assemblages which cities create,[14] they surely need to be central to our efforts to explain urban processes under global capitalism. On the other hand, and rather than assuming that urban policy circulations always set out to propagate the ambitions of global capitalism (or succeed in these efforts), we could reasonably expect Marxian analyses of various persuasions to consider the multiplicity of agendas jostling for space on the policy circulation superhighway, including humanitarian and developmental ambitions.[15]

To understand how the futures of specific, ordinary cities are being imagined and made across the world we would do better to consider a less oppositional theoretical landscape: somewhere between Marxian assumptions about the dominance of neoliberal capitalism in urban policy agendas, and Deleuzian attractions to the indefinable multiplicity of the circulation of technologies of rule, lies the distinctive political space of the city. We could certainly benefit from both sets of theoretical resources to determine whether and how different circulating policy agendas gain influence both in global urban policy networks and across the world of cities, and to explain how the politics, practices, and hopes of local governments and citizens shape decisions about whether or not to pursue these agendas. But we might also be inspired by the ways in which city dwellers and city governments, in association with the assembled elements of city life, and almost certainly not in conditions of their own choosing, continue to imagine and create their own futures.

Endnotes

1 D. Harvey, "The Right to the City," in *New Left Review*, 53 (2008), 23–40, here 39.
2 B. Latour, "Technology is Society Made Durable," in J. Law (ed.), *A Sociology of Monsters: Essays on Power, Technology and Domination* (London: Routledge, 1991), 103–31, here 103.
3 H. Lefebvre, *The Production of Space* (Oxford: Blackwell, 1991); L. Wirth, *Louis Wirth: On Cities and Social Life* (Chicago: University of Chicago Press, 1964).
4 A. Ong, "Worlding Cities, or the Art of being Global," in A. Ong, A. and A. Roy (eds.), *Worlding Cities* (Oxford: Blackwell, 2011), 1–26; C. McFarlane, "The city as assemblage: dwelling and urban space," in *Environment and Planning D: Society and Space* (forthcoming).
5 M.B. Aalbers, "The globalization and Europeanization of mortgage markets," in *International Journal of Urban and Regional Research* 33/2 (2009), 389–410.
6 M. Davis, *Planet of Slums* (London: Verso, 1996); S. Graham and S. Marvin, *Splintering Urbanism: Networked Infrastructures, Technological Mobilities and the Urban Condition* (London: Routledge, 2001).
7 A. Ong, *Neoliberalism as Exception: Mutations in Citizenship and Sovereignty* (Durham NC: Duke University Press, 2006).
8 McKinsey Global Institute, *Preparing for China's Urban Billion* (Shanghai: McKinsey and Company, 2009); McKinsey Global Institute, *India's Urban Awakening: Building Inclusive Cities, Sustaining Economic Growth* (Mumbai: McKinsey Global Institute, 2010); Monitor, *Africa from the Bottom up: Cities, Economic Growth and Prosperity in Sub-Saharan Africa* (Johannesburg and Boston: Monitor Group, 2009).
9 James Ferguson, "Global disconnect: abjection and the aftermath of modernism," in P. Geschiere, B. Meyer, and P. Pels (eds.), *Readings in Modernity in Africa* (2008), 8–16.
10 UNCHS, *State of African Cities* (Nairobi: UN-Habitat, 2010), 18.
11 Ibid., 20
12 F. D. Boeck, "Inhabiting Ocular Ground: Kinshasa's Future in the Light of Congo's Spectral Urban Politics," in *Cultural Anthropology*, 26 (2011), 263–286.
13 See Ong (2011) and McFarlane (2011)
14 McFarlane (2011)
15 J. Ferguson, " The Uses of Neoliberalism," in *Antipode* 41 (2010), 166–184.

CLASS, NATION, AND THE CHANGING POLITICAL DYNAMICS OF EUROPEAN CITIES

Patrick Le Galès

What sort of urban world do we live in? Within which urban constellations does class formation takes place? The current wave of massive urbanisation, linked to processes of globalisation—including economic turbulence—and emerging mobilities, seems to sketch a rather different urban world from the one we knew, dominated by "the West" and organised by nation-states, clearly defined classes, the impetus of industrialisation, or the effects of colonisation. Lively debates have emerged in relation to our intellectual tools, methods, and categories, to make sense of this new urban world. Developing different forms of new and innovative comparative research is a priority. As nation-states and cities are becoming more interdependent, comparing "independent units" rather than relations between spaces has largely become an illusion. Hence, the opening of avenues for trying all kinds of comparative research articulating different scales between a diversity of types of cities and neighbourhoods.[1] Another promising angle leads to the focus on theories of processes of urbanisation, making possible vast generalisation within less differentiated urban world. Some have gone further, generalising views of a Los Angeles based urban chaos, redefining a post-modern lexicon to make sense of widespread urbanisation, and embarking on the elusive quest for the Grail of urban research and the emergence of the "post-neo super metropolis" of 100 million inhabitants or more. Satellites maps and the rise of GIS are providing illuminating new representation of cities, relations among them, or within them. In a classic way, well known by the sociology of science, the development of new techniques of observation and representation lead to different conceptualisation of cities, metropolis, and the representation of a less differentiated urban world; but some questions are also set aside, such as class formation. New research methods based upon the exploitation of the material available on the web open fascinating new avenues to deal at the same time with individuals understood in terms of relations that may be mapped on the web. As Bruno Latour argues,[2] this set of data may be an opportunity to go beyond the analysis of individuals and/or institutions and organisations, and to think about social life as individuals who only make sense as part of a collective, as part as a set of networks, so that linking networks and class is one of the main tasks of urban sociology.[3]

This set of questions is particularly interesting for European cities with their long-term articulation of trade, culture, and forms of political autonomy integrated within nation-states following different trajectories. Of course, one may just look from the sky and identify a mega-European urban world, with a globalised core of London-Paris-Brussels-Rotterdam and shrinking medium-sized cities elsewhere. This is empirically inaccurate but interesting for urbanisation questions and dynamics. Indeed, progressively structured by nation-states,[4] their social structure and economic dynamics were strongly articulated towards politics and public policies.

For more than a hundred years now, European societies and cities have been strongly national-centred—even more with the decline of colonial empires—and were increasingly integrated within a national state and society. The German sociologist Max Weber suggested that the making of national societies relied upon two main mechanisms: the closure of borders and the making of interdependencies within each society. The first mechanism aimed at preventing external influence to play a role in the making of the national social and political order: the national elite tried to prevent transnational forces like religious organisations, international socialist movements, or international capitalists to play a structuring role in the national society. The second mechanism aimed at creating interdependence between the different social groups (classes and status groups), since this greater degree of social cohesion reinforced the feelings of belonging to the nation. Cities were progressively integrated within the national political order.

Now, national societies and nation-states continue to play a crucial role, but increasing mobility and changing scales have strongly eroded those two mechanisms. Class formations in European cities bring together a greater urban dimension along with the national scale, but also some elements of European and globalised societies. Discussing the making of European classes, the Spanish sociologist Juan Díez Medrano usefully sums us the discussion through four dimensions of a social structure derived from normative expectations, patterns of social interactions, shared subjective meanings and behaviour, and objective social positions.[5] Searching for European social groups requires the identification of "transnational groups of European citizens whose behaviour and consciousness denote solidarities that transcend national and sub-national affiliations."

Transnational influences mean that social groups and individuals are less interdependent, and they can more easily decide to exit from the national social and political order. These increased mobilities and horizontal interactions destabilise existing European cities and blur the frontiers of social groups. Global theorists[6] emphasise that flows, transactions, and the strategies of individuals and collective actors are being reshaped directly on a global scale, hence the making of a global society. Cultural practices, images and representations, social movements, and of course capitalism itself (or at least the vanguard forces of these processes) are said to become more and more disembedded. To these authors, the global scale becomes a new level for structuring major cultural and social conflicts of interest.

It is possible that these multiple mobilities and the global scale might indeed be a growing feature of the everyday lives of European citizens without them needing to physically move residence, or live and work in another country.[7] However, instead of focusing solely on mobility, understanding class formation may require us to study both the dynamics of mobility *and* those of rootedness.[8] This means looking both at the mobility experiences of individuals, and at the fixity of the place of residence (cities and neighbourhoods). In other words, the issue of class formation should combine both the mobility question, social networks, and the rootedness question.

The sociologist Mike Savage[9] has developed an interesting argument about the rise of "elective belonging" in social class formation and dynamics. Savage argues that the differentiation and overlapping of various scales of interactions for individuals beyond national frontiers has opened room for manoeuvre for individuals in terms of their choice of residence, of social practices, of identity claiming, of investment of different resources (including time and social capital) in different territories. One of the possible consequences is to blur settled national and urban logics of stratification and distinction. As societies become more complex and mobile, individuals become more privatised in their strategies and choices. These exit strategies in the different dimensions of leisure, work, sociability, education, and other areas are crossed with residential space choices. Residence has the greatest fixity in relation to the other dimensions of everyday life (leisure, work, sociability, and crucially education) in terms of defining one's sense of "social location."

Europeans are slowly becoming more mobile but they also have a day-to-day-life, they may have families, they often relate or belong to established social groups, and they have to use services: hospitals, transport, infrastructure, equipment, urban spaces that may be more or less exclusive, more or less public, more or less at a distance from other social or ethnic groups. Cases of extreme secession, such as gated communities, exist but these are not the norm. It is therefore essential to bring together the dynamics of exit within the urban fabric (the internal dimension) and the exit from the national society (the external dimension) to understand dynamics of social change and class formation.

Increasing market pressures on European cities, growing inequalities, tensions between ethnic groups, and complex dynamics between suburbanisation and embourgeoisement of the centre are making European cities less differentiated. The EU has marginalised the territorial and social component of the integration project, hence reinforcing competition and market logics. By contrast, the way Europeans organise their mobility in relation to their rootedness (including class relations) may remain very distinct in central and southern European cities. This combination may be crucial for the analysis of differences between European cities.

Endnotes

1   J. Robinson, "Cities in a world of cities: the comparative gesture," in *International Journal of Urban and Regional Research* 35/1 (2011), 1–23.
2   B. Latour, *Reassembling the social: an introduction to actor network theory* (Oxford: Oxford University Press, 2005).
3   T. Blockland and M. Savage, *Network Urbanism* (London: Routledge, 2008).
4   G. Esping Andersen, *Social classes* (London: Sage, 1992); P. Le Galès, *European cities, social conflicts and governance* (Oxford: Oxford University Press, 2002).
5   J. Medrano, "Social class and identity," A. Favell, V. Guiraudon (eds.), *Sociology of the European Union* (Basingstoke: Palgrave, 2011), 31.
6   For instance, J. Urry, *Mobilities* (Cambridge: Polity Press, 2007).
7   S. Mau, *Social Transnationalism: Lifeworlds beyond the Nation-State*, (London: Routledge, 2009); A. Favell and E. Recchi, *Pioneers of European Integration* (Cheltenham: Edward Elgar, 2008); N. Fligstein, *Euroclash* (Oxford: Oxford University Press, 2007).
8   A. Andreotti, P. Le Galès, and F. Moreno Fuentes, "Mobility, Transnationalism, and Rootedness of Middle Classes in European Cities," in *Global Networks* (forthcoming).
9   M. Savage et al., *Globalisation and Belonging* (London: Sage, 2005).

"EVERY REVOLUTION HAS ITS SQUARE": POLITICISING THE POST-POLITICAL CITY

Erik Swyngedouw

"… the people is those who, refusing to be the population, disrupt the system." [1]

Tiananmen Square, Place de la Bastille, Red Square, Alexanderplatz, Tahrir Square, Assaha-al-Khadra, Syntagma Square, Green Square, Wenceslas Square: these are just a few of the public spaces that have become engrained in our symbolic universe as emblematic sites of revolutionary geographies. Their names stand as *points de capiton* that quilt a chain of meaning through signifiers like democracy, revolution, freedom, being-in-common, solidarity, emancipation. The emergence of political space, these examples suggest, unfolds through a political act that stages collectively the presumption of equality and affirms the ability of "the People" to self-manage and organise its affairs. It is an active process of intervention through which (public) space is reconfigured and through which—if successful—a new socio-spatial order is inaugurated. The taking of urban public spaces has indeed always been—from the Athenian *ochlos* demanding to be part of the polis to the heroic struggle of the Tunisian people—the hallmark of emancipatory geopolitical trajectories.

Emblematically starting with the French urban revolts during the autumn of 2005, retaking streets and squares choreographed political struggle over the past few years as protests jumped around from Copenhagen to Rome and from London to Riga. In the spring and summer of 2011, *los indignados* [the outraged] occupied central urban squares in Madrid, Barcelona, and Athens, among other cities, to demand "democracy now." Urban revolts and passionate outbursts of discontent have indeed marked the urban scene over the past decade or so. Rarely in history have so many people voiced their discontent with the political and economic blueprints of the elite and signalled a desire for an alternative design of the city and the world, of the polis.

These urban insurrections are indeed telltale symptoms of the contemporary urban order, an order that began to implode, both physically and socially, with the onslaught, in the fall of 2007, of the deepest crisis of capitalism in the last seventy years, a crisis that finally exposed the flimsy basis on which the fantasy of a neoliberal design for the city and the world of the twenty-first century was based. We shall argue that, while the city is alive and thriving, at least in some of its spaces, the polis as the site for public political encounter and democratic negotiation, the spacing of (often radical) dissent, and disagreement, and the place where political subjectivation emerges, is performed and thus literally takes place, seems moribund. In other words, the polis as a "political" space is retreating while social space is increasingly colonised or sutured by consensual neo-liberal techno-managerial policies. Urban insurrections are the flipside of this evacuation of the properly political dimension from the urban—what will be described below as the post-political condition—and constitutes what I define as the ZERO-ground of politics.[2] The leitmotif of this contribution will indeed be the figure of a de-politicised post-political and post-democratic city and the retreating of the political through new forms of urban insurgency.

The contemporary urban condition is marked by a post-political police order of managing the spatial distribution and circulation of things and people within a consensually agreed neo-liberal arrangement.[3] Jacques Rancière associates this condition with the notion of *la police*, conceived as a heterogeneous set of technologies and strategies for ordering, distributing, and allocating people, things, and functions to designated places. These managerial practices and procedures colonise and evacuate the proper spaces of the political; *la police* is about hierarchy, ordering, and distribution.[4] Spatialised policies (planning, architecture, urban policies, etc.) are one of the core *dispositifs* of *la police*.

Politics, in contrast, inaugurate the repartitioning of the logic of *la police*, the reordering of what is visible and audible, registering as voice what was only registered as noise, and reframing what is regarded as political.[5] It occurs in places not allocated to the exercise of power or the instituted negotiation of recognised differences and interests. As Badiou insists, politics emerge as an event: the singular act of choreographing egalitarian appearance of being-in-common at a distance from the state.[6] Whereas any logic of *la police* is one of hierarchy and inequality, *le politique* is marked by the presumption of equality within an aristocratic order that invariably "wronged" this presumption.

It is within this aporia between Rancière's distinction of *la police* from *le politique* that urban insurrections can be framed. While much of the state's attempts to reorder the urban through mobilising discursively a set of signifiers of inclusiveness (social cohesion, inclusion, emancipation, self-reliance), well-worn clichés of urban doom (exclusion, danger, crisis, fear) are reproduced in practice. Attempts to produce "cohesive" cities revolve around choreographing distribution and circulation of activities, things, and people such that *la police* remains intact. While the state's discourse and policy recipes frame particular trajectories of "inclusion," they shy away from acknowledging division, polemic, dissensus and, above all,

1

from endorsing the assumption of equality on which the democratic political rests. Justice, equality, and communality are censored from the script of urban policy prescriptions.[7]

It is precisely this suturing process that suspends political litigation, voicing or staging dissent, or asserting polemical equality. These cut through *la police* and tentatively open up the spaces of the political again. The urban insurgents have no demands; they do not expect anything from the existing order. They have no program, no proclamations; neither leader nor party. Perhaps they are part of what Andrew Merrifield calls "The Imaginary Party," one that is called into being through resonance, viral infection, and affiliation, not through hierarchy, program, and structure.[8] They do not demand equality, they stage it; and, in doing so, produce, *pace* Etienne Balibar, equa-libertarian spaces.[9] This staging of equality and freedom, the interruption of the normalised geographical order of the sensible, exposes the aristocratic configuration and inegalitarian "wrongs" of the given, and invariably encounters the wrath of *la police*. Such exposition of equa-liberty cannot remain unnoticed: it either succeeds or meets with violence, the terror of the state that—in its violent acting—precisely affirms that some people are not part of "the people," that order of social being is indeed inegalitarian.

This constitutive gap between *la police* and *le politique* needs to be affirmed. *Le politique* cannot be reduced to managing and ordering space, to consensual pluralist and institutionalised policy-making. This is the terrain of *la police*; the ontic dimension of eve- ryday socio-spatial management. *Le politique*—as the staging of equality in the face of a wrong—

1 Democracia-real-ya,
Macrid (2011)
Source: Claudio Álverez, *El Pais*

is nothing else but the affirmation of impossibility of consensual management, of autocratic rule; it is an anarchic interruption that affirms the foundation of the democratic invention, i.e., the equality of each and every one qua speaking beings—a condition that is predicated upon affirming difference and the dissensual foundation of politics.

This notion of politics centres on division, conflict, and polemic. Politics appears as a practice of reorganising space under the aegis of equality. The key lesson to be learned from this intervention is, of course, that politics does not arise from the choreography of the social. On the contrary, *le politique* configures its own theatre, one that opens up a new spatiality within the given distribution of times and spaces; it appears from within the social and political order, but acts at a distance from the state of the situation; it emerges where it is not supposed to be, in public space. Such political events are interventions that transgress the symbolic order and mark a shift to a new situation that can no longer be thought of in terms of the old symbolic framings. Proper politics is thus about enunciating demands that lie beyond the symbolic order of *la police*; demands that cannot be symbolised within its frame of reference and, therefore, would necessitate a transformation in and of *la police* to permit symbolisation to occur. Therefore, the political act is, as Slavoj Žižek argues, "not simply something that works well within the framework of existing relations, but something that *changes the very framework that determines how things work* … it changes the very parameters of what is considered 'possible' in the existing constellation."[10] This constitutes a proper political sequence; one that can be thought and practised irrespective of any substantive social theorisation. It is *le politique* in itself at work. Such new symbolisations are where a possible repoliticisation of public civic space resides. These symbolisations should start from the premise that the presumption of equality on which democracy rests is "wronged" by the instituted oligarchic "police" order. It emerges where those who are uncounted and unnamed, whose fantasies are only registered as noise, produce their own metaphorical and material space. Such a claim to the Polis is what links the urban protests in the Middle East and the global North. It signals the ability of "the people" to take hold of their future.

Endnotes

1   M. Foucault, *Security, Territory, Population: Lectures at the Collège de France, 1977-78* (New York: Palgrave, 2007), 66.

2   E. Swyngedouw, "The Zero-Ground of Politics: Musings on the Post-Political City," in *NewGeographies—After Zero Theme Issue* 1 (Harvard University Design School, 2009), 52–61.

3   E. Swyngedouw, "Interrogating Post-Democracy: Reclaiming Egalitarian Political Spaces," in *Political Geography* (forthcoming).

4   J. Rancière, *Disagreement* (Minneapolis: Minnesota University Press, 1998).

5   M. Dikeç, *Badlands of the Republic* (Oxford: Blackwell, 2007).

6   A. Badiou, *The Communist Hypothesis* (London: Verso, 2010).

7   E. Swyngedouw, "Designing the Post-Political City and the Insurgent Polis," in *Civic City Cahier 5* (London: Bedford Press, 2011).

8   A. Merrifield, *Magical Marxism* (London: Pluto, 2011).

9   E. Balibar, *La Proposition de l'Egaliberte*. (Paris: Presses Universitaires de France, 2010).

10 S. Žižek, *The Ticklish Subject*. (London: Verso, 1999), 199.

A different version of this essay is forthcoming in *Political Geography.*

FRONTIERS OF URBAN POLITICAL ECOLOGY

Roger Keil

"The clientele of the Poissonnerie Shanahan is … by and large made up of suburbanites from Laval-les-Rapides, Chomedey or Duvernay. But one should not be fooled by the innocuous demeanour of these predators. According to some estimates, the bluefin tuna population in the Atlantic has declined by 87 per cent since 1970, a rate that matches quite closely the expansion of the suburbs over the same period. … It can thus be deduced," Maelo concludes, "that suburban development is very much in step with the movement of the tuna shoals." [1]

Maelo, Jean-Talon market fishmonger, and one of the key characters in Nicolas Dickner's novel, *Nikolski*, portrays Montreal's suburbs as suspended in a global web of political-ecological causality, which I will argue here is typical for our age. The frontiers of urban political ecology are now tested by the *realpolitik* of sustainability, the borderlessness of community, and the politics of resilience. [2]

Urban political ecology, a critical approach to the study of societal relationships with nature in cities,[3] concerns itself ultimately with urban sustainability, usually the domain of more technocratic, policy-oriented thought and practice. Talking about sustainable communities includes both *what* is to be sustained and *who* is to be sustained. Both questions are invariably tied up with concepts of spatial and social enclosure. Sustainability linked to socio-spatial community aims at the creation of a controllable spacetime, *Zeitraum*[4] from which societal relationships with nature can be reasonably constructed in such a way as to predict their functionality in the framework of current knowledge about ecological and social justice concerns. Sustainability is usually linked with time first. It is making claims about a different kind of future, i.e., it is a conscious attempt to make historical adjustment to the way we do things. Implicitly, the quest for sustainable communities makes assumptions about various types of spatial relationships in which sustainability is to be enacted and accomplished.

"Sustainable communities" are envisioned to be spatially bound, rationally experienced and governed, inhabited places in which humans and their actions dominate other species, and where human activity produces a certain physical landscape and metabolism and a certain institutional framework within which the work of sustainability is done. Often, a "sustainability fix" is sought in order to bring some institutional logic of action in line with real or imagined territorial boundaries and scalar perimeters.[5] The physical landscape is perceived on a continuum of sustainability-related development where, for example, urban sprawl is considered antithetical to sustainability goals, whereas compact cities are usually set up as the normative equivalent to sustainability agendas put forward by environmentalists and planners. Jonathan Franzen lets his environmentalist hero Walter Berglund nail this precisely: "…it was like having acid thrown in my face very time I passed the city limits. Not just the industrial farming but the sprawl, the sprawl, the sprawl. Low-density development is the *worst*. And SUVs everywhere, snowmobiles everywhere, Jet Skis everywhere, ATVs everywhere, two-acre lawns everywhere. The goddamned green monospecific chemical-drenched lawns."[6] The character's visceral reaction to "the sprawl" is typical for the ways in which we have collectively imagined how a particular real physical process, in this case suburbanisation, inhibits a pathway to a more sustainable urban life.

The societal relationships with nature—in both their material and cultural dimensions—that are encapsulated in "the sprawl" come with a particular kind of *realpolitik,* which enshrines certain practices as sustainable and others as unsustainable. Discourses on sustainability are now tied up inseparably with the making of urban realities and the politics associated with this process.[7] The urban political ecology of sustainability evokes a meaningful, yes even deliberate process, in which real people struggle to invent a politics of substance and empower functioning institutions in which sustainability has a home. This involves various degrees of a governmentality of restraint in matters of our use of natural resources from land to water to air. It also reifies both "community" and "sustainability" as *predictable* practices in bounded spaces. Certain questions are never asked in this real political or post-political game.[8] Principles and so-called best practices are established that reflect the momentary preferences and priorities of certain eco-operators who make their specific notion of community and sustainability the standard over others. Reference is being made here to mostly technocratically oriented, yet also neoliberally seduced, often movement-bred environmental entrepreneurs who sell or propagate one or the other artefact or process deemed "organic" or "eco." Increasingly, these eco-operators, captives of "defensible science" and the "triple bottom line," lose sight of the big picture of social and environmental change and get trapped in their worlds of efficiency and technological gadgets. After more than a quarter century of recycling, new urbanism and public transit expansion (to name just a few of the main avenues of real political sustainability), not much progress has been made. Municipal policies that are to create more sustainable urban communities, for example, are fickle and shaky in the face of development pressures, the demands of the creative economies, or the renewed call of growth after the dent the 2008 financial crisis made on the welfare of urban regions.

Secondly, then, instead of seeking boundaries that define socio-natural metabolisms and socio-political institutions, we need to recognise the reality of today's life under globalisation where all bets are off, where all borders are perforated. While containment is the metaphor of choice for community sustainability, here we encounter a different lexicon and register to be engaged with.

The transnationalised scales and topologies in which communities are produced, defined, and sustained force us to take a double step away from the deceptive normalisation of urban sustainability.[9] The first step is the acceptance that any notion of bounded action will be challenged by the inevitably fleeting character of interactions beyond local control. The added factor of nature's agency establishes a threatening framework for urban sustainability. The second step is more far-reaching. Here the notion of *contagion* in both its material and metaphorical sense is central.[10] The idea here is that sustainability of regularised socio-natural relations (in this instance the normal production cycle) is incapacitated by more than normal or *new* normal conditions in which infectious elements are introduced into an allegedly sound body (physical, economic, social, or political). That body is the agreed upon frame of operation for global capitalists and environmentalists alike. Contagion introduces a notion of agency that points to more-than-normal hazards, those that can only incompletely be captured by the logic of global supply chains or climate change simulations. It is remarkable how in both specialist discourse and common talk, contagion has now entered our daily conversation be it through recurring pandemic threats (nature's revenge) or crisis in the markets.

When we connect the practical and ethical considerations of community sustainability with the challenges of globalisation, a new frontier of urban political ecology opens up: what is community and what needs to be sustained? In an essay about the Frankfurt greenbelt, John Friedmann reminds us of a powerful concept in Nietzsche's thinking. The philosopher proposed the idea of *Fernstenliebe* [the love of those who are far away] partly as a head-on critique of the Christian notion of *Nächstenliebe* [the love of your neighbour].[11] Friedmann noted that the planning tool of a greenbelt contains an ethics of enclosure; the metaphor of the belt is one of control over flows. But how realistic and how sustainable is that in today's world? Resilience has been proposed by Ray Hudson among others as a powerful concept through which the trials of globalisation can be confronted by urban and regional actors.[12] This use of resilience implies the emphasis on regionally defined socio-spatial relations as the basis for resistance against the uprooting and decentering effects of larger scale processes of restructuring and change. Yet, instead of building defensive bulwarks against globalisation and its implied disturbances, resilience must be about sustaining open and creative relationships of humans among one another and with non-human nature. The reality of today's urban world offers a more differentiated landscape than the one suggested in the typical, caricatured, and widely used dichotomy of sprawl and compactness. The everyday lives we live in this complex landscape straddle the sustainable and the unsustainable all the time. What and who my communities are during one day and how they need to be sustained changes continuously. In order to find my way through the maze of relationships, I need to start where I am and not in an imaginary place that is either reviled (like sprawl) or celebrated (like the compact city). Suburbanisation, for example, is now the dominant way in which cities grow worldwide, but it comes in very different forms and has had a wide variety of histories both in terms of its built environment and social and political institutions. Next to the classical North American case, we include here all manner of peripheral urbanisation such as, for example, the squatter settlements of the global South or the high-rise suburbs of the former socialist countries in Eastern Europe.[13] Ultimately, life in the suburbs, or life in the expanding urban fringe is now the new reality in which strategies of sustainability are being negotiated. If we are moving away from the condemnation of sprawl and accepting its reality as a discursive plane on which negotiation over our future will have to take place, we are forced to act differently. Sprawl then becomes, as Michael Dear and Nicholas Dahman remind us, "an urban theoretical primitive, one of the most fundamental categories in our revised lexicon" through which we reposition "sustainability at the core of the urban question."[14] The normativity of sprawl versus compactness would be missing. Finally, let us return to Montreal and its suburban imagination. The voraciousness of the city's suburban appetites noted by Maelo, the fishmonger in the novel *Nikolski,* poses the problem of urbanisation today. It is a problem that has no outside. The Montreal band Arcade Fire has captured this in the lyric celebration of "The Sprawl" as memory and redemption: "Sometimes I wonder if the world's so small, that we can never get away from the sprawl!"[15] It is in the sprawl where sustainability, community, and the urban have to be found. It is there where we locate and ultimately transgress the frontiers of urban political ecology.

Endnotes

1 Nicolas Dickner, *Nikolski. A Novel* (Toronto: Vintage Canada, 2009), 84–85.

2 I would like to thank Alison Blay-Palmer who first asked me to articulate my thoughts on community sustainability for a panel she organized at the Seattle AAG in April 2011. Research underlying this short paper was supported by the Social Sciences and Humanities Research Council of Canada through funding from the Major Collaborative Research Project "Global suburbansims: governance, land, and infrastructure in the 21st century (2010-2017).

3 Roger Keil, "Progress Report 1: Urban Political Ecology," *Urban Geography* 24/8 (2003), 723–738.

4 I am taking this term freely from Walter Benjamin who calls the nineteenth century a "spacetime [*Zeitraum*] (a dreamtime, '*Zeit-traum*') in which the individual consciousness more and more secures itself in reflecting, while the collective consciousness sinks into ever deeper sleep." *The Arcades Project* (Cambridge and London: The Belknap Press of Harvard University Press, 389). I interpret this term to mean an opening for not yet fully understood possibilities of collective action in an environment of modernisation and uncertainty.

5 Adrian While, Andrew Jonas, and David Gibbs, "The Environment and the Entrepreneurial city: Searching for the Urban 'Sustainability Fix' in Manchester and Leeds," in *International Journal of Urban and Regional Research* 28/3 (2004), 549–569.

6 Jonathan Franzen, *Freedom* (Toronto: HarperCollins, 2010), 217.

7 Roger Keil and Mark Whitehead, "Cities and the Politics of Sustainability," Karen Mossberger, Susan E. Clarke, and Peter John (eds.), *Oxford Handbook of Urban Politics*, (forthcoming, Oxford University Press).

8 Erik Swyngedouw, "The Antinomies of the Postpolitical City: In Search of a Democratic Politics of Environmental Production," in *International Journal of Urban and Regional Research 33/3* (2009), 601–620.

9 Roger Keil, "Transnational urban political ecology: health, environment and infrastructure in the unbounded city," Gary Bridge and Sophie Watson (eds.), *The New Companion to the City*. 2nd Edition (Oxford: Wiley-Blackwell, 2010).

10 "Japan and the global supply chain. Broken links: The disruption to manufacturers worldwide from Japan's disasters will force a rethink of how they manage production," *The Economist*, 31 Mar 2011 http://www.economist.com/node/18486015/print; last accessed 4 April 2011.

11 John Friedmann, "Wem gehört er?" in *Kommune* 9/6 (June 1991), 36.

12 Ray Hudson, "Resilient regions in an uncertain world: wishful thinking or a practical reality?" in *Cambridge Journal of Regions, Economy and Society* 2009, 1–15.

13 Roger Keil, "Globale Suburbanisierung: Die Herausforderung der Verstädterung im 21. Jahrhundert," *Dérive*, 40/41, October–December, 6-10, 2010 and http://www.yorku.ca/city/?page_id=222 for more information.

14 Michael Dear and Nicholas Dahmann, "Urban Politics and the Los Angeles School of Urbanism," Dennis R. Judd and Dick Simpson (eds.), *The City Revisited: Urban Theory from Chicago, Los Angeles, New York* (Minneapolis: University of Minnesota Press, 2011), 74.

15 Arcade Fire, "Sprawl II (Mountains Beyond Mountains)," from the CD *The Suburbs*, 2010.

OTHERWORLDLINESS

Benedikte Zitouni

Capitalism is no longer boasting and bragging as it was in the 1990s. It now seems at best, a necessary evil, and at worst, more lucidly, a catastrophic way of existence. Financial as well as ecological disasters leave no doubt as to the destructive nature of current metabolic regimes.[1] Except for some wishful think-tanks perhaps, and even there, candid optimism is out. The End of Cold War is finally over. The years since 2000 have evened the score. For as much as the previous decade condemned us anti-capitalists to live in a monolithic era, bereaved us, and left us floundering in a no-choice zone, the past decade has given us a confident inkling that the future is ours to reclaim. With a world heading to calamity, the need for change is more often acknowledged. Our present-day is pushing for alternative ways.[2] And in the meantime, over the last couple of years, we ourselves have been transformed and are better prepared to the task. We've become otherworldly.[3]

Metamorphosis started in November 1999. Alter-globalists breached the defences of the World Trade Organisation summit and declared to the world that "Another world is possible!"[4] For a while, Seattle was the word. It disturbed the expected course of events, it showed an awe-inspiring opposition (no more condoling please), and last but not least, it instilled a new sense of struggle.[5] For class consciousness was not the only force at work. Seattle's battle was fought on many fronts at once. The choice was no longer between whales or workers, women's rights or healthy food, as only a collective assault would make the monolith stagger. And there's more to it than mere tactics. Such solidarity or connectivity was possible, precisely, because the future is so indeterminate and because—that's the feat— alter-globalists *claimed* that indeterminateness.

We do not know any longer—if we ever did—where exactly change must come from. All kinds of events may sign promising points of no return and so we've learned to place our bets on many fronts at once.[6] Claiming the future's indeterminateness means, thus, calling on the collective. It establishes a sense of multifariousness. We do not have to conform to the right ideological stances anymore, holding out one doctrine over the others but, rather, we must learn to live in a realm where no one has the ultimate answers and where all of us are trying to make valuable changes.[7] Connectivity, then, becomes vital. Only the relaying of our attempts will give rise to partial strongholds.[8] Or, inversely, *all* of our attempts are reclaims, taking back terrain from the monolith. The "us" is diversified, active, and branching out.[9] Realising this has been the first step, out of three, of our becoming otherworldly.

The next step is an earthly one. Lately, the issue of climate change has disrupted the elementary configurations drawn by the 1972 Club of Rome's Report, which stated the depletion of natural resources and pleaded for limiting growth,[10] by introducing two radical premises. One, the Planet is about to go awry, ready to run wild. Two, there are global and hence elusive Rubicons not to be crossed. Jumpiness and thresholds were added to finiteness and, together, they've overturned our existential mappings. We are no longer living in a world that can be drawn with arrows of aims and means, rarity and remedy, extraction and consumption, but are engulfed by billions of bonds, thrown into the maze of inter-specific and atmospheric reliances.[11] Rarity itself—as Peak Oil shows—is now part of our earthly, virtuous, or vicious circling.[12] We're not taking care of it any longer; we're in it.

But what's to be "in it"? What's the bonding about? Many of us who are involved in social sciences—in contemporary cultural mapping, so to speak—are looking for answers by reinvigorating perception. We're forging new words and brains. "Technonatures," "naturecultures," and "zoopolises" signal our enmeshment.[13] Fish "work," organs "feel," dunes "sing," or with an urban tinge, wastes "metabolise," streets and metros lead "virtual" or "atmospheric" lives because we are training our senses.[14] In order to get our bearings, we're learning how to be *emulated* by earthly reliances (rather than just accepting them).[15] We're redistributing active qualities, reconsidering passive ones, and infusing the entire maze with lively bustle so that we can become part of it, i.e., act within the maze.[16] That's the second step: we're (re)connecting and turning our backs on human exceptionalism.

When fish work and dunes sing, anti-capitalism has indeed changed. Today, perhaps, we have come to a point where we can acknowledge that 1989 did not only launch capitalism into a state of frenzy (1990s) before it fell into catalepsy (2000s), but that it also launched and freed us. Retrospectively, what then felt like defeatism and helplessness on our part now looks more like the flailing tentacles of aspiring brains and bodies set loose. The sudden collapse of the Eastern Bloc, the surging desire witnessed in Berlin and Tiananmen, cracked up our own rigid intellectual framing.[17] This is maybe the most important change: we've let go of scientism, of knowledgeable and structuralist disdain. No more do we put the future into the hands of (our) thinkers. No more do we want scientists to discriminate between the different options. No expert nor intellectual will do, for collective desire has come into play.[18]

This is not to say that desire overrules science but rather that it gets into science. All knowledge-making is motivated, and luckily so. The Left never claimed otherwise but it has (had) a harder time accepting the next point made by the sudden surges of desire: nothing is structurally determined; all is want and subjectivity-in-the-making; only collective practices matter; or, in sum, desire, thinking, and action coincide and they're everywhere. We're all think-doers, players, practitioners and none of us can tell others what to think-do without exposing ourselves and offering alliances first.[19] Exit the avant-garde. Exit the intellectual framing.[20] If we take that point, we can learn how to strengthen our practitioners' locales, wherever they are, be it by brainy, hands-on, experimental, or traditional means. All registers are open to us for the deterministic Left has loosened its grip.[21] That's the third and maybe most recent step.

To conclude, then, we might take a look at the emerging current decade. Whatever its outcome, the Arab Spring has already marked an epochal change. Uprisings do happen. From there on, anti-capitalism or what can now be called otherworldliness might take yet another step. After the transversal reclaiming, the plunge into earthly reliances and the spread of think-doing, non-Western and non-Christian heritages might hold our fourth mutation.[22] And this says something about otherworldliness. "How is 'becoming with' a practice of becoming worldly?"[23] "What change are we capable of when we encounter others?"[24] Otherworldliness consists of continually enriching our relations with the world.[25] It is a way of adding issues to our concern and letting ourselves be activated by it. Perhaps, its subtitle should be "The Rehabilitation of Our Experimental Capacities" or maybe it should declare "The End of Sitting Upon Our Laurels." For we're not waiting anymore. We're exposed, and that's the least we can say.

Endnotes

1 Isabelle Stengers, *Au temps des catastrophes: Résister à la barbarie qui vient* (Paris: La Découverte, 2009); Jared Diamond, *Collapse: How Societies Choose to Fail or Survive* (New York: Viking Penguin, 2005); Franz Broswimmer, *Ecocide: A Short History of the Mass Extinction of Species* (London: Pluto Press, 2002); Mike Davis, *Dead Cities and Other Tales* (New York: The New Press, 2002).

2 See radio series such as: "Terre à terre" ("2004, France Culture, led by Ruth Stegassy) and "Objecteurs de croissance" ("2006, Radio Panik in Belgium), literally meaning "Down to Earth" and "Growth Objectors." Or written accounts of recent movements such as in: David Vercauteren, *Micropolitiques des groupes: pour une écologie des pratiques collectives* (Mayenne, France: HB éditions, 2007). Or exhibitions such as: "Bêtes et Hommes," curated by Vinciane Despret, Yolande Bacot and Catherine Mariette at La Villette, Paris, from 12 September 2007 until 20 January 2008; "Making Things Public. Atmospheres of Democracy," curated by Bruno Latour and Peter Weibel at ZKM—Center for Art and Media Karlsruhe, Germany, from 20 March until 3 October 2005. These are but a few inspiring instances, others will be mentioned in the following notes.

3 The word "otherworldliness" is inspired by Donna Haraway, *When Species Meet* (Minneapolis: University of Minnesota Press, 2008)—at the end of the text, I mention more, but suffice to say here that the word is inspired by the French and Spanish "alter-globalisation" (rather than anti-globalisation). Other than that, this article is based on Felix Guattari, *Chaosmosis: An Ethico-Aesthetic Paradigm* (Bloomington: In-

diana University Press, 1995) (or. Fr. 1992). The reading of the book was done collectively, by the GECo - Group of Constructivist Studies reading group at the University of Brussels (ULB) during 2010–11. I would particularly like to thank Sophie Auby, Julie Colaiacovo, Fleur Courtois-l'Heureux, Serge Hayez, Ardalan Kalantaran, Nicolas Prignot, Isabelle Rouquette, Isabelle Stengers, and Willy Wolsztajn for this shared learning.

4 Philippe Pignarre and Isabelle Stengers, *La Sorcellerie Capitaliste: Pratiques de désenvoûtement* (Paris: La Découverte, 2005) the title of which deserves translation: *Bewitching Capitalism: How to Break its Spell.*

5 Starhawk, "How We Really Shut Down the WTO," December 1999, available on www.starhawk.org. Starhawk, *Web of Powers: Notes from the Global Uprising* (Gabriola Isl, Canada: New Society Publishers, 2002). On the importance of considering all-pervasive struggle, see: Géraldine Brausch, "Un detour par les stratèges de Jullien pour relire les analyses stratégiques de Foucault," in *Dissensus* 4 (2011), 80–118, 2011. For a new sense of struggle, see also: Michael Hardt & Toni Negri, *Empire* (Cambridge, MA: Harvard University Press, 2000); Michael Hardt and Toni Negri, *Multitude: War and Democracy in the Age of Empire* (London: Penguin, 2005); or recent documentaries such as "Marx Reloaded" (Arte, April 2011) and ongoing meetings such as the European Social Forums (2002).

6 On the importance of placing the bets, see American Pragmatist

Philosophy in general and more particularly: William James, *The Will to Believe & Human Immortality* (Mineola, NY: Dover Publications, 1956); or films by Frank Capra such as *Mr Smith Goes to Washington* (1939), *Meet John Doe* (1941), or *It's a Wonderful Life* (1946).

7   Vinciane Despret, "En finir avec l'innocence. Dialogue avec Isabelle Stengers et Donna Haraway," Eva Rodriguez (ed.), *A propos de Donna Haraway* (working title) (Paris: Presses Universitaires de France, forthcoming). In the same book, see also my text: " '*With whose blood were my eyes crafted*' (D. Haraway) Les savoirs situés comme la proposition d'une autre objectivité."

8   For relays and connexions between different struggles, see Michel Foucault & Gilles Deleuze "Les intellectuels et le pouvoir," in *L'Arc* 49 (1972), 3–10. Republished in Foucault's *Dits et Ecrits* (1994, 2001).

9   The tactic of defining the "us" as being variegated and already active on the ground, be it by sometimes mundane but nevertheless decisive acts, is inspired by the way in which Virginia Woolf brings on the "Society of the Marginals" in *Three Guineas* (London: The Hogarth Press, 1938).

10 See their website: www.cluboforome.org > history.

11 On atmospheric reliances, see: Peter Sloterdijk, *Ecumes, Sphères III* (Paris: Hachette, 2006) (first translation 2005, or. Germ. 2003, and the English translation is forthcoming by Semiotext(e) editions); Peter Sloterdijk, *Neither Sun nor Death* (New York: Semiotext(e), 2011) (or. Germ. 2001). For the difference between elementary configurations and the maze of interspecific reliances, see: Reviel Netz, *Barbed Wire, an ecology of modernity* (Wesleyan University Press: 2004) and especially his critique of Soviet agricultural planning; James Lovelock, *The Revenge of Gaia: Earth's Climate Crisis and the Fate of Humanity* (New York: Basic Books, 2006); Bruno Latour, "A Plea for Earthly Sciences," keynote lecture for the annual meeting of the British Sociological Association, London, April 2007 (online www.bruno-latour.fr).

12 On Peak Oil, see: Rob Hopkins, *The Transition Handbook: From oil dependency to local resilience* (White River Junction, Vermont: Chelsea Green Publishing, 2008); Giovanna Borasi and Miro Zardini, dir., *Désolé plus d'essence: L'innovation architecturale en réponse à la crise pétrolière de 1973* (Montreal & Mantova: Centre Canadien d'architecture & Corraini Edizioni, 2007); James Howard Kunstler, *The Long Emergency: Surviving the Converging Catastrophes of the Twentieth Century* (Boston: Atlantic Monthly Press, 2005).

13 Damian White and Chris Wilbert, *Technonatures: Environments, Technologies, Spaces, and Places in the Twenty-First Century* (Waterloo: Wilfrid Laurier University Press, 2009). For natureculture, see: Bruno Latour, *We Have Never Been Modern* (Cambridge, MA.: Harvard University Press, 1993) (or. Fr. 1991). Jennifer Wolch, "Zoöpolis," Jennifer Wolch and Jody Emel(eds.), *Animal Geographies: Place, Politics, and Identity in the Nature-Culture Borderlands* (London and New York: Verso, 1998). See also my article: "L'écologie urbaine: mode d'existence? mode de revendication?" in *Cosmopolitiques–Cahiers théoriques pour l'écologie politique* 7 (2004), 137–148.

14 For the fish, see: Richard White, *The Organic Machine: The Remaking of the Columbia River* (New York: Hill and Wang, 1995); Christelle Gramaglia, "Passions et savoirs contrariés comme préalables à la constitution d'une cause environnementale. Mobilisations de pêcheurs et de juristes pour la protection des rivières," in *Anthropologie des connaissances* 3/3 406–431. For the organs, see: Katrin Solhdju, *Selbstexperimente: Die Suche nach der Innenperspektive und ihre epistemologischen Folgen* (München: Finke, 2011). For the dunes, see: Stéphane, Douady, *Le chant des dunes* (Paris: Gallimard, 2006). On wastes metabolising, see: Matthew Gandy, "Rethinking urban metabolism: water, space and the modern city", in *City* 8/3 (2004), 381–387. On the streets' virtual life, see my book: *Agglomérer: Une anatomie de l'extension bruxelloise (1828-1915)* (Brussels: ASP & VUB Brussels University Press). On the metros' atmospheric existence, see work by Olivier Thiery: "Diagnostiquer les devenirs du métro à travers 'Meteor': Ethnologie et prospective avec Isaac Joseph," Daniel Cefaï en Carole Saturno, *Isaac Joseph: Itinéraires d'un pragmatiste* (Paris: Economica, 2007); "Ethnographie des atmosphères, ethnographie atmosphérique. Eléments pour une reconfiguration de l'enquête anthropologique avec Peter Sloterdijk," in *Ethnographiques.org* 5 (2004).

15 This emulation by non-humans was taught to me by Bruno Latour, as is the case for many other researchers who have followed his doctoral seminars. See for instance the following collection of recently published essays, Sophie Houdart and Olivier Thiery, dir., *Humains non Humains: Comment repeupler les sciences sociales* (Paris: La Découverte,

2011). Otherwise: Isabelle Stengers, *The Invention of Modern Science* (Minneapolis: University of Minnesota Press, 2000) (or. Fr. 1993); Vinciane Despret, *Quand le loup habitera avec l'agneau* (Paris: La Découverte & Seuil, 2002). In a more hands-on and collectively brainy manner, see the group Rotor (www.rotordb.org), who initially worked on wastes and reuse only and who now, more broadly speaking, brings connections to everyday materials. See our collaboration at the Architecture Biennale of Venice and also two of their other books: Rotor, Ariane d'Hoop and Benedikte Zitouni, *Usus / usures: How Things Stand* (Bruxelles: éditions de la Communauté française de Belgique, 2010); Rotor, Coproduction (Brussels: CIVA & A16, 2010); Chus Martinez and Katja Schroeder (eds.), *Deutschland im Herbst*, a project by Rotor (Kraichtal: Ursula Blickle Foundation, 2008).

16 On the redistribution or reconsideration of the active and passive qualities, see: Bruno Latour, *On the Cult of the Factish Gods* followed by *Iconoclash* (Duke University Press, in press) (or. Fr. 2009); Didier Debaise (ed.), *Philosophie des possessions* (Paris: Presses du Réel, forthcoming).

17 See also Félix Guattari, *Chaosmosis, op. cit*, on surging desire, historical subjectivity and the events of Berlin and Tiananmen as being, amongst others, the starting point for his book.

18 Desire is an upcoming theme in political movements and collective claims. See, for example, an anonymous and collective leaflet: *Choming Out: Les désirs ne chômont pas* (Bruxelles: Editions d'une Certaine Gaieté, 2011). It literally means "Coming Out" as "Chomeurs", i.e., jobless people who advocate the right to be jobless and to choose the activities and engagements they're involved in, as well as claiming and redefining the solidarity between workers in a more general sense. Apparently, the title was taken from the following article: Valérie Marange, "Le désir ne chôme pas", *Chimères* 3 (1998). See also the part on "Elles voulaient plus," in Vinciane Despret and Isabelle Stengers, *Les faiseuses d'hsitoires: Que font les femmes à la pensée* (Paris: La Découverte, 2011).

19 See the "Ecology of Practices" developed in: Isabelle Stengers, *Cosmopolitiques: Pour en finir avec la tolérance (partie 7)* (Paris: La Découverte, 1997). English translation is forthcoming at the University of Minnesota Press; the first three parts have already been published in one single volume.

20 On the difficult and even hateful relationship of intellectuals with the masses, on the disdain for popular knowledges, see: Jacques Rancière, *La Haine de la démocratie* (Paris: Fabrica, 2005).

21 Especially in France, Deterministic or Structuralist or what is also called Systemic Left have been poignantly present. I remember being a student and participating in a seminar at the EHESS—Ecole des hautes études en sciences sociales in Paris, at the end of the 1990s, where it was impossible to object to the precise and timed predictions of Capitalist Downfall given by Immanuel Wallerstein without being accused of betraying the ideals of Science and of Marx. It is not surprising that Félix Guattari, in *Chaosmosis, op. cit.*, felt compelled to criticise structuralist and deterministic thinking and pleaded for a transition from the Scientist Paradigm to the Ethic-Aesthetic Paradigm. In other words, this part of the article should be put into a French, Continental, context where Deterministic, Structuralist and Systemic thinking have been extremely important for the Left.

22 This might again take an English or American audience by surprise. But it must be said that in French or Francophone Belgian academic and political thinking, very few non-Western, non-Christian heritages are at work or explicitly taken on. Just to take an example: the world-known ecofeminist Vandana Shiva or the as well-known alter-globalist Arundathi Roy, both women living in India, are simply ignored in French-speaking academia. This is to say that the fourth mutation is an urgent one and will, quite probably, be a slow one in some cultural settings.

23 Donna Haraway, *When Species ..., op. cit.*, 3.

24 Taken from a recent conference paper by the anthropologist Graziella Vella on her work on slaughterhouses and architecture, where she refers to Vinciane Despret saying: "La lecture par contraste n'est pas tant d'interroger les autres qu'une façon d'interroger ce que peut notre culture quand elle les rencontre et ce que cette rencontre suscite comme invention," taken from Vinciane Despret, *Ces émotions qui nous fabriquent: Ethnopsychologie des émotions* (Paris: Le Seuil & La Découverte, 1999) (translated into English: *Our Emotional Makeup: Ethnopsychology and Selfhood*).

25 This is directly inspired by a sentence in Félix Guattari, *Chaosmose* (Paris: Galilée, 2005): "La seule finalité acceptable des activités humaines est la production d'une subjectivité auto-enrichissant de façon continu son rapport au monde" (38).

URBAN INTRUSIONS: A REFLECTION ON SUBNATURE

David Gissen

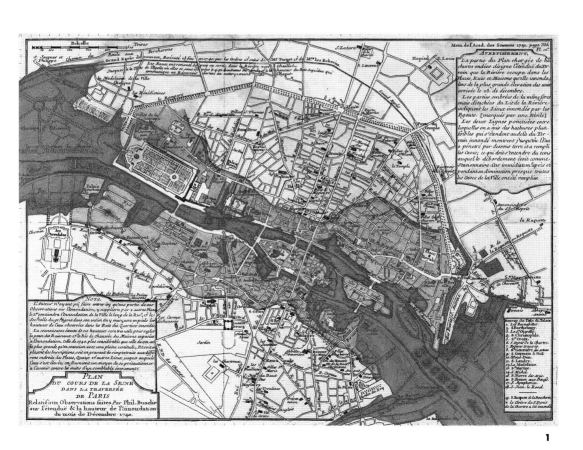

1 Phiippe Buache, Map of the 1740 Paris Flood, 1741. This early example of an urban cartography focused on the

city's inadequate drainage cnd ventilation, continues into the present.

Source: Reproduced by, and courtesy of *Bibliothèque National*, Paris.

1

Echelle de   1   2   3   4 Toises

2

Within the body of writings, drawings, and photographs that constitute the theory of architecture and urbanism, nature appears in at least three iterations: as the supernatural, the natural, and the subnatural. These may not be the only three categories, but they dominate.[1] Similarly, stating them in this order is not intended as a way of uncritically validating their separation or suggesting that they have some type of hierarchy. These three forms of nature move through the writings of surviving medieval texts on architecture, Renaissance architectural theories and drawings, eighteenth-century Romanticist and Picturesque theories and images, and Modern and late-Modern architectural theories, manifestos, and photographs. They appear in the writings and images of Villard de Honnecourt, Leon Battista Alberti, Richard Payne Knight, Le Corbusier, and Hundertwasser, among many others. The subnatural is the only one of these three that is not named as such in the texts, being a recent coinage. It was first used to describe the plays and sets of Samuel Beckett—the sense of utter natural collapse one sees in the dialogue, but also more literally in heaps of mud, rubble, and barren trees.[2] Only recently has it been explored in an explicitly architectural

2 Pierre Patte, Proposed Section of a Street, from *Mèmoires sur les objets plus importants de l'architecture*, Paris, 1769. This is the first section that shows a city's buildings and subsurface as a totality. It also emphasises the management of urban effluvia, particularly in the city's sewers.

Source: Reproduced by, and courtesy of Peabody Library, Rare Book and Manuscript Collection, Johns Hopkins University

context (see note 1 below). Once you know what to look for in subnature, you begin seeing its distant history. More important, unlike the other terms, it contains the most potent possibilities within a future architecture and for those that imagine the cities within which buildings are set.

The supernatural is the most distant to us. The supernatural is the superhuman world of miracles; a world that we cannot know or see, except—according to the religious—after death. We don't live in a time when architects write about supernatural phenomena, but it still appears as a physical, representational residue in certain religiously and phenomenologically oriented projects that attempt to represent the Christian god with effects of light and space. If we consider the supernatural a religious world of superhuman beings and forms, then the earliest surviving work of architectural theory that portrays the supernatural is most likely the "lodge-book" of Villard de Honnecourt, a medieval master builder. Here, a fantasia of strange animals entangles the different elements of cathedrals, some are recognisable but others from fictional or mythological worlds.[3] In contrast to the distance of supernatural concepts and representations, the natural might be one of the most commonly represented and discussed within architecture and urbanism. The architectural historian Adrian Forty traces the concept of nature to the early modern architectural theories of the renaissance. Nature was a concept as much as a thing, an external ideal that represented geometric perfection and the perfection of god. Within the Picturesque aesthetics of the late-eighteenth and early-nineteenth century, nature took on additional material dimensions as a setting within which architecture could harmoniously appear. In this way, as Robin Middleton and David Watkin argue, contemporary architectural environmentalism that seeks to nestle buildings within nature may be traced back to the picturesque movement.[4]

If we use the term "supernatural" to describe a world of superhuman objects and miracles, and the term "natural" to describe the setting and material within which human experience is historically set, then "subnatural" describes a setting and a thing that cannot support human society as we currently conceive it. Subnature is a type of disturbing thing that is produced by human society, yet doesn't provide any obvious material benefit to society. Within architectural thought, the subnatural is potentially threatening to inhabitants or to the material formations and ideas that constitute architecture. Subnatures are those forms of nature deemed primitive (mud and dankness), filthy (smoke, dust, and exhaust), fearsome (inundations, gas, or debris), or uncontrollable (weeds, insects, and pigeons). We can contrast these subnatures to those seemingly central and desirable forms of nature—the sun, clouds, trees, and wind. These latter forces are generally worked into the forms, practices, and ideas that constitute the primary realisation of nature within architecture and the city.

Within the history of architecture and urbanism, the subnatural can be found in many places, but we might detect the earliest reflections on this condition within writings and drawings that consider the urban ground—literally the earth beneath city dwellers' feet.[5]

Within rapidly modernising cities, the urban ground emerged as a new problem, a new site of contention. The ground of early-modern Paris and London seethed with miasmatic gasses, exhalations, and various vapourous and liquid stagnations. Within these cities, new forms of urban cartography mixed architectural and geographical forms of representation, charting the repulsive matter that clung to the urban subsurface. In the face of the city's subnature, architects and urbanists began conceptualising their discipline's engagement with these materials and spaces. If the eighteenth-century "street" was once merely the left-over space between buildings, architects suddenly conceptualised it as a space of flow. Here within buildings and the streets outside them, the unwanted matter of the city would be sent away in conduits and channels. At first, this was a representational project, as in the famous street sections of Pierre Patte, but it soon became actualised within the grand pro-jects of nineteenth-century European cities—in their sewer and water networks. What was left of a pre-modern ground—its wetness and dankness—was simply mythologised within eighteenth- and nineteenth-century architectural writings on grottos. Here the last tastes of the earth could be experienced in well-formed spaces in cities.[6]

This rethinking of the urban ground within urbanism also influenced architecture via re-flections on the house and its engagement with the earth. Le Corbusier was one architect who railed against cellars as "mediocre spaces, dark or poorly lit and generally damp."[7] His interest in modern materials, forms, and construction techniques emerged from a spiritually infused vision of modernity, but it also reflected a more materialist disdain for the city's stag-nancies. The basement was an archaic space relative to a new modern world, but it also was a space that literally lay outside the modernist milieu of light and air. Any remaining orien-tations to the vapours and smells of the ground in architectural thought were dismissed as largely historicist, sentimental, and counter-modern.

The post-war reaction against the rationalism of modernist architects and planners such as Le Corbusier is well known, but it is almost always portrayed as a return to the historical fabric of the city or a turn towards Situtationist human play (*Homo ludens*). Less understood are the recoveries of the subnatural that also attacked certain strands of modernity. The writings on space by Gaston Bachelard incorporate various recoveries of the smell of the earth and the space of the domestic basement as a way to think outside a modernist aban-donment of ancestral, geologically situated space.[8] At roughly the same time as Bachelard's writings, the artist/architect Hundertwasser called for a non-modern architecture in *The Mould Manifesto*.[9] Here, mould was both literal and figurative as the unwanted growths that emerge from the ground and overwhelm modern architecture and planning. More recently, architects reawaken the taste of the earth in more direct, but equally intriguing ways. In his underground house for Vasivierre, the architect Philippe Rahm created a house with an enormous cellar open to the rooms above it. For Rahm, the room has the sole purpose of pulling "an earthy taste, a slightly brownish tone" out of the ground and into the house—a new (or old) form of domestic experience reawakened out of the history of modernity.[10]

With each of the above post-war thinkers, we witness how the subnatural that engages with our preconceptions about modernity is a bit abject, but much more significantly, is intensely historical, too. Subnatures are not simply denigrated matter and experiences, but things that require recovery. They are forms of nature from our past that we might learn to cultivate and ultimately adore, however difficult that may be.

We've already been led away from many of the most intense realisations of architectural modernity, architectural theorists dismissed supernatural aesthetics long ago, so where does a concept of subnature lead us today? Ultimately, a concept of subnature promotes a concept of nature within architecture that lacks the passivity and asocial qualities often attributed to architecture's "natural" environment; it might challenge the reductive and naturalistic aspects of contemporary environmentalist spatial aesthetics; such aesthetics imagine buildings as sites of natural flux—simple conduits of air, sun, and water; finally, a concept of subnature might help us understand any concept of nature as historically driven, especially how certain ideas about nature appear to be produced through the history of architecture. Ultimately, *subnature* is not about what is natural to architecture, but about the natures that we produce through our most radical concepts of architecture.

Endnotes

1   For an excellent overview on the concept of "nature" in architecture, see Adrian Forty, *Words and Buildings: A Vocabulary of Modern Architecture* (London: Thames and Hudson, 2002), 220–239. On the "supernatural" in architecture, see the recent collection Renata Hejduk (ed.), *The Religious Imagination in Modern Architecture: A Reader* (London: Routledge, 2010). On "Subnature" see David Gissen, *Subnature: Architecture's Other Environments* (New York: Princeton Architectural Press, 2009).

2   Robert Scholes, *Structuralism in Literature* (New Haven: Yale University Press, 1975), 119–120.

3   See Carl F. Barnes, *The Portfolio of Villard de Honnecourt: A New Critical Edition and Color* (London: Ashgate, 2009; facs. edn.).

4   Robin Middleton and David Watkins, *Neoclassical and 19th Century Architecture* (New York: Rizzoli, 1977), 37–46.

5   For overviews on some of this literature, see: Alain Corbin, *The Foul and the Fragrant: Odor and the French Social Imagination* (Cambridge, MA: Harvard, 1986); Rodolfe El-Khoury, "Polish and Deodorize: Paving the City in Late-Eighteenth Century France," in Assemblage 31

(1997), 6–15; Matthew Gandy "The Paris Sewers and the Rationalization of Urban Space," in *Transactions of the Institute of British Geographers* 24/1(1999), 23–44; Antoine Picon, "Nineteenth-Century Urban Cartography and the Scientific Ideal: The Case of Paris," in *Osiris*, Vol. 18 (2003), 135–149.

6   On the development of the grotto, see Naomi Miller, *Heavenly Caves: Reflections on the Garden Grotto* (New York: George Braziller, 1982).

7   Le Corbusier, *Precisions: On the Present State of Architecture and City Planning*, trans. Edith Schreiber Aujame (Cambridge, MA: MIT Press, 1991), 38

8   See for example, Gaston Bachelard, *The Poetics of Space*, trans. Maria Jolas (Boston: Beacon, 1994), 23.

9   Hundertwasser, "Mould Manifesto Against Rationalism in Architecture," in Ulrich Conrads (ed.), *Programs and Manifestoes in Modern Architecture* (Cambridge, MA: The MIT Press, 1986), 157–160 (originally published in 1958).

10 Philippe Rahm, *Underground House*, Board from the exhibition "Anxious Climate," 2007.

2

CRISES AND PERTURBATIONS

THE WORK OF ARCHITECTURE IN THE AGE OF STRUCTURED FINANCE

Louis Moreno

"The most compelling evidence that we are going through a crisis is that we have already redefined the meaning of words and symbols that were part of our cultural archetypes." [1]

Since the demise of the gold standard in 1971,[2] *architecture* has become a powerful keyword signifying the idea that contemporary capitalism is underpinned by a stable, secure, and durable basis. As confidence is essential to markets, and free-floating exchanges are by their nature complex and volatile, the idea that finance possesses an "architecture"—a structural and symbolic form of organisation—has become central to global economic debates.[3] Moreover, the extraordinary parallel growth of both urbanisation and financialisation during this period has reinforced the sense of a deep and problematic relationship between the economic space of capital and the social space of cities. Yet, despite copious references to "structure" and "engineering" in contemporary finance, we do not have a clear conception of the "practical influence" of capital and capitalism on the form and function of urban space today.[4]

The ambiguity is perhaps surprising considering the extent of urban imagery the fall of Lehman Brothers left in its wake. In a survey of the 2008 recession-scape, *The Economist* magazine argued that more than the "ghost estates of Ireland [or] the foreclosure signs on American homes … as a symbol of the property cycle that still distorts the world economy the Burj Khalifa takes some beating."[5] Named in honour of the Abu Dhabi monarch who bailed out Dubai, the half-a-mile-high structure symbolises to economic commentators the connection between asset bubbles and the production of the built environment.[6] However, perhaps the greater historical significance of Burj Khalifa, is not just that it represents another swing of the business cycle; but that its architecture manifests the globalisation of a mode of urban economic engineering pioneered over a century ago in Chicago.

Prior to 1880, few buildings in Chicago exceeded eight storeys. Due to combined land, engineering, and financial factors, tall structures were limited by physics and economics. In 1884, however, a corner was turned when the engineer William Le Baron Jenney employed a steel frame for the Home Insurance Building. Although on its opening few recognised the significance of the skeleton frame, its structure set in motion a commercial revolution. As the real estate economist Homer Hoyt noted in 1933, the "architects had hit upon a principle that was to revolutionise office construction. The weight of the upper floors was no longer to rest upon the first floor, but a steel frame like a basket supported each floor at its own level, so that the masonry on the top of the steel frame could be built first if desired."[7] Since physics no longer formed an absolute barrier the "chief limitations" to reaching new altitudes were now largely economic.

By the time the World's Fair landed in Chicago, anything seemed possible. In 1893, the World's Columbian Exposition set out to show Europe how the New World envisioned the city of the future. But it was the "wild speculative" boom going on beyond the fair that would have a more enduring legacy.[8] A decade earlier a downtown "flat fever" had set a precedent for urban living with an "invasion of fashionable residential districts by the apartment building."[9] Now, since "vertical rather than lateral expansion became the order of the day,"[10] a skyscraper "craze" was running at full tilt.[11] In just a decade since the steel frame hit the streets, a "wave of high buildings over the downtown area" had crystallised the modern central business district's form. During this time of feverish speculation, a group of local architects were given licence to research, develop, and refine the commercial applications of the tall building.

While the Chicago School of Sociology would define the industrial city's "ecology," and the Chicago School of Economics would construct a neoclassical ideology for the free market, it was the Chicago School of Louis Sullivan, Daniel Burnham, John Root, and others that first gave urban accumulation a structural form. In the mid-1950s, a reassessment of the legacy of the Chicago School began, and the architectural theorist Colin Rowe noted that the "authenticity" of buildings like The Reliance and Wainwright was owed precisely "to their being no more than the rationalisation of business requirements."[12] In these terms, the Chicago School not only manifested a new style of commercial design, they instantiated a new mode of architectural conduct. As the critic Montgomery Schuyler wrote in 1895, what distinguished the Chicago School was their "compulsion" to "frankly accep[t] the conditions imposed by the speculator."[13] Sullivan himself freely attributed their success to a capacity to tune the steel frame to the demands of the American marketplace:

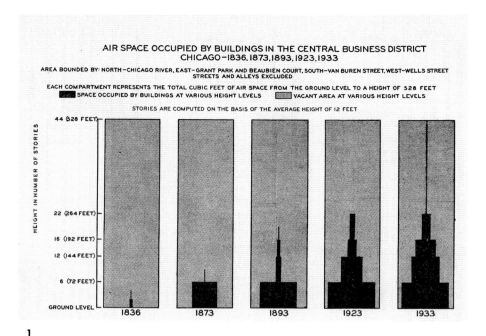

AIR SPACE OCCUPIED BY BUILDINGS IN THE CENTRAL BUSINESS DISTRICT
CHICAGO—1836, 1873, 1893, 1923, 1933

AREA BOUNDED BY: NORTH—CHICAGO RIVER, EAST—GRANT PARK AND BEAUBIEN COURT, SOUTH—VAN BUREN STREET, WEST—WELLS STREET
STREETS AND ALLEYS EXCLUDED

EACH COMPARTMENT REPRESENTS THE TOTAL CUBIC FEET OF AIR SPACE FROM THE GROUND LEVEL TO A HEIGHT OF 528 FEET
SPACE OCCUPIED BY BUILDINGS AT VARIOUS HEIGHT LEVELS   VACANT AREA AT VARIOUS HEIGHT LEVELS

STORIES ARE COMPUTED ON THE BASIS OF THE AVERAGE HEIGHT OF 12 FEET

HEIGHT IN NUMBER OF STORIES

44 (528 FEET)
22 (264 FEET)
16 (192 FEET)
12 (144 FEET)
6 (72 FEET)
GROUND LEVEL

1836   1873   1893   1923   1933

1

The passion to sell … is the impelling power of American life. Manufacturing is subsidiary and adventitious. But selling must be based on a semblance of service—the satisfaction of a need. The need was there, the capacity to satisfy was there, but contact was not there. Then there came the flash of imagination which saw the single thing. The trick was turned and there swiftly came into being something new under the sun.[14]

Rowe suggested that just as the column generated the Classical temple, and the Gothic cathedral sprung from the extension of the vaulting bay, the Chicago frame was the "constituent element" of a new urban order. "The frame has been the catalyst of an architecture; but one might notice that the frame has also *become* architecture, that contemporary architecture is almost inconceivable in its absence."[15] By contrast, the European frame, Rowe argued, had a very different project and destiny. Free of the commercial compulsion of the American architecture of "the Loop," Le Corbusier's Ville Radieuse was to be a revolutionary model of social reform. But, so the story goes, this vision was obliterated with the destruction of Pruitt Igoe on 15 July 1972 at 3:23 pm (or thereabouts).[16] However, in Rowe's terms what had fallen away was merely the moral pretensions of the International Style. From its inception, concluded Rowe, the frame was never social architecture, it was economic engineering.

1 The creeping monetisation of cxygen: Hoyt's graph demonstrates the way Chicago Loop buildings "tapped" the value of "successively higher layers of air" (1933: 329). Source: Hoyt (1933: 332). Reproduced courtesy of University of Chicago Press.

2

Contradicting the assertion that American lives have no second act, Chicago modernism was resurrected almost as soon as the International Style was pronounced dead. In 1973, Skidmore, Owings and Merrill's 108-storey Sears Tower re-engineered the Chicago frame for a new era of capitalism. So successful was the Chicago growth machine that by the beginning of the twenty-first century, Fazlur Khan's neo-Chicago frame was exported worldwide, actuating the record-breaking altitude of Burj Khalifa (another SOM product). But, according to office architect Frank Duffy, the by-product of the frame's ease of replication is the emergence of an "intellectually bankrupt" global city form. Looking at contemporary Shanghai, Duffy despairs that in spite of the epochal transformation Chinese urbanisation represents, the city's fabric "is a ghost of the explosion of innovation in those [US] cities 100 years ago. Exhaustion and entropy have become the norm. … The city's future is being compromised by an … office typology that is in terminal decline."[17]

Synthesising the analysis of Hoyt and Rowe, we can piece together a pathology for this structural inertia. Ever since the steel frame was erected on the Chicago corner of LaSalle and Adams Street, the culture of architecture was suborned to the culture of economic growth. The real objective, the *ethos* of the frame, was to fuel capital accumulation by ac-

2 Bank of China Tower, Hong Kong, architect I.M. Pei
Source: Jun Keung Cheung (2009)

celerating the escalation of land value. And as developers needed quality tall buildings to generate high rents from occupiers, steel producers wanted to supply frames to developers; and occupiers were fascinated by the new possibilities of living and working in the air—architecture, Louis Sullivan said, was the point of "contact" in a new circuit of metropolitan supply and demand. What the Chicago School produced, "imposed by the speculator," was "not so much architecture as ... equipment"[18]; a form of production specified by Eastern US rolling mills to exploit the growing demand for steel frames from land speculators.[19]

In the neoliberal era of global capital flows and institutional investment, the rolling debt plants of Wall Street have pump primed a global building boom. In doing so, Sullivan's "point of contact" between market forces has been assumed by a different kind of architecture. The establishment of "currency futures" in 1972 by Leo Melamed (at the Chicago Mercantile Exchange) and Eugene Fama's 1970 research on the Efficient Market Hypothesis (at the University of Chicago) have had a much deeper impact than Khan's engineering on the architecture of contemporary capitalism. Currency futures provided the means to speculate—using derivatives—on the contingency of floating exchange rates,[20] and the Efficient Market Hypothesis[21] asserted that open financial markets were "informationally efficient." Both these innovations had a far-reaching influence on the predominance of "structured finance"[22]; a practice that generated an almost unlimited source of capital through products like mortgage-backed securities, and whose alchemy consoled governments and investors that debt production was a sound and rational basis to economic growth.[23]

Further, the growing financialisation of property markets physically compounded the fallacies of structured finance, entwining financial and property markets in a global real estate bubble.[24] In such terms, buildings attained the condition of investment *equipment*; notionally securing asset speculation and spatially fixing cities into the vectors of capital flow. In this state, where the production of actual structures serves the requirements of financial engineering, it is not surprising that the typology of Shanghai's commercial district has been *derived* from another historical and geographical source. It was as if the dual inventions of late nineteenth-century Chicago, the frame and the derivative,[25] had co-evolved into a new International Style of architecture; one in which the landscape of cities could be conceptually manipulated like a financial asset.[26]

Walter Benjamin once argued that in the nineteenth-century, "construction play[ed] the role of the subconscious."[27] While this may have been true in a time when one city could claim to be the capital of the world, today construction plays a necessary but insufficient role in capitalism's understanding of its global self. Updating Rowe's hypothesis, we could say that financial derivatives have not only been the investment catalyst for architecture, derivatives have *become* the architecture of contemporary capitalism. But if the basis to the floating economy still depends on some sense (however residual) that confidence in capitalism resides in its architecture, the continuous "coin clipping" of the urban fabric may wear away the concept's inherent value. Leaving only the sound and fury of an architecture that signifies nothing.

Endnotes

1 A Wall Street fixed-income broker quoted in *The Financial Times*, 11 March 2008.
2 According to *The Economist's* "A short history of modern finance," the 2008 financial crisis "all began with floating currencies. In 1971, Richard Nixon sought to solve the mounting crisis of a large trade deficit and a costly war in Vietnam by suspending the dollar's convertibility into gold. In effect, that put an end to the Bretton Woods system of fixed exchange rates, which had been created at the end of the second world war. ... Once currencies could float, the world changed. Companies with costs in one currency and revenues in another needed to hedge exchange-rate risk." http://www.economist.com/node/12415730—last accessed 14 June 2011.
3 On its website, the World Bank states that contemporary finance requires an architecture to "help manage crises and even prevent them from occurring." (cf. http://www.worldbank/ifa—last accessed 13 June 2011). Following the Asian crisis of the late 1990s, the US House of Representatives held an inquiry inviting Treasury Secretary and ex-Goldman Sachs CEO Robert Rubin and Federal Reserve Chairman Alan Greenspan to advise on improving the "architecture" of the international financial system (see http://commdocs.house.gov/committees/bank/hba57053.000/hba57053_0f.htm). Also, for a comparative discussion of the Bretton Woods and post-1970s neoliberal architecture, see Michael Pryke, "Making Finance, Making Worlds," Nigel Clark, Doreen Massey, and Philip Sarre (eds.), *Material Geographies: A World in the Making* (London: SAGE, 2009).
4 "Few people would reject the idea that capital and capitalism 'influence' practical matters relating to space, from the construction of buildings to the distribution of investments and the worldwide division of labour. But it is not clear what is meant by 'capitalism' and 'influence.'" Henri Lefebvre, *The Production of Space*, (Hoboken, NJ: Wiley, 1991) pp. 9–10.
5 Andrew Palmer, "Bricks and slaughter: a special report on property," in *The Economist* 5 March 2011 (3)1.
6 "According to Andrew Lawrence of Barclays Capital, the construction of tall buildings is a reliable indicator of economic crises in the making." Ibid.
7 Homer Hoyt, *One Hundred Years of Land Values in Chicago: The relationship of the growth of Chicago to the rise in its land values 1830–1933* (Chicago: University of Chicago Press, 1933), 150.
8 Ibid., 195.
9 Ibid.,136.
10 Ibid., 152.
11 "The financial success of these new skyscrapers was, until the end of the World's Fair in 1893, greater than might have been anticipated. Tenants poured out of the old buildings, now rapidly obsolete, into the new and more modern quarters that had better elevator service, more ornate fixtures, and more light and air" (Ibid., 151).
12 Colin Rowe, "Chicago Frame," in *The Mathematics of the Ideal Villa and Other Essays* (Cambridge, MA: MIT Press, 1987), 103. Rowe's essay, was originally published in *The Architectural Review* in 1956. The article preceded by a year the republication of Sullivan's 1896 article "The Tall Office Building Artistically Considered." See Reinhold Martin, *The Organization Complex: Architecture, Media, and Corporate Space* (Cambridge, MA: MIT Press, 2003), 82–85.
13 Rowe, 103.
14 Sullivan, quoted in Rowe, 103.
15 Rowe, 90.
16 Charles Jencks, *The Language of Post-Modernism: The New Paradigm in Architecture* (New Haven CT: Yale University Press, 2002), 9.
17 Frank Duffy, "The Death and Life of the Urban Office," Ricky Burdett and Deyan Sudjic (eds.), *Endless City* (London: Phaidon Press, 2008), 332.
18 Rowe, 105
19 "... it was *they*, [Sullivan] says, who conceived of the idea of a skeleton, which would carry the entire weight of thee building" Rowe, 103.
20 "Leo Melamed was clever enough to see a business [in floating currency exchanges] and launched currency futures on the Chicago Mercantile Exchange ... Mr. Melamed saw that financial futures would one day be far larger than the commodities market. Today's complex derivatives are direct descendants of those early currency trades." *The Economist*, "A short history of modern finance." For a discussion of the creation of the modern currency futures derivatives market, also see Donald MacKenzie, *Material Markets: How Economic Agents are Constructed* (Oxford: Oxford University Press, 2009).
21 The *Oxford Dictionary of Finance and Banking* calls the Efficient Market Hypothesis (EMH) "a central theory of modern financial theory" (2008, 138); and Clark and Wojcik call EMH the "intellectual scaffolding" of finance , Gordon L. Clark and Dariusz Wojcik, *The Geography of Finance: Corporate Governance in the Global Marketplace* (Oxford: Oxford University Press, (2007:), 182.
22 Structured finance is defined by the *Oxford Dictionary of Finance* as "the creation of complex debt instruments by securitisation or the addition of derivatives to existing instruments" (2008, 426).
23 Alan Greenspan's 20 May 1999 testimony to the US House of Representatives focused on the innovations of structured finance as central to understanding capitalism's "architecture": "financial instruments of a bygone era ... have been augmented by a vast array of complex hybrid financial products that has led to a far more efficient financial system." (see http://www.federalreserve.gov/BOARDDOCS/TESTI-MONY/1999/19990520.htm—last accessed 14 June 2011)
24 For a prescient analysis of the dangers inherent in the integration of financial and property markets, see J. Coakley, "The Integration of Property and Financial Markets," in *Environment and Planning A* 26 (1994), 697–713. For more recent analyses of property market instability see Colin Lizieri, *Towers of Capital: Office Markets and International Financial Services* (Hoboken, NJ: Wiley-Blackwell, 2009); and Richard Barras, *Building Cycles: Growth and Instability* (Hoboken, NJ: Wiley-Blackwell, (2009).
25 Although derivatives were not invented in Chicago, the creation of the Chicago Board of Trade in 1848 is cited as a key event in the history of US futures markets. See Don M. Chance, "A Brief History of Derivatives," in *Essays in Derivatives: Risk-transfer Tools and Topics Made Easy* (Hoboken, NJ: Wiley Finance, 2008).
26 In the 1970s and 1980s, David Harvey developed a neo-Marxian analysis (indebted to Karl Polanyi) of a trend in capitalism towards the fictitious commodification of land as a financial asset, see: David Harvey, *The Limits to Capital* (London: Verso Press, 2006); David Harvey, *Social Justice and the City* (revised edn.; Athens: University of Georgia Press, 2009). For a concise survey of this debate, see Anne Haila, "Land as Financial Asset: The Theory of Urban Rent as a Mirror of Economic Transformation," in *Antipode* 20/2 (1988), 79–101.
27 From, Walter Benjamin, "Paris, Capital of the Nineteenth Century," in *The Arcades Project* (Cambridge, MA: Harvard University Press, 1999),16. Benjamin took this quote from Sigfried Giedion, who also provided Colin Rowe with the concept "constituent element."

VERTICAL ACCUMULATION AND ACCELERATED URBANISM: THE EAST ASIAN EXPERIENCE

Hyun Bang Shin

1   Seoul, South Korea (2006)
Source: Photo by Hyun Bang
Shin

When visitors from outside East Asia arrive at a city like Seoul or Hong Kong, a short drive from the airport takes them to a cluster of high-rise buildings, giving the impression that they have arrived at the city's central business district. They soon realise, however, that they are mistaken; continuing their drive, they face more, sometimes endless, strings of high-rise building clusters. What has driven this overwhelmingly vertical cityscape is a decades-long compressed urban accumulation process built upon massive investment in property development in many East Asian economies that share some particular characteristics: strong developmental states; weak civil societies; export orientation; rapid industrialisation and urbanisation; and heavy investment in human and fixed capital.

Those highly industrialised East Asian economies, which rose from poverty-stricken conditions, have been heavily dependent on the real-estate sector, resulting in often speculative property development booms. This phenomenon prevails not only in advanced capitalist cities like Seoul, but also in mainland Chinese cities in transition. For nearly three decades since China opened its door for economic policy experimentation, Chinese cities have also found themselves at the heart of a property boom. The frenzy of property development initially occupied cities in eastern provinces,[1] but the zeal has spread out to other inland cities such as Nanjing and Chongqing. A favourable environment for sustained investment has been sought after by strong states in East Asia, which support the promotion of urban development and accelerated urbanism.

From this perspective, it may be possible to draw out distinctive commonalities to establish some sort of "Asian urbanism" in the shaping of East Asian urban morphology. Despite each city's disparate political, economic, and socio-cultural backgrounds compounded by historic events and institutional innovations, the neo-Marxian political economic perspective on capital accumulation processes provide the following three aspects that stand out prominently as East Asia's shared urban accumulation experience: (i) the acquisition of property-related revenues; (ii) strong developmental states; and (iii) the prominence of real-estate capital built on speculative home-ownership aspirations.

The finance of city development in East Asia relies heavily on the use of property-related revenues. This is particularly obvious where state ownership of urban land has been firmly established. In Hong Kong, for instance, studies suggest that between 1970 and 1991, land and lease revenues accounted for 20 per cent of the total government incomes and financed 80 per cent of the total infrastructure expenditures. In Singapore, these rates were about 19 per cent and 62 per cent respectively.[2] Chengri Ding reports that the revenues generated from land conveyance fees and loans from using land as collateral "accounted for 40 to 50 per cent of the municipal government's Year 2002 budget in Hangzhou, a city located south-west of Shanghai; in turn these revenues were used to fund more than two-thirds of the city's investments in infrastructure and urban services."[3]

East Asian states have been known for their developmentalist approaches to economic development, with heavy investment in the built environment.[4] The developmental states commonly emphasised national economic stability and expansionary economic performance often at the cost of redistribution. They have established close ties with business interests and performed strong state intervention during investment decision-making. For example, the development path of urban China has seen a surge of state-sector investment in fixed assets, including those in the real estate sector, in order to lay the foundations for further economic growth. In national accounts, fixed assets refer to those production assets that are used continuously in production processes without full exhaustion, and include tangible assets such as buildings, houses, equipment, and infrastructure provision (such as railways, roads and airports). In Beijing, the share of gross fixed capital formation (hereafter, GFCF)—that is net investment in fixed assets—in the city's regional GDP was around 60 per cent for the second half of the 1990s about 30–40 per cent of the GFCF went into real estate.[5] In the case of Hong Kong, about a quarter of the city's GDP has been invested in the construction and real estate sectors since 1980.[6] East Asia as a whole has seen a strong presence of state entrepreneurialism fuelling the urban accumulation process.[7]

Finally, real estate capital in East Asia has been prominently accumulated upon home-ownership aspiration. The desire for asset increase is shared by an extensive range of property-based interests, which include prospective home-buyers, speculators, private- and public-sector developers, as well as states. States, in particular, make strong interventions in overall housing systems through regulating land supply and taking control of financial institutions, while working closely with construction firms and developers.[8] The rush towards real-estate markets where the availability of land is limited is illustrated by the connection between speculation and mass construction of high-rise buildings, spearheaded by Hong Kong and Singapore. South Korea and mainland China also joined the dominant trend, while Taiwan was involved to a much lesser extent, being prone to earthquakes. In Korea, government statistics indicate that the majority of new housing construction has been in the form of high-rise apartments since the mid-1980s; in 2005, their share even reached 90 per cent of the dwellings approved for construction. This situation was supported by a housing policy oriented towards home-ownership.[9] As a result, modern high-rise apartments have been identified as the means of asset-building as well as the loci of an urban way of living. A vicious circle of capital investment and reinvestment has been paired with a repeated, compressed cycle of property-led development and redevelopment in the urban landscape to achieve what could be termed as "vertical accumulation."

Now, the question is, does this property-led development and vertical accumulation in East Asia have a viable future? Until recently, the region was successful in sustaining its economic development, inducing its surplus capital as well as foreign capital into the built environment. It may be worth noting that even in times of economic difficulties, particularly since the 1997 Asian financial crisis, many East Asian states tried to use their power to facilitate more investment in fixed assets and the built environment as an effort to keep their momentum of economic growth. The long-term prospect of the cities in the region, however, is

subject to more intrinsic challenges. Three aspects can be highlighted: (i) property speculation and over-accumulation; (ii) aggravating inequalities and debt-financing; and (iii) the
sustainability of development.

Japan's experience of property boom and bust in the late twentieth century provides a
striking example of the vulnerability of a national economy closely linked with property
speculation. Nonetheless, lessons do not seem to have been learnt by other East Asian states
where the property sector is intertwined with economic development, public finances, and
people's asset-building aspirations. Even during the 1997 Asian financial crisis, states were
more interested in keeping their growth momentum leveraged by property markets. The
consequence was over-accumulation in the built environment. One of the striking examples
would be so-called ghost towns in China, where unleashed local state actions have led to
the construction of new towns with scarce occupants. In spite of various warning signals of
an overheated market, curbing over-accumulation in the property sector seems a daunting
task for East Asian states whose GDPs are substantially generated from the property con-

2

2 Guangzhou, China (2010)
Source: Photo by Hyun Bang
Shin

struction market. For example, 13 per cent of China's GDP is reportedly from the property sector.[10]

The recent crisis generated by the collapse of the US sub-prime mortgage market illustrates the vulnerability of a speculative property market financed by debt.[11] East Asia's speculative property markets have also seen debt-financing expand for housing production and consumption. The very speculative nature of East Asia's property markets is now failing an increasing number of prospective buyers unable to meet their housing needs and aspirations. Intergenerational inequality or difference is also increasingly envisaged in the ways and capacities housing needs are met. Ray Forrest and Yosuke Hirayama[12] persuasively argue that the younger generation in contemporary Japan and Britain has not been able to become homeowners in the way their previous generation was able to manage. High levels of economic inequality aggravate the situation. Singapore and China are known for their high-income inequality, with their Gini index reaching 0.43 in 1998 and 0.47 in 2004 respectively.[13] Hong Kong has recorded a much higher figure, 0.533 in 2006, based on monthly household income.[14] These income inequality figures exceed those of the USA (0.41 in 2000) and the UK (0.36 in 1999). Where locals face increasing difficulties in financing their properties, overseas investors or ex-pat populations play prominent roles. For example, Hong Kong has seen the influx of mainland Chinese buyers to the city in recent years. The situation poses a potential to fuel dissatisfaction that may damage the legitimacy of the ruling regimes as well as the viability of the property-led development and urban accumulation model in East Asia.

Examples from former industrial centres and boom cities of the twentieth century (such as Detroit and Leipzig) suggest that cities go through cycles of historical and geographical uneven development in the global expansion of capital accumulation. This point is particularly applicable to Chinese cities that experienced the "concrete revolution" in recent decades, taking massive densification and so-called creative destruction as part of the development process. This transformation has been facilitated by "obsolescence" and "deterioration" of the buildings built prior to the 1990s. Those buildings are facing demolition well before reaching their usual design life cycle, experiencing compressed cycles of demolition and reconstruction for maximising returns on investment. The sheer amount of construction work in a short time frame also signals a possibility of poor building quality. It is apparent that Chinese cities will sooner or later face the urgent task of upgrading and reconstruction. But how will the upgrading and reconstruction be made possible? Will the Chinese economy keep its current rate of growth in the future? The Singaporean government first introduced its main upgrading programme in 1990 in order to arrest the degradation of buildings that are twenty years old or more.[15] If Chinese cities are to follow the same footsteps and make use of existing dwellings instead of wholesale reconstruction, they will need to immediately start working on devising a similar upgrading programme.

East Asian cities differ from one another in terms of their historical experience of urbanisation, not to mention the geopolitical position derived from the World War II and Cold War period. Nevertheless, they share many aspects in their developmental paths that could be considered vertical accumulation. Accelerated cycles of creative destruction and concentrated investment in fixed assets, including real estate, have been central to the sustaining the economic growth of cities. This process has created a myriad of networks and a spectrum of property-based interests, to an extent that the rapid growth and modernisation process of East Asian cities could be termed a "concrete revolution." However, concrete does not last forever. The East Asian model of property-led development and urban accumulation evolved during the region's rapid industrialisation and urbanisation is seeing the rise of more challenges and greater burdens, created by the model's very own success. Property speculation and over-accumulation built on aggravating socio-economic inequalities create conditions for long-term fragilities, suggesting that the existing East Asian model will not be able to dictate future cities in the same way.

Endnotes

1   A. Haila, "Why is Shanghai building a giant speculative property bubble?" in *International Journal of Urban and Regional Research* 23/3 (1999), 583–588.

2   Y-H. Hong, (1996) "Can leasing public land be an alternative source of local public finance?" Working Paper (Lincoln Institute of Land Policy, 1996).

3   C. Ding, "Property tax development in China," in *Land Lines* 17/3 (2005) URL: http://www.lincolninst.edu/pubs/1041_Property-Tax-Development-in-China

4   R. Groves, et al., "The property owning welfare state," Groves, R. et al. (eds.), *Housing and the new welfare state* (2007).

5   NBS China (various years) China statistical yearbook. National Bureau of Statistics.

6   A. Haila, "Real estate in global cities: Singapore and Hong Kong as property states," in *Urban Studies* 37/12 (2000), 2241–2256.

7   J. R. Schiffer, "State policy and economic growth: A note on the Hong Kong model," in *International Journal of Urban and Regional Research* 15/2 (1991), 180–196; E. B. Shin, "Residential redevelopment and entrepreneurial local state: The implications of Beijing's shifting emphasis on urban redevelopment policies," in *Urban Studies* 46/13 (2009), 2815–2839; T. F. Yu, "Entrepreneurial state: The role of government in the economic development of the Asian newly industrialising economies," in *Development Policy Review* 15 (1997) 47–64.

8   J. Lee, R. Forrest, and W. K. Tam, "Home-ownership in East and Southeast Asia: market, state and institution," R. Forrest, R. and J. Lee (eds.), *Housing and social change* (London: Routledge, 2003), 20–45;

H. B. Shin, "Property-based redevelopment and gentrification: the case of Seoul, South Korea," in *Geoforum* 40/5 (2009), 906–917.

9   H. B. Shin, "Living on the edge: Financing post-displacement housing in urban redevelopment projects in Seoul," in *Environment and Urbanization* 20/2 (2008), 411–426.

10   B. Davis, "The great property bubble of China may be popping," *The Wall Street Journal* 9 June 2011.

11   M. B. Aalbers, "The financialization of home and the mortgage market crisis," in *Competition & Change* 12/2 (2008), 148–166.

12   R. Forrest and Y. Hirayama, "The uneven impact of neoliberalism on housing opportunities," in *International Journal of Urban and Regional Research* 33/4 (2009), 998–1013.

13   UN-Habitat, *Planning for sustainable cities: Global report on human settlements* 2009 (London: Earthscan, 2009). See Table B-6

14   Census and Statistics Department, *2006 Population by-census thematic report: Household income distribution in HK* (Hong Kong: The Census and Statistics Department, Hong Kong Special Administrative Region Government, 2007). See p.14

15   D. K. H. Ho, et al., "Asset value enhancement of Singapore's public housing main upgrading programme (MUP) policy: A real option analysis approach," in *Urban Studies* 46/11 (2009), 2329–2361.

The author would like to thank Chris S.J. Lee for help with clarifying the arguments presented in this paper. Thanks are also due to Matthew Gandy for constructive suggestions.

LONDON FOR SALE: TOWARDS THE RADICAL MARKETISATION OF URBAN SPACE

Michael Edwards

London is the capital of the most class-stratified (unequal) nation-state in western Europe, second only to Portugal.[1] Britain never experienced the bourgeois or socialist revolutions that modernised the state and land ownership elsewhere, and it pioneered capitalism through a distinctive evolution of earlier feudal relations, expelling the people from the land and forging the first urban working class. The elite of Britain became dominant over a vast empire and that dominance has evolved into a powerful set of financial, professional, and cultural institutions that still exercise influence (and make money) on a world scale. London is a place where the world's elite come for education, medical treatment, shopping, consultancy advice on privatisation, money laundering, and business management: important parts of the city's economy make up a global clearing house for the practices of neoliberalism.[2]

London is characterised by the dominance of landed interests. The Crown and the aristocratic Westminster and Grosvenor Estates act alongside corporate giants such as Land Securities and British Land in the control and management of London's land. The dominance of property has recently been reinforced by the unintended consequences of an urban planning system that protects areas of "high amenity" for property owners—an owner-occupying majority in the housing system as well as hereditary, corporate, and developer owners—allowing house building companies to build at the (slow) rate that best suits their profitability. Through the decades since 1975, when salaried workers in all the OECD countries have received declining shares of the growing social product, the flow of funds into land and property acquisition has been boosted, especially since 2000, to the point where the "value" of housing, commercial properties, land, and infrastructure reached 87 per cent of the national stock of tangible assets in the UK economy.[3] This process has been fuelled by easy credit for households and corporate buyers, and was reinforced by the collapse of confidence in collective forms of pension provision, which led families to pour their savings into housing as an individualised strategy of wealth accumulation. The geography of this process has focused land value growth increasingly in London and in the surrounding regions so that the lower quartile price of a dwelling in London reached nine times the lower quartile London household income by 2008.[4]

A third particularity of London has been crucial in helping to bridge the contradiction of low-paid people surviving in a high-rent city: the struggles for housing in the twentieth century, which led to a large stock of social housing, publicly owned and let at manageable rents to nearly half (at peak) of ordinary Londoners—three quarters in some districts. Along with rent controls on private landlords, this had stabilised the patchwork of fine-grain social (and ethnic) mixing across more of the city than would be expected. If the phrase "sustainable communities" has meant anything in London it has been the scope for working class, as well as richer communities, to reproduce themselves from generation to generation in most neighbourhoods.

That has all been changing since the 1980s, as the social housing sector has shrunk through privatisation, incomes have increasingly polarised, de-industrialisation has destroyed mid-level jobs and an unregulated private landlord sector has captured a quarter of the stock. This private stock houses high-, middle-, and low-income people offering flexibility to the growing flows of educated migrants and students, but also some of the worst value-for-money and most crowded conditions for the poorest households.

In the labour market millions are employed at (or below) the national minimum wage, on which it is not possible to live decently in London. This has prompted a strong movement, London Citizens, linking local and religious organisations with precarious and low-paid workers' groups to demand a "London living wage." The campaign has brought gains to workers, initially in public bodies, then to some of the banks and universities who were shamed into compliance.

The labour market requires far more, both in quantity and quality of workers, than can be reproduced within London, sucking in 750,000 daily commuters and major migration flows of qualified and other workers from other regions, from the rest of Europe, and the world. It is an economy sustainable only by denuding other regions and nations of their expensively trained people.[5]

The third sphere where stresses are powerful is in the welfare system, which covers much of the gap between low income and high London rents for working and non-working households, private and social tenants. These benefits have become a target for the new Conservative-led coalition government at national level and their proposed cuts would greatly shrink the proportion of London in which lower income people can afford to live. Tens of thousands will have to move to the cheapest parts of the city, or to other towns and regions. The more central or salubrious districts will become entirely unaffordable and homelessness will escalate. The city will rapidly become even more segregated.[6]

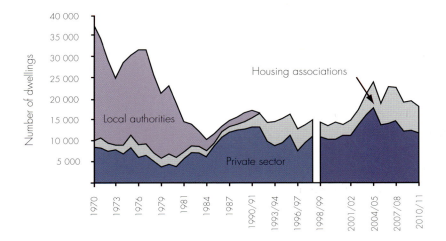

40 000
35 000
30 000
25 000
20 000
15 000
10 000
5 000

Number of dwellings

Housing associations

Local authorities

Private sector

1970 1973 1976 1979 1981 1984 1987 1990/91 1993/94 1996/97 1998/99 2001/02 2004/05 2007/08 2010/11

1

Since the 1990s, areas exhibiting strong concentrations of deprivation have been designated for "regeneration" and this slippery word is used to legitimise almost every construction project. The evidence is now very strong that public funds and agencies carry much of the risk while the gains flow to property owners and investors. The "deprived" residents in whose name the "regeneration" is launched often get displaced or priced out as their areas cease to be viable locations for mixed-income residence or the businesses they need.

The pressure on London has been increased by the appeal its housing offers to the elite and investors from around the world, so that foreign buyers now make up a majority of all buyers in some districts. Some have second or multiple homes, others are simply speculating in what is seen as a safe market (and may not even have their apartments occupied), while others again are buying as investments for renting. It is reported that, in the "prime" London housing market, the average price paid ranges from £6.2 million by Russian buyers to £1.3 million by Latin American buyers, with price fluctuations correlating strongly with the numbers of new billionaires being created in each continent.[7] A substantial part of the housing stock is thus going to meet international luxury consumption and investment demand. This makes a nonsense of the planning system in which demographic and economic studies of need and demand have long influenced how housing capacity is allocated. Not any more: it is the market that increasingly determines what gets built, where, and for whom. Even the relatively progressive mayor Ken Livingstone (2000–8) struggled to secure modest outputs of new social rented housing on land that he could extract from private developers in the boom.[8]

The penetration of financial capital into unexpected parts of society has recently been dramatised by breakdowns in the sale and leaseback of "assets" that exist to serve collective public needs. The London fire service turns out to have transferred the ownership of its fire engines to a private company, Assetco, from which it leases them. This became problematic when

1 Greater London, annual completions of new dwellings by type of developer 1970–2011
Source: CLG and GLA data

Assetco got into financial difficulties and it looked as though London might suddenly have no fire engines. A similar potential disaster has emerged in the care homes sector where a lot of private companies are now contracted to care for elderly and other dependent people, often at public expense. A large chain of care homes, Southern Cross, turned out to have done a sale-and-leaseback with private equity companies, on terms that embodied upward-only rent reviews and indexation to inflation. This means that as Southern Cross gets into financial difficulties, it—and the residents for whom it cares—risk eviction from their buildings. Even London's City Hall is on a lease from the developers More London. The concept of public buildings is slipping away.

Perhaps most pernicious of the expanding set of market relations in London is the role now played by the housing market in regulating access to good state schools. In such an unequal society, primary and secondary schools are very different in the character of their intakes, in how they educate and socialise their children, and in how they are perceived by parents. Policies of successive governments since the 1980s have undermined measures that made the system somewhat egalitarian and emphasised "choice" for parents. In this context, parents compete for places in what are seen as the better primary schools which in turn help gain access to better secondary schools. Since access to popular schools nowadays tends to be limited by catchment area boundaries, there is competition for housing mediated through local price premiums, which may run to tens of thousands of pounds.[9] Thus class differences, and their spatial expression, get further hardened between generations.

The popular version of the 1945 County of London Plan was introduced with the proud statement, "So when the LCC plans for London it is not merely planning these things in an abstracted way *for* Londoners; it is London's own people through their own democratic government, planning themselves."[10] That plan clearly assumed that business interests (which it referred to as "vested interests") would be subordinated to the plan. By contrast, the latest London Plan, published in 2011, implicitly assumes we are all subordinated to capital.[11] That is what is meant by today's legal requirement that a plan must be "viable" to be "sound."

Endnotes

1   Richard Wilkinson and Kate Pickett, *The Spirit Level: why more equal societies almost always do better* (London: Allen Lane, 2009).

2   Doreen Massey, *World City*, (Cambridge: Polity Press, 2007).

3   ONS data and see Michael Edwards (2011 in progress) "Towards better urban development." Draft at http://societycould.wordpress.com

4   Department of Communities and Local Government data, in GLA Economics, *Economic Evidence Base to support the public consultation drafts of the London Plan* (London: GLA, 2009) Fig. 7.2.

5   Massey op. cit.

6   A. Fenton, "Housing Benefit reform and the spatial segregation of low-income households in London," working paper 34, (Cambridge: Department of Land Economy, 2011).

7   Savills, "The World in London: how London's residential resale market attracts capital from across the globe" (London: Savills, 2011) http://pdf.euro.savills.co.uk/uk/residential---other/the-world-in-london---summer-2011.pdf

8   This is the core issue for the Just Space Network of community groups pressing for changes to the London Plan, http://justspace2010.wordpress.com; and see Michael Edwards (2010 October) "Do Londoners make their own plan?" in K Scanlon and B Kochan (eds.), *London: coping with austerity* (London: LSE London Series, 2010 Octoboer; paperback, 978-0-85328-459-8), chapter 5, 57–71. Eprint http://eprints.ucl.ac.uk/20241/ Whole book is a free download at http://www.lse.ac.uk/collections/LSELondon

9   P. Cheshire and S. Sheppard, "Capitalising the Value of Free Schools: The Impact of Supply Characteristics and Uncertainty," in *Economic Journal* 114/499 (2004), F397–424.

10 E. J. Carter and Ernö Goldfinger, *The County of London Plan explained*, (West Drayton: Penguin, 1945).

11 Mayor of London, *London Plan*, (London: GLA, 2011).

THE POLITICS OF
THE *BANLIEUE*

Mustafa Dikeç

1 21 June 2005: a vast police operation in La Courneuve, Paris.

Source: Sebastien Dufour/ GAMMA

Since the 1980s, the *banlieues* of French cities have increasingly become matters of concern. These housing estates at the peripheral areas of French cities are much more diverse than the singular term "*banlieue*" deceptively suggests, covering a variety of social, economic, demographic, and architectural characteristics. However, in common parlance, the term banlieue refers to the deprived social housing estates of popular neighbourhoods at the urban peripheries, associated with a number of problems ranging from threats to "French identity" to terrorism.

This is not to say, however, that the banlieues have acquired a negative image only from the 1980s. Their image as a sort of "feared outside" long predates the 1980s. Here we can think about the *faubourgs* beyond the walls of the city, "the Apaches" of Belleville at the turn of the twentieth century, the *banlieue* rouge of the 1960s, and the *loubards* [hooligans] of the 1970s. What happened in the 1980s was that the "problem of banlieues" has become associated with the "problem of immigration," evoking concerns about the "integration" of non-European immigrants and their descendants into French society.

This was a novelty compared to the previous decade. In 1977, for example, a commission was established to find solutions to what was seen to be a "sudden rise" in violence in France. The results were published under the title *Responses to Violence* (2 volumes), known also as the "Peyrefitte Report." Three *morales en marge* [morals at the margins] were identified: gangs, the underworld, and a category referred to as a new form of marginality. What was the "new marginal" like then? "The marginal searches," suggested the report, "for the lost paradise—replacement of monetary economy by barter economy; substitution of a creative, freely accepted, non-polluting work for 'alienating' work; oriental religions—and sometimes for artificial paradise: drugs, alcohol…"[1]

We have come a long way since the Peyrefitte Report's environmentally friendly marginals. The banlieues of the 1980s evoked the problem of immigration, the banlieues of the 1990s added Islam to the mix, and since then "the banlieue" has become shorthand for perceived menaces to French society. This was not merely the product of lazy journalistic accounts, but more importantly, of the state's various practices of articulation—policies, official discourses, reports, statistics, mappings. These articulations consolidated an image of banlieues as misfits in an otherwise (allegedly) cohesive society, threatening its peace and identity as an unwelcome intruder from beyond the city gates.[2]

It is true that there are problems in the banlieues, but one problem, in particular, seems to preoccupy state officials: violence (or "urban violence," as it is sometimes referred to). The French state's responses to incidents of violence have been typically harsh in recent years. The spontaneous revolts of 2005 were repressed by the declaration of a state of emergency, an unprecedented measure as far as mainland France is concerned. In July 2010, after revolts in a banlieue of Grenoble, French President Nicolas Sarkozy put the blame on "insufficiently controlled immigration" and declared that foreign-born criminals would be stripped of their French nationality.

So it all comes down to this: the problem in the banlieues is one of immigrants and violence. But there are other forms of violence that the banlieue inhabitants disproportionately suffer from. One major, and persistent, problem is mass unemployment. In the deprived social housing estates of banlieues targeted by urban policy—or, by what is left of it—unemployment levels reach 25 per cent. The young population is particularly hit by this problem, with 30 per cent of the young people living in these areas without jobs, even reaching 40 per cent in some areas.

Another form of violence that disproportionately hits the banlieue inhabitants is discrimination. The banlieues are marked by a strong territorial stigmatisation, and this creates a situation in which where one lives becomes a handicap (notably in job applications). Although it is quite common to hear anecdotes about the negative effects of such stigmatisation, the issue of discrimination took an interesting turn in 2009 when a notorious banlieue, La Courneuve, took action to press charges against the government for *territorial discrimination*, and referred the matter to the High Authority for the Struggle against Discrimination and for Equality.[3] The argument was that the injustices suffered by the inhabitants of this banlieue were *actually produced* by public policies and discourses. We must remember that this is the banlieue that Nicolas Sarkozy had promised to clean with power hoses. A former working-class banlieue located to the north-east of Paris, La Courneuve was hard hit by economic restructuring in the 1970s and 1980s, and has never really recovered since, with about one in every four people unemployed (and even higher for young people).

Yet another form of violence that the state officials rarely, if ever, talk about is police violence. Despite recurrent incidents of police violence, marked much more in the banlieues than in other areas, this issue is mainly overlooked by state officials. The issue here is not to defend the "good" banlieue inhabitants against the "bad" police; it is no secret that there are no obvious goodies and baddies here, and that the relations between the banlieue youth and the police are particularly tense. However, part of the resentment of the youth comes from what is perceived as the impunity of the police in relation to whatever they do. It would help to remember that of the forty-eight large-scale revolts in the 1990s, thirty-four of them were provoked by the killing of a banlieue youth, and in thirty of those, the police were implicated. Several other revolts in the 2000s were triggered by similar reasons, including the revolts in the autumn of 2005.

Seen from this perspective, the banlieue revolts look more like manifestations of discontent than mindless looting and burning. To be sure, they contain an element of violence, but it would be simplistic to suggest that this is for violence's sake only. As President Sarkozy put it in his speech in Lorient on 3 April 2007: "When people here demonstrate, when they use violence, it's not to have fun, it's never to harm anybody, it's because they're desperate, because they no longer have any option, and they feel condemned to economic and social death." Sarkozy, however, was not talking about the banlieues, but the Breton fishermen.

"Fishermen don't cheat," he stated, and then went on to argue that their violence is a sign of desperation, not of merely violent inclinations.

The banlieue revolts, however, have never been interpreted this way. This difference in political (and media) treatment was also observed by Azouz Begag writing in the wake of the 1990 Vaulx-en-Velin revolts, unprecedented in terms of their scale at the time: "The young people of Vaulx-en-Velin who burn and ransack stores are '*casseurs*'[4]; farmers who destroy railway lines are 'angry.'"[5] This political denial is significant and ironic given that many French politicians, including Sarkozy, celebrated the so-called Arab Spring as the voice of "the people" expressing their discontent and wishes. The Republic, it seems, fails to recognise its own people when they manifest discontent, mistaking them for *racaille* [scum] rather than "the people."

Endnotes

1   Peyrefitte Alain, *Réponses à la violence. Rapport du comité d'études sur la violence, la criminalité et la délinquance, 2 vols* (Paris: La Documentation française, 1977), vol. II, 143.
2   Mustafa Dikeç, *Badlands of the Republic: Space, Politics and Urban Policy* (London: Blackwell, 2007).
3   Interestingly, the HALDE has just been dismantled in favour of a much watered-down *défenseur des droits* (ombudsman).
4   *Le Robert & Collin*s dictionary translates this term as "demonstrator who damages property," or "rioting demonstrator." Literally it means "breaker."
5   Azouz Begag, 1990 "La révolte des lascars contre l'oubli à Vaulx-en-Velin," in *Les Annales de la recherche urbaine* 49 (1990), 114.

SPLINTERED URBANISMS: WATER, URBAN INFRASTRUCTURE, AND THE MODERN SOCIAL IMAGINARY

Karen Bakker

Consider the following fictional account of three neighbours, living on the outskirts of a megacity in the global South. Their story illustrates the claim that utility services—distributed as incomplete "archipelagos" rather than comprehensive networks across urban space—are both material emblems and cultural signifiers of social citizenship.

Ani lives in a gated community. Like her neighbours, she used to be connected to the municipal water supply system, but then became frustrated by frequent cut-offs, low pressure, and the often murky, smelly water. So together with her neighbours she decided to create a "water co-operative." The co-operative drilled a series of deep wells, which was expensive, but the water is free and so plentiful that Ani has recently installed an imported whirlpool bathtub and plans on building a swimming pool in her backyard. Bottled water from a local company that taps several springs in the hills above the city (much to the distress of local farmers, who are thus deprived of their customary water sources) satisfies the family's daily drinking water needs. For guests, and as a special treat, Ani buys mineral water imported from Europe.

Mira lives in a small house just outside the gates of Ani's neighbourhood, and makes a living selling bottled drinks to passing drivers on the busy road. She considers herself lucky to have a connection to the municipal water supply network, but has experienced the same water problems as Ani. So, every few days, Mira straps twenty-litre water jugs onto the back of the family scooter and drives to the private microtreatment plant down the road. She knows that the plant is un-

regulated, and she worries about the quality of the water she buys, but this is all she can afford since her husband lost his job during the recent economic downturn. For additional income, Mira sells water to her poorer neighbours, who bring empty plastic bottles they have scavenged from the nearby dump.

Alia is one of Mira's regular customers. She lives with her family in a small, self-built shack, illegally occupying the thin strip of land between Mira's house and the river—one of the main sources for the city's water supply network, and also the neighbourhood's open sewer. The most impoverished households scavenge wood scraps to construct "helicopter toilets" over the river to provide themselves with a minimum of privacy and comfort. Downstream, the water is so polluted that local farmers have had to stop using it. And the neighbourhood's groundwater has become predictably polluted. Nonetheless, Alia uses her family's shallow hand-dug well for washing and bathing water, as she cannot afford to buy bottled water for all of their household needs. When the dry season comes, or when Mira has no more tap water to sell (which happens frequently), Alia buys from a water vendor, who delivers twenty-litre jugs in a wheelbarrow from the nearest "public" water tap (over a mile away). The drier the weather, the higher the prices demanded by the local "chief" in charge of the ostensibly public tap. At the height of the dry season, Alia pays up to ten times more per litre than Mira pays for her tap water.

This story mirrors the daily reality of many urban residents around the world. Both rich and poor households, on any given day, use several different types of water: groundwater for bathing, bottled water for drinking, and rainwater for washing laundry. They interact with a range of different water providers: the municipal water supply network, the tanker-truck driver, the local water vendor, and the bottled water seller. And they use a variety of supply technologies, from highly industrialised to artisanal: individual household wells or rainwater collection systems, reticulated water networks, water pumps, gravity-fed roof tanks. Acquiring water is a complex and time-consuming task, and it requires intimate knowledge of the political ecology of the city's water: where it flows at different times of year, and how cost and quality vary across time and space.

This suggests that the term "network," and the interconnectedness it evokes, is a poor descriptor of water supply systems in many cities. Rather, the metaphor of the archipelago—spatially separated but linked "islands" of networked supply in the urban fabric—is more accurate than the term "network." Inequality of access is literally embodied in urban infrastructure, access to which is highly fragmented in large cities around the world.

Why is this fragmentation of urban water supply networks so persistent in cities in developing countries? This question presupposes an assumption that fragmentation is an aberrant and perhaps recent phenomenon. To cite an influential example, Stephen Graham and Simon Marvin argue in *Splintering Urbanism* that the fragmentation of access (and pricing) of urban services has recently occurred, along with the restructuring of utility networks, embedded in wider changes in aid and financial flows, technological innovation, and governance. Their analysis is representative of conventional thinking about cities and public services, according to which services are fragmenting because of macroeconomic and political trends, such as high levels of debt, that reduce the fiscal capacity of states to provide and extend government services. Neoliberalisation thus creates the ideal conditions for "vulture capitalists" (like private water companies from the North) to aggressively seek out new markets.

Urban theorists of the global South (Appadurai, Chatterjee, Roy, Stoler, and others) have explored alternative frameworks for understanding fragmentation of access to urban services. What if urban infrastructure was inherently "splintered," rather than "splintering"? Most governments, after all, do not provide (and indeed have never provided) universal public services. In most cities of the developing world, "public goods"—from health care to water supply, from education to electricity—are circumscribed to the elite. Partha Chatterjee argues that urban services pose a conundrum for developmental states, which seek to extend public services as a means of shoring up political legitimacy, but are typically unable to extend public services to the entire population. Fiscal constraints, managerial shortcomings, governance processes, clientelism, corruption, patronage (and networks of reciprocity associated with ethnicity and identity) all shape the state's capacity to act. More often than not, exclusion is literally hardwired into the network. Splintered urbanism is an urban condition, rather than a recent phenomenon.

As a result, access to urban infrastructure is often a locus of political struggle. It is also a site for intense, often undocumented innovation. Private individuals, non-governmental organisations, political movements, and (mostly small-scale) businesses seek to fill the substantial gap. Alternative strategies of service provision emerge, from the "comrade plumbers" of South Africa's townships to the community co-operatives of Buenos Aires. All of these are "private" (in the sense of non-governmental) strategies, which provide water to and by members of the "public."

Urban water also raises questions regarding scales and practices of provision. This is particularly urgent in light of the partial retreat of private infrastructure companies from poorer cities, neighbourhoods, and countries, over the past few years, as a result of which "community" management has become the default for many urban residents around the world. But community provision—the new darling of the aid community—presents us with a dilemma: in celebrating community resourcefulness and promoting community-run water supply systems, we risk condoning both government inaction and corporate misconduct, while depriving low-income communities of the services that wealthier communities already enjoy.

Urban water thus challenges our definitions of "public" and "private," and disrupts simplistic models of urban development. Like other utility services, water occupies the interstices between our categories and analytical frameworks. The incorporation of water—as urban nature—into urban infrastructure and spaces thus challenges basic tenets of what Charles Taylor terms our "modern social imaginary."

DISRUPTIONS

Stephen Graham

"The secret ambition of design is to become invisible, to be taken up into a culture, absorbed into the background.… The highest order of success in design is to achieve ubiquity, to become banal." [1]

"Cities are the summation and densest expressions of infrastructure," write urban historians, Robert Herman and Jesse Ausubel. "Or, more accurately, a set of infrastructures, working sometimes in harmony, sometimes with frustrating discord, to provide us with shelter, contact, energy, water and means to meet other human needs." [2]

By sustaining flows of water, waste, energy, information, people, commodities, and signs, massive complexes of contemporary urban infrastructure are the embodiment of western Enlightenment dreams of the social control of nature through advances in technology and science. They are a prerequisite to any notion of modern "civilisation." They are at the heart of the ways in which cities act as the main centres of wealth creation and capital accumulation through extending their control and appropriation of labour power and of resources over distant territories, people, and ecosystems. They have tended to become inexorably woven into notions of the modern state and modern identities associated with nationhood. And infrastructure networks are always at the centre of discussions about urban futurity and the "impacts" that new waves of technological innovation will have on our rapidly urbanising planet.

The everyday life of the world's swelling population of urbanites is increasingly sustained by vast and unknowably complex systems of infrastructure and technology stretching across geographic space. Immobilised in space, they continually bring into being the mobilities and circulations of the city and the world. Energy networks connect the heating, cooling, and energising of urban life through infrastructure to both far-off energy reserves and global circuits of pollution and global warming. Huge water systems sate the city's insatiable thirst whilst wastewater and sewerage remove human and organic wastes from the urban scene (at least partially).

Within cities, dense water, sewerage, food, and waste distribution systems continually link human bodies and their metabolisms to the broader metabolic processes through which attempts are made to maintain public health. Global agricultural, shipping, and trade complexes furnish the city's millions with food. Highway, airline, train, and road complexes support the complex and multi-scaled flows of commuters, migrants, tourists, and refugees, as well as materials and commodities, within and through the global urban system and its links with hinterlands and peripheries. And electronic communications systems provide a universe of digitally mediated information, transaction, interaction, and entertainment, which is the very lifeblood of digital capitalism and which is increasingly assembled based on assumptions of always being "on." The vital material bases for "cyberspace" are largely invisible and subterranean. They also link intimately both to the electrical infrastructures that allow it to function, and to the other infrastructural circuits of the city as they themselves become organised through digital media.

Whilst sometimes taken for granted—at least when they work or amongst wealthier or more privileged users—energy, water, sewerage, transport, trade, finance, and communication infrastructures allow modern urban life to exist. Their pipes, ducts, servers, wires, conduits, electronic transmissions, and tunnels sustain the flows, connections, and metabolisms that are intrinsic to contemporary cities. Through their endless technological agency, these systems help transform the natural into the cultural, the social, and the urban.

As the great demographic and geographic shift of global urbanisation intensifies, humankind will become ever more reliant on functioning systems of urban infrastructure. Indeed, the very nature of urbanisation means that every aspect of people's lives tends to become more dependent on the infrastructural circuits of the city to sustain individual and collective health, security, economic opportunity, social well-being, and biological life. Moreover, because they rely on the continuous agency of infrastructure to eat, wash, heat, cook, light, work, travel, communicate, and remove dangerous or poisonous wastes from their living place, urbanites often have few or no real alternatives when the complex infrastructures that sometimes manage to achieve this are removed or disrupted.

Infrastructural edifices thus provide the fundamental background to modern urban everyday life. This background is often hidden, assumed, even naturalised. This is most common in wealthier, western cities where basic access to a suite of communication, energy, water, and transport systems have been to some extent universalised as the basis for modern, urban, citizenship. Once initially completed and universalised, the water, sewerage, and electricity systems of the city tended to "[become] buried underground, invisible, banalised, and relegated to an apparently marginal, subterranean urban world."[3]

In conditions where continuous access to key infrastructure circuits has been broadly universalised, anthropologists Geoffrey Bowker and Susan Leigh Star stress that "good, usable [infrastructure] systems, disappear almost by definition. The easier they are to use the harder they are to see. As well, most of the time, the bigger they are, the harder they are to see."[4] Within social scientific writing about cities, especially, the vast infrastructural circuits of the city have often emerged as little more than "the forgotten, the background, the frozen in place"[5]—a merely technical backdrop that is the preserve of engineers only. Bowker and Leigh Star offer the banal and often universal experience of uninterrupted electricity services to power a simple, reading light as an example of how infrastructures have a tendency to become taken for granted. "Unless we are electricians or building inspectors," they write, "we rarely think about the myriad of databases, standards, and inspection manuals subtending our reading lamps, much less about the politics of the electric grid that they tap into."[6]

When infrastructure achieves such a status as a "black box," few modern urbanites venture to understand the inner workings of the technology or the giant lattices of connection and flow that link these network access points seamlessly to distant elsewheres. How many of the world's burgeoning billions of urbanites, after all, routinely consider the extraordinary assemblages of fuel sources, generating stations, transmission wires, and transformers that push electrons through the myriad electrical artefacts of contemporary urban life? Or the mass of servers, satellites, glass fibres, routers—and, indeed, electrical systems—that bring our "virtual" worlds of play, socialising, e-commerce, or communication into being? Or the globe-straddling systems of communication, data processing, financial transaction, or risk profiling that bring airliners into the sky? Or the vast subterranean worlds that bring the fresh water to the tap or faucet or remove the human waste from the toilet once flushed? Or the global supply chains that populate supermarket shelves with produce, or fill the gas or petrol station with the hydrocarbon products of the fossilised bodies of billions of ancient life forms?

In many cities of the global South, in contrast, access to energy, water, waste, communications, and transport services is anything but assumed—enormous efforts at continuous innovation mean that basic infrastructural politics infuse urban life in such contexts. It is crucial to stress that, beyond the discourses of the powerful, infrastructure services have "always been foregrounded in the lives of more precarious social groups—i.e., those with reduced access or without access or who have been disconnected, as a result either of socio-spatial differentiation strategies or infrastructure crises or collapse."[7]

It is equally important that western histories, whereby relatively standardised and ubiquitous infrastructure grids have been more or less constructed, are not generalised as an inevitable trajectory or history for all cities everywhere. In many cities of the global South, for example, access to networked infrastructures has always been highly fragmented, highly unreliable, and problematic—even for relatively wealthy or powerful groups and neighbourhoods.

In contemporary Mumbai, for example, many upper middle-class residents have to deal with water or power supplies that operate for only a few hours per day. Their efforts to move into gated communities are often motivated as much by their desire for continuous power and water supplies as by hopes for better security. The pervasiveness of such infrastructure disruptions in Mumbai is in turn used by the city's boosters to invoke major infrastructural edifices and massive demolitions of informal settlements as they strive to overcome continuous infrastructural disruptions and so become "more global" or "the next Shanghai."

This means that, in many cities, infrastructural circulations are not rendered as mere "technical" issues that merge into the urban background. Far from it: their politics dominate urban life and urban political discourses to a powerful extent. Colin McFarlane and Jonathan Rutherford write that "it is clear that from the viewpoint of Bombay or Ulan-Ude [in Russia] infrastructures have rarely, if ever, been concealed or technical issues."[8]

The startling point about the rendering of taken for granted energy, communication, transport, and water grids as "normal," culturally banal, invisible, even boring is that it takes the sudden interruption or disruption to such systems to make them visible on the urban scene. Such events render the huge material systems of infrastructure as instant, albeit often temporary, ruins of modernity. When the website is not available, the volcanic ash prevents the airline from flying, electricity is blacked out, the fuel is unavailable for the food supply, water pumps or school run, the subways fail to move, or the tap fails to deliver clean water, the infrastructural backstage of urban life becomes startlingly visible. Whether through technical malfunctions, interruptions in resource supplies, wars, terrorist attacks, public health crises, labour strikes, sabotage, network theft, extreme weather, and other events

1

1 "Because electricity can't be stored in large quantities, modern urban life is stalked by the prospect of electrical blackouts— whether through technical failure, natural disaster, or, as with this North American ice storm, extreme weather conditions."

Source: Courtesy of Kenn W. Kiser, MorgueFile.

usually considered to be "natural" (such as floods, earthquakes and tsunamis), disruptions to the flows of energy, water, transportation, communication, and waste that are the very lifeblood of the contemporary city quickly breed a sense of emergency. The "black box" of the infrastructure system is thus momentarily opened; the politics of infrastructural assemblages become a sudden preoccupation within media and public debate.[9]

It is worth considering a few examples to help illustrate this point. In Spring 2010, the interruption of global airline systems by the Icelandic volcanic eruption filled the world's newspapers with detailed technical analyses of how jet engines deal with ingested dust. The cascading disruptions and devastations of urban Japan through the earthquake-tsunami-nuclear catastrophe a year later filled the same newspapers with detailed cross-sections of different styles of nuclear reactors, highlighting their various levels of resilience to power outages. And the unintentional severing of a transoceanic optic fibre line off the coast of Egypt by an Egyptian fishing trawler in February, 2008—which instantly brought to a halt much of the digitally mediated economy of Dubai, Mumbai and beyond—fleetingly revealed the global strands of interurban glass which bring the supposedly "virtual" world of the Internet into being.

As well as being experiences that tend to destroy any prevailing myths about the "technical" nature of infrastructure, infrastructure disruptions render the arcane worlds of technology momentarily visible and highly political. But infrastructure disruptions also present a major opportunity to understand cities better. For by removing the complex, stretched-out flows that continually sustain modern urbanism, such events, paradoxically, work to make such flows more visible—before they are rendered into the urban background once "normal" service is resumed. Critical analysis of city life needs, therefore, to exploit infrastructure disruptions as what sociologists call "heuristic devices"—opportunities for learning in ways that render the banal and ordinary as contested worlds of dynamism and action that are absolutely crucial in constituting the contemporary city as a process.[10]

Endnotes

1   Bruce Mau, *Massive Change* (London: Phaidon, 2003), 3–4.
2   Robert Herman and Jesse Ausubel, *Cities and Their Vital Systems—Infrastructure Past, Present And Future* (Washington: National Academy Press, 1988).
3   Maria Kaika and Eric Swyngedouw, "Fetishising the modern city: The phantasmagoria of urban technological networks," in *International Journal of Urban and Regional Research* 24/1 (2000), 122–148, here 122.
4   Geoffrey Bowler and Susan Leigh Star, *Sorting Things Out: Classification and its Consequences* (Cambridge, MA: MIT Press, 2000).
5   Susan Leigh-Star, "The ethnography of infrastructure," in *American Behavioral Scientist*, 43/3 (1999), 377–391, here 379.

6   Geoffrey Bowler and Susan Leigh Star, *Sorting Things Out: Classification and its Consequences* (Cambridge, MA: MIT Press, 2000), 33.
7   Colin McFarlane and Jonathan Rutherford, "Political Infrastructures: Governing and Experiencing the Fabric of the City," in *International Journal of Urban and Regional Research*, 32/2 (June 2008), 363–74.
8   Ibid.
9   Bowker and Leigh-Star even define the tendency to "becomes visible upon breakdown" as one of the eight characteristic of technologies that are socially constructed to be "infrastructure." See Geoffrey Bowler and Susan Leigh Star, *Sorting Things Out: Classification and its Consequences* (Cambridge, MA: MIT Press, 2000).
10 See the author's recent edited book, which seeks to do exactly that: Stephen Graham (ed.), *Disrupted Cities: When Infrastructures Fail* (New York: Routledge, 2009).

SYSTEM CITY: URBAN AMPLIFICATION AND INEFFICIENT ENGINEERING

Sarah Bell

"*Those who use the machine when they need to react to life directly or employ the humane arts, are as completely lacking in efficiency as if they studied metaphysics in order to learn how to bake bread.*"
Lewis Mumford, *Technics and Civilization*, 1934

"*An urban operating system—how audacious is that?*"
Living PlanIT website, 2011

The smart city has arrived. Networked sensor technologies monitor how people move, communicate, and consume; provide information to improve how engineers design, operate, and maintain infrastructure; measure the quality of air, water, and the environment; and collect data for education, healthcare, and security services. In the future, the smart city will be efficient, sustainable, and liveable. Sensor networks will bring intelligence to the familiar urban networks of transport, energy, water, retail, security, economy, policy, culture, and society. Modern urban lifestyles will be supported and made more sustainable as resources are utilised more efficiently through technological interventions that are largely invisible yet ever present.

This Promethean view of the city characterises the enthusiastic propositions of IBM, Cisco, Microsoft, Oracle, and other major technology companies as they map out their contributions to solving the challenges of urbanisation and shape new markets for their products and services.[1] Multimedia websites promoting smart city initiatives variously describe cities as machines, organisms, and systems of systems that can be made smarter and more efficient through the application of ubiquitous sensor, network, and information technologies.

1   Tania Cobham *Natural Façade* (2011)
Source: Courtesy of the artist

Systems metaphors are common in urban studies. Systems ideas can be found, for example, in the relatively straightforward analysis of resource and energy flows in urban metabolisms,[2] the futurism of cyber-cities,[3] and the critical deployment of the cyborg as a trope for exploring urban political ecology.[4] The smart cities agenda takes the idea of urban systems literally. The smart city is at once an engineering proposition to build and operate the next generation of urban networks, and at the same time is an ontological standpoint that frames all urban questions as essentially engineering problems to be analysed and solved using empirical, preferably quantitative, methods. As such, it represents what Carl Mitcham has described as an "engineering philosophy of technology—or analyses of technology from within, and oriented towards an understanding of the technological way of being-in-the-world as paradigmatic for other kinds of thought and action."[5]

The smart city depends on ubiquitous data collection, including networks of urban sensors to collect data on almost every measurable urban activity or phenomenon including air quality, retail activity, hospital cleanliness, room temperature, mobile phone use, and transport. Smart city proponents claim that such data, supported by good information systems and visualisation, can improve the quality of technical and democratic decision-making in cities and improve the basic efficiency of services and systems. However, it necessarily gives pre-eminence to urban phenomena that can be measured and are deemed important enough to measure.

Urban sensor networks conform to Don Ihde's early phenomenological analysis of technology mediated relations in terms of amplification-reduction structures. Urban sensors amplify the phenomena that are measured in the city with a necessary reduction in the overall field of vision or concern, obscuring that which is not measured. The sensors or instruments themselves are central to this structure with the consequence that "the instrument mediated entity is one which, in comparison with in the flesh relations, appears with a different perspective."[6]

Managing demand for energy and improving energy efficiency through the smart grid and building management is a common exemplar of the sustainability credentials of smart city technologies. Sensor networks in buildings together with software analysing user preferences can purportedly lead to better prediction of demand and more efficient energy systems. Analysing user needs in buildings using sensor technologies amplifies measurable phenomena and reduces "fleshy" human experiences. For instance, office building management systems based on sensor technologies simplify human comfort to the measurable phenomena of temperature and humidity. A standard temperature control range for office buildings has emerged around twenty-one to twenty-three degrees Celsius, corresponding to the most comfortable temperature to wear a business suit, with much engineering and design attention paid to finding the most efficient means of maintaining temperature in this narrow range.[7] The wider experience of human comfort is reduced to a particular experience of temperature for a specific group of building users, resulting in high energy consumption to maintain constant yearly indoor "comfort." An alternative approach to managing comfort in buildings might consider changing cultural norms of business dress, allowing a wider variation in clothing along with seasonal variations in temperature, enabling an extension of the "comfort" range to eighteen to twenty-five degrees, with considerable savings in building heating and cooling. Such possibilities for cultural change to achieve sustainability exist beyond the sensor networks of "smart" building management systems. This is not to say that temperature sensors and building management systems should not be as efficient as possible, but to highlight the narrowness of vision that is a consequence of reducing urban questions to engineering problems to be solved by ubiquitous measurement and intelligent control systems.

Ihde contrasts the "full sensory world of mundane experience" and the "monosensory 'world' of what is instrumentally mediated."[8] The ubiquitous sensors of the smart city provide engineers and urban decision makers with a "multi-sensory" experience of the world, which none-the-less remains partial and limited. In the excitement over new possibilities for knowledge from the terabytes of urban data now available to researchers and policy makers, there is a risk that an "instrumental realism" may come to dominate, whereby the "instrumentally constituted 'world' becomes the 'real' world" and the "mundane" world of the city is forgotten and downgraded.[9]

Cities have always been "smart." The intelligence of cities lies in the individual and collective minds of people who live there, not merely in the technologies they deploy. Engineers have been central in the development of technologies and systems that support and shape urban life and the intelligent application of technology is crucial in addressing many urban problems. However, cities cannot be reduced to measurable phenomena to be captured by sensor networks. Smart city technologies can provide useful knowledge about urban services and systems, but intelligent implementation requires critical understanding of what they amplify and what they reduce. The full potential of engineering and technology to contribute to more sustainable cities will not be achieved by reducing all urban questions to engineering problems. Amplifying the technical and reducing the cultural experience of cities is ultimately inefficient. Engineers, technology providers, and their clients should heed Mumford's warning and be judicious in determining when to reach for technological systems and when to "react to life directly."[10]

Endnotes

1   See for example IBM Smarter Cities www.ibm.com/smartercities, Oracle's Solutions for Smart Cities http://www.oracle.com/us/industries/public-sector/smart-cities.htm, Living PlanIT (a partnership including Microsoft and Cisco) www.living-planit.com, all accessed 19 May 2011.
2   H. Giradet, *The Gaia Atlas of Cities* (London: Gaia Books, 1992).
3   W. J. Mitchell, *Me++* (Cambridge: MIT Press, 2004).
4   M. Gandy, "Cyborg Urbanization: Complexity and Monstrosity in the Contemporary City," in *International Journal of Urban and Regional Research* 29/1 (2005), 26–49.
5   C. Mitcham, *Thinking Through Technology* (Chicago: University of Chicago Press, 1993) 39.
6   D. Ihde, *Technics and Praxis* (Dortrect: D. Reidel Publishing Company, 1979), 21.
7   H. Chappells and E. Shove, "Debating the future of comfort: environmental sustainability, energy consumption and the indoor environment," in *Building Research and Information*, 33/1 (2005), 32–40.
8   Ihde, 46.
9   Ibid.
10 L. Mumford, *Technics and Civilization* (New York: Harcourt, Brace and Company, 1934) 319.

ZOONOSES: TOWARDS AN URBAN EPIDEMIOLOGY

Meike Wolf

1 People wearing surgical masks enter the general hospital in Mexico City following the outbreak of swine flu in 2009.

Source: Dario Lopez-Mills/ Associated Press

To no longer ask if a severe global flu pandemic could occur but rather to enquire *when* it will occur has become commonplace among public health experts. This kind of pandemic awareness is by no means self-evident: infectious diseases seemed to constitute a public health problem in the time of industrialisation when urban populations were exposed to a variety of health threats, ranging from malnutrition, inadequate housing, and poor sanitary conditions to polluted drinking water and a high population density. While by the end of the nineteenth century many of these diseases had declined due to on-going improvements in urban hygiene and sanitation and the emergence of bacteriological knowledge, they have nevertheless gained in importance in recent years. Currently, infectious diseases such as AIDS, tuberculosis, and malaria remain one of the world's leading causes of death, especially in the global South. Among them, zoonoses (infections spreading between animal and human bodies) play a key role in international attempts to prevent, manage, and abolish infectious diseases.[1] The empirical cases of SARS, avian flu, and 2009 H1N1 influenza have illustrated that ongoing urbanisation and globalisation processes show an accelerated effect on the development and spread of emerging new zoonoses.

Since urban environments and infectious disease are very closely related—as perspectives from epidemiology, medical history, and the social sciences have convincingly shown[2]—and as an ever-growing proportion of the world's population lives in cities, this invites the assumption that the study of urban health has much to contribute in shaping individual and population health, both on a global and a local scale.[3] Whereas there is substantial literature on the multiple ways in which infectious diseases are embedded in a broader social, cultural, political, biological, and economical context (calling into question the entire conception of zoonoses as mere biological or "natural" phenomena[4]), not much research has yet been done on the specific *urban* aspects of emerging infectious diseases.[5]

First, from the perspective of cultural anthropology, there is a need for studies that seek to determine the impact of microbial globalisation[6] on preventive practices, technologies, and moralities—and thereby on everyday urban life in general. It is acknowledged, however, that the structure of urban health governance exerts a massive influence on differing responses to infectious disease outbreaks[7]—as places of transnational connectivity and bulwarks of disease control, cities may contribute to the surveillance, management, and monitoring of human movements, as the paradigmatic examples of SARS and influenza have shown. Post-Foucault, it has been recognised that technologies, discourses, and practices of prevention and health promotion are constitutive of the construction of subjectivities, social order, and rationality.[8] A constantly increasing interest in prevention and health promotion—no longer restricted to biomedical and public health experts alone—has diffused into the (bio-)political constitution of cities.

In understanding this process, it might be useful to distinguish between classical preventive approaches and the concept of *(bio-)preparedness*, as anthropologist Andrew Lakoff suggests. Based on a comparison between nineteenth-century urban hygiene and mid-twentieth-century swine flu, Lakoff outlines that current pandemic preparedness runs into a specific form of security, which aims to sustain critical urban infrastructure rather than protect the security of the population. Whereas traditional attempts to prevent infectious diseases (such as vaccination) focused on specific threats, relied on statistical calculation, and targeted the national population, current forms of pandemic preparedness are orientated to potentially catastrophic threats, feature imaginative enactment rather than risk calculation, and seek to gauge the vulnerability of the public health infrastructure—including elements like staff protection, the supply of equipment, pandemic surveillance systems, or the maintenance of essential services such as food distribution or transport.[9] In order to identify vulnerabilities and to generate knowledge about possible responses to ongoing pandemic and bioterrorist threats in the absence of actual events, as Lakoff describes, imaginative enactment features scenario-based exercises on imaginary disease outbreaks as a central tool, bringing together government officials and national security experts as participants in the exercise.

These observations may contribute to the analysis of alliances between biomedical and non-medical forms of prevention and preparedness and their impact on everyday urban life (such as the surveillance of mobility and transport or the distribution of antiviral drugs and vaccines)—and to emerging neoliberal forms of governance more generally.[10] In this sense, it is of vital importance that zoonoses are conceptualised not as a specific and singular threat, but as encompassing, ongoing and generic.

And second, not much is yet known about how the interaction between urban environments and zoonotic diseases is carried out.[11] Cities serve as entry points for new infectious diseases, and their spread is facilitated by—among other factors—a high population density, a sustainable chain of transmission, a lack of exposure to livestock in early childhood, enhanced infections due to the interaction of coexisting diseases (like asthma and respiratory infections) within particular settings ("syndemic effects"[12]), selective pressure caused by clinical or laboratory disinfection practices, and poverty that is characteristic of cities. It is now considered proven that agricultural "high-risk" practices such as poultry farming, live bird markets, the close proximity of different species, and factory farming contribute to the emergence of new zoonoses—many of which are often attributed to a "pre-modern elsewhere."[13] But, as scholars like Steve Hinchliffe and Nick Bingham aptly illustrate, there are no impregnable walls between this imaginary "elsewhere" and a modern world city—rather, cities and rural hinterlands are organised within the same network of interaction and disease transmission.

Hence, zoonoses are closely linked to human practices, routines, technologies, and bodies and may even be considered an integral part of human life and human "nature" itself (for example, it is assumed that the influenza virus has become endemic in Southeast Asia where it seems to have found a permanent ecological niche in ducks and domestic poultry). What further complicates the situation is the fact that zoonotic agents live in a borderless world: microbes like the SARS- or influenza-virus travel along transnational trade routes connecting global cities and mobility hubs with one another[14]—the spread of zoonoses could only occur if certain socio-technical practices (e.g., the use of agricultural antibiotics, climate change, air conditioning), environments (e.g., human-animal interfaces, built environments, chicken farms), and connections (e.g., air routes, animal migration, consumption patterns) were in place. As deeply liminal agents, zoonoses witness ongoing transformation processes and fall in between established structures, they revise traditional dichotomies of urban and rural, modern and pre-modern, human and non-human.[15] As such, zoonoses question our ways of categorising "natural" (or "cultural") environments—and dispute the construction of cities as settings where "nature" is strictly separated from human life. Seen from this point of view, conceptualisations of zoonotic agents as the threatening "other" of the human body must be called into question, especially since discourses on emerging infectious diseases are always constituted in relation to policies of inclusion and exclusion.[16] But how can we deal with the multi-dimensional and complex issues of urban health and zoonotic disease? Epidemiological research that merely concerns itself with objectively verifiable "hard" data, statistical analysis, and risk calculation fails to shed light on cultural influences shaping disease patterns (like differing explanatory models, self-treatment strategies, gender roles, personal hygiene, or leisure pursuits).[17] And vice versa, anthropological research on urban health that is blind to biological and epidemiological determinants in disease etiology runs the risk of postulating simple "culturalistic" cause-effect relationships.[18] Research on the interrelation of zoonoses and urban environments forces engagement with cultural, biomedical, and epidemiological theory: zoonoses must be analysed as a mobile, transgressive, and non-territorial phenomenon, which challenges traditional, limited concepts of urban space, the human body, culture, and prevention. As neither mere "natural" facts nor "cultural" constructions, zoonoses have much to say about the social construction of urban space and future risks, about emerging forms of urban governance and preparedness, and about social inequalities.

In addition, no conclusion can yet be drawn as to which type of city is affected most by emerging infectious diseases and their associated disease burden. Due to the complexity and multitude of the dynamics involved, the specific problems these cities may face show similarities *and* differences. There is a growing need for co-operation between the social and the biomedical sciences in order to develop an improved understanding of urban health. However, zoonoses are always a reminder of the material dimensions of urban environments that are inhabited by both human and non-human residents.

Endnotes

1   World Health Organization. 2011. *Health topics: infectious diseases*. < http://www.who.int/topics/infectious_diseases/en/>

2   Alfons Labisch, *Homo Hygienicus. Gesundheit und Medizin in der Neuzeit* (Frankfurt am Main: Campus, 1992); Matthew Gandy, "The bacteriological city and its discontents," in *Historical Geography* 34 (2006), 14–25.

3   Sandro Galea and David Vlahov, "Urban Health. Populations, Methods, and Practice," Sandro Galea and David Vlahov (eds.), *Handbook of Urban Health. Populations, Methods, and Practice* (New York: Springer, 2005), 1–15.

4   Paul Farmer, "Social Inequalities and Emerging Infectious Diseases," Peter Brown (ed.) *Understanding and Applying Medical Anthropology* (Mountain View: Mayfield, 1998), 98–107; Stacy Lockerbie and Ann D. Herring, "Global Panic, Local Repercussions: Economic and Nutritional Effects of Bird Flu in Vietnam," Robert A. Hahn and Marcia C. Inhorn (eds.), *Anthropology and Public Health. Bridging Differences in Culture and Society* (Oxford: Oxford University Press, 2009), 566–587; Brigitte Nerlich and Christopher Halliday, "Avian flu: the creation of expectations in the interplay between science and the media," in *Sociology of Health & Illness* 29/1 (2007), 46–65; Merrill Singer, "Pathogens Gone Wild? Medical Anthropology and the 'Swine Flu' Pandemic," in *Medical Anthropology* 28/3 (2009), 199–206.

5   S. Harris Ali and Roger Keil (eds.), *Networked Disease. Emerging Infections in the Global City* (Malden: Blackwell, 2008).

6   Kathryn White and Maria Branda, *Building Trust, Taking Responsibility. Civil Society as Partners in Global Health Governance* (United Nations Association in Canada, 2006),< http://www.unac.org/en/library/unacresearch/2006Avian_CivilSociety.pdf>

7   Roger Keil and S. Harris Ali, "SARS and the Restructuring of Health Governance in Toronto," S. Harris Ali and Roger Keil (eds.), *Networked Disease. Emerging Infections in the Global City* (Malden, MA: Blackwell, 2008), 55–59; Mee Kam Ng, "Globalization of SARS and Health Governance in Hong Kong under 'One Country, Two Systems,'" S. Harris Ali and Roger Keil (eds.), *Networked Disease. Emerging Infections in the Global City* (Malden, MA: Blackwell, 2008), 70–85.

8   Deborah Lupton, T*he Imperative of Health. Public Health and the Regulated Body* (London: SAGE, 1995); Friedrich Schorb, *Kreuzzug gegen Fette. Sozialwissenschaftliche Aspekte des gesellschaftlichen Umgangs mit Übergewicht und Adipositas* (Wiesbaden: VS Verlag für Sozialwissenschaften, 2009).

9   Andrew Lakoff, "The generic biothreat, or, how we became unprepared," in *Cultural Anthropology* 23/3 (2008), 399–428.

10 Thomas Lemke, "Beyond Foucault: from biopolitics to the government of life," Ulrich Bröckling, Susanne Krasmann and Thomas Lemke (eds.), *Governmentality: Current Issues and Future Challenges*. (New York: Routledge, 2010), 165–184.

11 Galea and Vlahov, 2005.

12 Merrill Singer and Scott Clair, "Syndemics and Public Health: Reconceptualizing Disease in Bio-Social Context," in *Medical Anthropology Quarterly* 17/4 (2003), 423–441.

13 Steve Hinchliffe and Nick Bingham, 2008. "People, animals, and biosecurity in and through cities," S. Harris Ali and Roger Keil (eds.), *Networked disease. Emerging infections in the global city* (Malden: Blackwell, 2008), 214–227.

14 Ali and Keil, 2008; Arthur Kleinman and James L. Watson (eds.), *SARS in China. Prelude to pandemic?* (Stanford, CA: Stanford University Press, 2006).

15 On the concept of liminality, see Victor Turner, *The ritual process. Structure and anti-structure* (1969; repr. Hawthorne: Aldine de Gruyter, [1995]).

16 Arthur Kleinman and Sing Lee, "SARS and the problem of social stigma," Arthur Kleinman and James L. Watson (eds.), *SARS in China. Prelude to pandemic?* (Stanford: Stanford University Press, 2006), 173–195.

17 Cecil G. Helman, "Cultural Factors in Epidemiology," Cecil B. Helman (ed.), *Culture, Health and Illness. Fifth Edition* (Oxford: Hodder Arnold, 2007), 372–391.

18 On biocultural approaches, see Melissa K. Melby, Margaret Lock, and Patricia Kaufert. "Culture and symptom reporting at menopause," in *Human Reproduction Update* 11/5 (2005), 495–512.

3

EXCURSIONS

Ulrike Mohr

Martin Kohler

Köbberling & Kaltwasser

Laura Oldfield Ford

Lara Almarcegui

Ulrike Mohr

Restgrün (2006)

Ulrike Mohr's investigations of the ecological dimensions to urban entropy raise important questions about the intersection between science and aesthetics. Mohr plays on the boundary of human intervention in nature in two ways: first, by simply observing nature its meaning and significance change; and second, by focusing on one element of nature and performing simple modifications, we contend with the scope and complexity of our relations with nature as an extension of ourselves.

Schwarzpappel
Populus nigra

Weidengewächse (Salicaceae)
Populus
nigra, Pionierbaumart

Herkunft: Palast der Republik, 4. April 2006

Neue Nachbarn (2008)

Martin Kohler

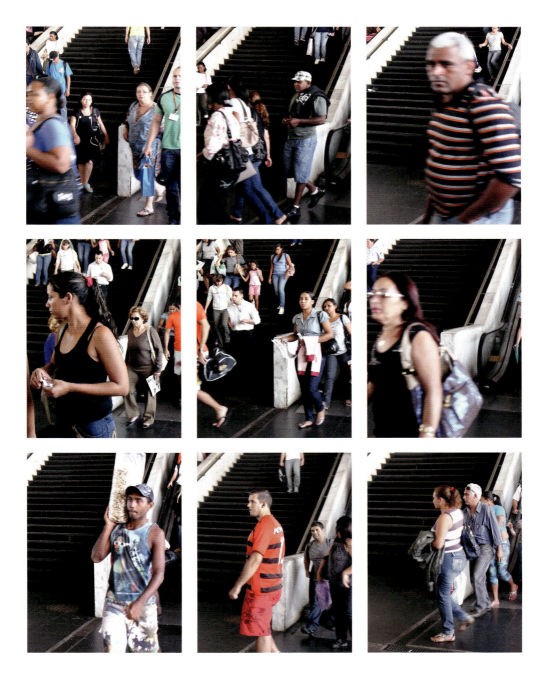

Escalator sequence: Brasília (2010)

The project is inspired by the Brazilian anthropologist Darcy Riberiro. In his book *O Povo Brasileiro* Riberiro claims that the Brazilian people represent a novel kind of hybrid ethnicity resulting from the Portuguese invaders mixing with indigenous peoples and African slaves, as well as the subsequent "Brazilianisation" of European, Asian, and Arab immigrants during the nineteenth and twentieth centuries. Merging from the beginning, these different ethnic matrices have dissolved into a new kind of syncretic culture. This series of 18 photographs, taken over thirty seconds at the end of an elevator in the central bus station of Brasília, shows the composite character of Brazilian society.

The Games are open (2010)

In the summer of 2010, following the Olympic Vancouver Winter Games, the artist team of Folke Köbberling and Martin Kaltwasser created a sculpture from materials salvaged from the Athletes' Village on nearby interim lands awaiting future development. Taking the form of a larger-than-life bulldozer, a machine usually associated with fast and drastic change, the wheat board construction was intentionally made from materials that would slowly break down when exposed to the weather and the passage of time. The project presents a kind of decay in the face of rapid and seemingly unstoppable urban change.

Laura Oldfield Ford

Laura Oldfield Ford's drawings, mainly from London but also featuring other British cites, combine seemingly disparate elements into a form of collage as cultural critique. There is a particular emphasis on places or communities that have been cut adrift or face erasure though processes of urban regeneration and speculative development.

Lara Almarcegui

1 An empty terrain in the Dan-
shui River, Taipei (2008)

2 To open a wasteland,
Brussels (2000)

3

4

3 A Guide to the Wastelands of the Lea Valley. Twelve empty spaces await the London Olympics (Barbican Gallery 2009)

4 A wasteland in Rotterdam port (2003–2018)

All photographs by Lara Almarcegui

4

PLACES AND SPACES

URBAN COMPLEXITY: AN INSTANCE

AbdouMaliq Simone

Fifteen years ago, Pademangan Timur in North Jakarta was cleared out, its 10,000 residents evicted, no matter the documents in their possession. If you were to look across North Jakarta's vast patchwork of tens of thousands of mostly single-household pavilions from the elevated ringroad, the district would be indiscernible. There are miles of tightly compacted tin roofs, roads bearing everything, and a fundamental ambiguity among efficacy, decay, repair, dissolution, work, residence, downward and upward trajectories. Situated along the intersection of two major thoroughfares, the district was considered prime land for the insatiable appetite of the presidential family, but then the revolt of 1998 came along and these aspirations were put to rest. For five years, the area lay fallow and then some urban farmers started to grow rice, and soon after, the "resurrection" of the district began with mostly a new generation of settlers.

Whenever a district seems to put itself together from scratch, a range of strategic calculations have to be made, possible scenarios played out, and a certain resilience deployed in order to adapt to incessant contingencies. Specific manoeuvres generate unanticipated effects, and anticipation, itself a necessary practice of inhabitation, risks mirroring self-fulfilling prophecies. As nascent inhabitants have no recourse to legal frameworks they continuously have to hedge their bets. The pay-off for the risk of settling in a place where theoretically one could be evicted at any time is the area's locational advantage—close to work, transportation, and markets. As residency in cities like Jakarta usually entails selling something in addition to whatever jobs the household does, it is advantageous to be close to already settled areas and transportation routes; this is why some settlers will initially instantiate themselves at the area's access points. This, however, makes the emerging settlement visible—not only to the authorities—but to a wide range of other potential inhabitants whose incoming might overwhelm the possibility of a more gradual and ordered occupation. As a result, some initial residents may choose to stake their claims further in, also anticipating a more centralised, and thus more secure and commercially dominant position, once the area grows.

Then there are considerations as to how much territory a household will actually claim. On the one hand, a sizeable chunk of land could be subdivided into various plots and eventually sold off to support the household. Alternately, land could be reserved for relatives or associates thus guaranteeing a measure of security in the composition of neighbours. But without legal title, any claim ultimately has to be backed up with the capacity to defend it by various means of persuasion—all of which are labour intensive and can actually provoke displays of greater force by others, thus weakening a household's long-term bargaining power. Then there is the question as to whether a household wants to surround itself with relatives. Even as they provide almost ready-made networks of support and cheap labour, they also entail obligations and reciprocities that are often more efficiently distributed across diverse spaces rather than in tightly wound contiguous relationships. The resourcefulness of potential neighbours rests not only in their capacity to reiterate shared values and coexist with a minimum of negotiation over everyday management procedures but in the various networks, information, and positions they bring with them. In districts where people are usually always on the hunt for various opportunities to get ahead, households need highly differentiated channels of access to the wider city. As such, common familial bonds and ethnicity are the driving factors behind the initial composition of "neighbourhoods" within Pademangan Timur, but only to a point.

The everyday toing and froing of residents across the expanse of the space, propel efforts of the initial residents to work out lines of convergence among these clusters—establishing pathways, and designating "representatives" to conduct various transactions, such as the provision of water, power, and sanitation. This rehearsal of articulation thus provides some initial structuring as the area "fills in" further with new inhabitants. Some reference to common background in the composition of these initial clusters also provides a basis for an initial enclosure or folding in, as groups of households demarcate a zone of familiarity, a sense that this is the constellation that will be relevant to manage on a day-to-day basis. But once established and plots subdivided, a newer generation of residents usually will not share that common reference, providing the sense of differentiation for the "neighbourhood."

Once land starts being marketised there is the question about the price and to whom land is to be sold. Once an area starts being developed, no matter how illegal the process may be, there are always those interested in quick profit-taking and have the cash to start buying up plots put up for sale by the various initial claimants, consolidating them, and then availing them to criminal networks who need temporary spaces for various activities, in turn drawing unwanted attention to the district and making vulnerable the residencies of the majority. Widely divergent prices in plot sales also jeopardise emerging calibrations among inhabitants that are needed in order to consolidate a working sense of unified purpose that will be required in order to better secure the area and preclude debilitating internal conflicts and manipulations by outsiders. Marketising land not only secures income for households but attempts to regulate the densification necessary in order to attain lower costs for service provision. Even though Pademangan Timur is an "illegal" settlement, water and power companies will provide bulk service to such areas as long as consumption covers the requisite costs. Even though many households may live off unofficial attachments to the provision grids, a certain density of consumers is needed in order to access water and power at an affordable price.

Given the legal status of the area, how much then do households invest in it? While most Jakarta residents will continue to build incrementally over time with progressive improvements to conditions, the inhabitants of Pademangan Timur potentially could lose everything at any given time. On the other hand, there is the inclination to establish "facts on the ground"—where the less provisional an area looks, the more difficult it may be for authorities to move against it, especially if any subsequent negotiations around eviction entail formulas for compensation. Then there are considerations as to the extent to which the area attempts to perform itself as a "regular" district, with its devices of governance and accountability—thus mirroring, in this instance, the formal districts of Pademangan and Sunter next door. Alternately, its long-term survival is enhanced by providing space for powerful actors in these neighbouring districts to do things they otherwise would not do within their districts.

What, then, on the surface may look to be a fairly homogenous, simply ordered area of now some 2,000 households, is a surface full of granular textures, varied exposures and folds, intersecting and not always reconcilable calculations that continuously push residents in provisional adjustments in this complex urban world.

ASSEMBLING MODERNITIES: CONCRETE IMAGINATIONS IN BUENOS AIRES

Leandro Minuchin

"The building under construction produces in our spirits a sense of amazement that cannot be compared with any other human industrial creation … the impressive sight of metallic skeletons; the extraordinary forms made out of reinforced concrete, and masonries filling the frame's empty flanks … Construction is the most visible way through which progress materialises." This is the opening paragraph from the first issue of the journal *Nuestra Arquitectura*, published in August 1929. It reflects the perception of architects and engineers, absorbed by the promises and imagery of a technological and constructive revolution that was, from the beginning of the 1920s, transforming the urban fabric of Buenos Aires.[1] In the copious pages of specialised journals that disseminated the virtues of novel materials and depicted the spectacle of cranes colonising the urban skyline, construction, modernity, and progress were often uncritically entangled as indistinguishable components of a technical and scientific manifestation destined to dismantle the remains of an inherited colonial grid.

For part of the emergent *porteño* technical elite, often young professionals influenced by European avant-gardes and modernist experiments, construction was a means to attend—and ultimately overcome—the pressing social disparities and necessities of a cosmopolitan metropolis, traversed by the intricacies and tensions caused by immigration, commercial expansion, and the growing demands of the urban middle class. For the advocates of new architecture, the transformation of the city's material fabric was presented as a mechanism, not only to dream and plan the city's possible futures, but also to reinstate a lost sense of urban order.

However, construction sites and the building fever that multiplied them across the city not only served to consolidate and empower a technical vision that associated the unfolding of the process of modernisation with the rational alteration of the city's material landscape. It also prompted the emergence of a contrasting material sensibility that used the proliferation of building sites and the growing speculative drive steering the construction industry, to reflect a side of Buenos Aires those glorifying the endless "emergence of the new" often overlooked. Sceptical architects and insightful urban essayists mobilised the city's changing material conditions to depict modernity's corrosive and inconclusive nature. For writers like Ezequiel Martínez Estrada and Roberto Arlt, the interest in examining the proliferation of construction sites and unfinished buildings, lay not in registering the material

1

1 Horacio Coppola. Avenida del trabajo, Buenos Aires (1936). Source: Coppola + Zuviría: Buenos Aires. Pictures by Horacio Coppola and Facundo Zuviría, texts by Adrián Gorelik. Published in Buenos Aires by *Ediciones Larivière*.

2

signs of expansive public or private investments, but in exposing the conflictive reality of a novel material landscape they viewed as being inherent to the process of modernisation: the ghostly emergence of disconnected networks, the precarious transitory architectures of a growing periphery, and the changing textures of industrial communities trying to penetrate the networks of survivability in the metropolis.[2] The half-built structures and the improvised shelters populating the outskirts of the city, stood as a material repertoire to illustrate the silent and disruptive forces driving the process of transformation. For those explorers of the metropolitan condition, the moment of construction, with its ensemble of knowledges, materials, and multiple forms of solidarities and associations, represented an entry point into an urban world dominated by the sudden appearance of social types that contrasted with the rational and orderly depictions attached to modernity's technical dreams. In Arlt's novels and contributions to *El Mundo* newspaper, Buenos Aires—assembled as a complex set of mechanical and chemical processes—is occupied by urban vagabonds, failed inventors strolling through the hectic night consumed by melancholy and temporary unemployment and part-time revolutionaries dreaming of a technological insurgency.[3]

Despite their opposing interpretations of the constructive transformation altering the fabric of the city, these two contrasting sensibilities found in the constellation of novel building materials a tool and a means to articulate their respective descriptions and projections for

2 Horacio Coppola. Calle
Saavedra, Buenos Aires (1936)
Source: Coppola + Zuviría:
Buenos Aires. Pictures by

Horacio Coppola and Facundo
Zuviría, texts by Adrián Gorelik.
Published in Buenos Aires by
Ediciones Larivière.

Buenos Aires. Structural to their consolidation, was the multiplication of concrete structures across the city's landscape and the increased utilisation of cement. During the 1930s, nationalist policies sponsored a fragile process of industrialisation. Different governments protected and encouraged cement production, enabling Argentina to become virtually self-sufficient, with eleven Portland cement plants by 1938.[4] The state configured and displayed its new role and presence through the manipulation of cement and impressive concrete inscriptions. In Buenos Aires, the national government was involved in building the new grain elevators; colossal structures, which together with the 9th of July Avenue and its futuristic underground parking, defined what engineers referred to as a "new modern monumentality."[5] The state also embarked on the construction of the General Paz ring road: a concrete belt that strengthened the cultural and economic barriers separating the capital from its expanding metropolitan fringes.

This association of concrete with the consecration of circulation and order as archetypical modern ideals, was fuelled by CIAM-inspired architectural imaginations.[6] Le Corbusier himself, when projecting the future Buenos Aires, dreamt of an intricate network of elevated urban highways. The master plan, finally published in 1947, contained the layout for a complex distribution of concrete surfaces crafted to re-engineer the modes of linking the body with the city. For Le Corbusier, the combination of elevated thoroughfares and a sequence of vast concrete columns would help to liberate the city's congested grid and secure the inscription of a new urban logic of circulation.[7]

But concrete not only served to project state-led visions of modernisation or assemble rationalist programmes for urban transformation. For architects and urban critics concerned with the social implications of the rapid process of urbanisation, concrete emerged as an accurate aesthetic instrument to describe a metropolis in transition. It reflected, through its multiple infrastructural applications, modernity's limits and shortfalls in universalising the virtues of technology, reform, and progress. In the work of Martínez Estrada, the unfolding of the city's ring road, rather than revealing modernity's transformative and emancipatory potentials, showcased the distance separating the visions of a planned and regularised urban setting with the reality of changing and precarious architectures piling up on the fringes of the metropolis; an ephemeral material landscape of heterogeneous elements where settlers strive to negotiate their access to "the modern world."[8] For the author of *X-Ray of the Pampa* and other explorers of the material conditions of Buenos Aires, concrete was not only associated with cracks in the technical and bureaucratic visions of modernity. It also served to assert the presence, visibility, and projection of alternative urban experiences. In his Marxist analysis of the material state of Buenos Aires, Russian-born architect Wladimiro Acosta uses concrete to assemble a revolutionary urban transformation. In his book *Vivienda y Ciudad*, Acosta proposes a complete dismantling of the city's oppressive grid and the construction of a lineal city made out of imposing "integral building blocks" that would penetrate and meander through the pampas.[9]

The contrasting imaginations surrounding the use and appropriation of cement, expose the multiple ideals of modernity circulating in a metropolis caught in a rapid process of transformation. In modern Buenos Aires, concrete allows for the articulation of different urban political visions: from the emancipatory ideals associated with early experimentations to the disfigured modernity of a military rule that sought in the construction of a Corbusian network of urban highways, the means to discipline and administer the forms of circulation in the metropolis. Novel materials play a structural role, not only in the assembling of alternative and futuristic urban projects, but also in the consolidation of different forms of social associations. Tracing and recuperating the ways in which different architects, engineers, and urban critics use and manipulate the city's material reality reveals the tension between modernising idealists and the critical voices depicting the marginal and peripheral figures that struggle to assemble their distinct material insertion into the modern metropolis. By exploring alterations in the practice of construction and the materials that serve to structure and project different modes of appearing in the city, we open up the possibility of crafting an alternative urban history: one that focuses on socio-material entanglements to unveil the assembling of different political imaginations.

Endnotes

1 J. Perla, "La edificación de Buenos Aires," in *La Ingeniería* (1936), 242.

2 See R. Arlt, *Obra completa* (Buenos Aires: Planeta-Carlos Lohlé, 1991); E. Martínez Estrada, *La Cabeza de Goliat* (Madrid: Ediciones Castilla, 1970).

3 R. Arlt, *Los siete locos* (Buenos Aires: Losada, 1958).

4 E. Díaz Molano and P. Cristia, "Hacia la solución integral del problema del cemento portland," in *Revista Construcciones*, 89 (1952), 146–151.

5 F. Zamboni, "Obras de la Avenida 9 de Julio," in *La Ingeniería*, (1937), 837–859.

6 The *Congrès internationaux d'architecture modern* (International Congress of Modern Architecture) funded in 1928. For a history of the influence of the International style in Buenos Aires see, J. Liernur and P. Pschepiurca, *La red austral: Obras y Proyectos de Le Corbusier y sus discípulos en la Argentina (1924–1965)* (Buenos Aires: Prometeo, 2008).

7 Le Corbusier, "Plan Director de Buenos Aires," in *La Arquitectura de Hoy* 1 (1947), 1–65.

8 E. Martínez Estrada, *Radiografía de la Pampa* (Buenos Aires: Losada, 2001).

9 W. Acosta, *Vivienda y Ciudad* (Buenos Aires: Anaconda, 1947); and "El City-Block integral: un estudio de urbanismo práctico," in *Nuestra Arquitectura* Agosto (1931), 20–27.

LAGOS: CITY OF CONCRETE

Giles Omezi

"… *Elvis did not pay too much attention to the cars that in spite of their speed wove between each other like careful threads of a tapestry. The motorways were the only means of getting across the series of towns that made up Lagos. Intent on reaching their destinations, pedestrians dodged between the speeding vehicles as they crossed the wide motorways. It was dangerous, and every day at least ten people were killed trying to cross the road. If they didn't die when the first car hit them, subsequent cars finished the job. The curious thing, though was that there were hundreds of overhead pedestrian bridges, but people ignored them. Some even walked up to the bridges and then crossed underneath them.*" [1]

Lagos sits on topography dominated by ubiquitous marshlands and a vast lagoon draining several rivers north of the city. It thus presents the road engineer with the dilemma of how to stitch this rapidly expanding city together to aid movement between its constituent parts over such challenging terrain. Over twenty-five years, specifically between 1967 and 1992, the combined efforts of the Federal Government and Lagos State roped the city together using a system of fast expressways, which were viewed as the solution to the traffic problem that was becoming apparent as a major issue as far back as the late 1950s. At this point, the population of the city hovered just below the million mark, today estimates put it at close to eighteen million people. [2]

The city's expressway system consists of three north-south axial roads that connect the island of Lagos with the mainland of Lagos and sets up a language that fuses a vocabulary of multiple lanes, cloverleaf interchanges, and bridges to aid mobility of the car. The most westerly arterial road, known as the Western Avenue System begins at the western tip of Lagos Island as the Eko Bridge, rising over the swamps of Ijora and Iganmu, through the residential district of Surulere and heads off north. After a kink in its alignment, it passes through

Mushin becoming the ten-lane Agege Motor Road, which leads eventually to the old town of Abeokuta north of Lagos. The next arterial is the Ikorodu Road, which as a continuation of the Carter Bridge and Murtala Mohamed Way, cuts through the older districts on the mainland and beyond on its way to Ikorodu and the Ijebu towns north of the Lagos Lagoon. The last of these arterial roads is the Third Mainland Bridge, which floats over the Lagos Lagoon detached from the its western bank. Described as the longest bridge in Africa at twelve kilometres, the Third Mainland Bridge enables the affluent residents of the districts of Ikoyi and Victoria Island to bypass much of Lagos as they head north via Ibadan and Ilorin, or to the ancient city of Benin, and the merchant cities beyond the River Niger to the east. At the foot of Lagos, a western corridor of development spawned by the Badagry Expressway takes traffic to the border town of Seme. This horizontal band of city hemmed in by marshlands and creeks is balanced by the Lekki Expressway system east of Victoria Island, which has similarly fuelled a corridor of linear developments comprised mainly of large residential estates. The latter road opens up the reclaimed sandbar of the Lekki peninsula arching up over a relatively short span bridge over the eastern reaches of the lagoon at Epe to complete a ring road of sorts around the Lagos Lagoon. The former straddles the creek system leading to the old slaving port of Badagry and Porto Novo in Benin Republic vividly rendered in *The Water House*, Antonio Olinto's novel on nineteenth- and twentieth-century Lagos.

Two ring-road systems traverse the east-west and north-south roads; the Apapa Oworonshoki looping westwards from a spur off the Third Mainland Bridge, intersecting Ikorodu Road, Agege Motor Road, Badagry Expressway, terminating at the port complex in Apapa. Here, the ring road seems caught in decades of indecision on the best way to bridge the gap between the Quays at Apapa and the ghosts of the old wharves along Marina Street on Lagos Island. The unbuilt city plans hesitantly pondered this gap, proposing a tunnel in one iteration and bridges at different locations to complete the ring. A German-built inner ring road system encircles the island in a necklace of fast, elevated, concrete road sections, interrupted by complex interchanges that appear to have been configured to connect strategic destinations when Lagos still held sway as the federal capital. Short bursts of speed are interrupted by sweeping intersection after intersection, as the road is elevated above the corrugated asbestos roofscape of old colonial offices and the tropical patina on the modernist buildings of the post-colonial state. The destinations are the old Federal Secretariat, the short spurs leading into Ikoyi Road and the old seat of government, Dodan Barracks, tucked behind Obalende, the commercial district of Lagos Island, and the leafy residential areas of Ikoyi. The latter area, a layout planned on Garden City principles, quietly morphed in description from an exclusive *European Reservation Area* to a post-independence *Government Reservation Area*. The exclusivity maintained in classic Fanonesque terms for the new ruling elite or as Fanon puts it "the petit bourgeoisie."

The inner-ring-road system—built in the 1970s to relieve traffic—obstructs and obliterates the once picturesque promenade of Marina Street, which was reconfigured as the northern edge of a vast car park. This feat was achieved by sand filling the waters on the northern bank of Lagos Harbour adjacent to the old colonial era trading houses and wharves. The reclaimed land acts as a support platform for the elevated expressway and slip roads below, which now define the new coastline of Lagos Island before turning north over the Macgregor Canal to complete the fast expressway ring. The city of Lagos pushes up hard against this system of expressways, onto which it spills its rapidly growing population and disengages from it when forced to—either by the marshlands yet to be reclaimed, or by the large expanses of water. Consequently, the road engineers' response to the dual challenge of the topography and mobility needs of Lagos has created a typology of urban spaces: static intersections, appropriated spaces beneath bridges and a system of undulating linear expressways; the latter best experienced before the weekly Sunday morning church service traffic.

The expressways of Lagos order this city, providing a movement system that has dictated the urban footprint of the city since independence in 1960. The ordering is clear in the instance of the Agege Motor Road/Western Avenue, which in mimicking the colonial railway alignment up to the tough neighbourhood of Mushin rises to avoid the Ojuelegba junction, skirting the National Stadium to the east, and climaxes at the intersection where the relic of the National Theatre nestles, as the expressway forks in a dizzying spaghetti of complex elevated intersections, ramps, and roundabouts leading to the Apapa Port and Eko Bridge.

1

1 Vehicles at a standstill on the Carter Bridge in Lagos as Federal troops check identities (25 September 1967).

Source: Keystone/Getty Images.

The marshlands of Ijora and Iganmu are avoided by the road system, despite holding the centre of national culture, built at the height of the petro dollar boom of the 1970s: the National Theatre. The building itself is a curious mimesis of the Palace of Culture and sports in Varna, Bulgaria, which somehow in its appropriated guise served to reinforce the projection of Nigerian nationalist aspirations. Concrete spokes radiating out skyward and suggestively converging the energies of the black world into its womb as the centrepiece of the 1977 Second Festival of Black Arts and Culture commonly referred to as FESTAC 77. The National Theatre's collision with the expressway system created an ambiguous space that combined high culture, industrial detritus and marshlands enclosed somewhat by the slender columns of the elevated expressways. The two-speed city shaped by concrete is present at its most extreme here. The German-engineered bridge piers and road deck shade an assortment of commercial activity in a somewhat unorthodox landscape of appropriation, which is as much a metaphor for the polarised economic realities as the juxtaposition of the rulers' will against that of the ruled, rural space versus urban space, tradition versus modernity. These binaries unwittingly burden Lagos with a complexity often read superficially as simply chaotic, rather than a work in progress where the aspired modernity of post-colonial Nigeria is being resolved and reworked.

The iconography of the concrete expressway underscores Nigeria's modern aspirations forged by the post-colonial state. The expressway network was placed at the core of a nationalist modernisation project that sought to incorporate and subsume space at the scale of the city, nation, and the continent, all requiring "integration" into the sphere of Nigerian Federal military power.[3] The quasi-militaristic undertones of fast armoured mobility that the expressway recalls—tested for instance during the brutal quelling of the 1990 coup that saw armour pouring out of the Ikeja Cantonment on the mainland and racing down Ikorodu Road towards Lagos Island to relieve a besieged Dodan Barracks.[4] The ownership by the military of the two key five-year development plans from which these roads were built makes it difficult to regard the Third Mainland Bridge simply as a bypass road, and it is tempting to speculate more cynically perhaps from beneath the shadow of the military junta planning for the avoidance of military ambush. The road engineers detached this elevated expressway completely from the city thereby establishing a corridor for a high-speed sprint (traffic permitting) from the leafy suburb of Ikoyi to the safety of the airport in Ikeja in the event of the inevitable mutiny of junior officers.

The static intersections of the city run contrary to their intended purposes, that of permitting free traffic flow; instead, the congealed mass of vehicles provide the footfall for trade and commercial activity and reconfigure the sense of the city with the emergence of new destinations yelled out by the conductors from the ubiquitous Danfo and Molue buses: "Oshodi, Oshodi !!!" "… Ojuelegba, Ojuelegba …!!!" The modernist aspirations evoked in the narrative of the Otto Koenigsberger led government planning team have been tested and reinterpreted; the pristine modernist imagery of orderly workers and vehicles rendering the space of this newly independent nation rudely disrupted by its people. His words echo from the text of the 1964 study: "This road is a super expressway, and should be flanked on both sides by parallel access or service roads, bicycle tracks, and pedestrian walks. Where crossing is necessary, the motorway can be elevated or on the mainland where elevation permits it, depressed below the street level with service roads crossing over it. Where it is on the same level as access roads, it should be fenced off; for a motorway is designed for a speed of 50 to 60 mph or even higher."[5] They are largely ignored by the citizens of Lagos, who view the congealed traffic on the surface of the road system as fertile ground for the trading activities that have proliferated across the city.

The concrete expressways of Lagos heralded the arrival of the post-colonial Nigerian state. This transition is apparent in the texture of urban literature on Lagos from the 1960s and 1980s: Cyprian Ekwensi's classic novel, *Jagua Nana*, evokes a quaint colonial town with the sounds of trains being shunted in the now derelict yards of Ebutte Metta, truncheon-wielding police constables, and shopping days to Kingsway on the Marina, set against the hard grit of concrete post-oil-boom Lagos sketched by Ben Okri of Molue buses falling off bridges into the lagoon; or the slum settlement of Bridge City under a bridge from Chris Abani's *Graceland*, set in Lagos during the early 1980s.

The concrete of Lagos defines its aspirations but ultimately works as the substrate for the city population to appropriate and redefine notions of modernity as crafted by the ruling elite of the early post-colonial state. The city is being rediscovered and revealed, however, as the Lagos state administration reasserts its claim to the public realm through interventions of landscape beautification for "slack spaces" around the static nodes of the expressway system. As the Nigerian state seeks to restate its claim to relevance for its citizenry, led by the current administration of Babatunde Fashola, the city has become the laboratory for a series of public-private partnership initiatives established in the last decade to deliver urban services such as transport, utilities, and waste management. Thus, the city is emerging as the site where the citizen is being re-engaged, as municipal authorities seek to regain their trust and perhaps instil wider aspirations to make Lagos the most dynamic megacity in sub-Saharan Africa.

Endnotes

1 Chris Abani, *Graceland* (New York: Picador, 2004).
2 The Lagos State Government disputed the Federal Government 2007 census population figures of just over nine million, preferring to use their own estimates of seventeen million for planning purposes.
3 The post-civil-war military government increased control of highways under direct federal control from just over 5,000 kilometres to close to 25,000 kilometres in the mid-1970s, and set out planning and building a network to better integrate the country. This action was a direct consequence of the fragmenting of the administrative units from four semi-autonomous regions in 1966 to twelve states in 1967.

The purpose of state creation was to prevent any one single unit from dominating the centre. See Allison Ayida, *The Nigerian Revolution*, and F. Okunnu, *In Service of the Nation*.
4 Omoigui n.d.
5 Otto Koenigsberger, Charles Abrams, Susumu Kobe, Maurice Shapiro, and Michael Wheeler, *Metropolitan Lagos* (New York: United Nations Technical Assistance Programme, 1964). See also Max Siollun, *Oil, Politics and Violence: Nigeria's Military Coup Culture 1966–1976* (New York: Algora Publishing, 2009).

VERTICAL URBANISM: FLYOVERS AND SKYWALKS IN MUMBAI

Andrew Harris

1

1   Bandra East skywalk,
Mumbai (2009)
Source: Photo by Andrew
Harris

The critical, architectural, and popular imaginations of contemporary urbanisation have rarely featured flyovers and skywalks in Mumbai.[1] This is because they are relatively new: most flyovers (elevated road highways) were built in Mumbai after 1998, while the first sky-walk (elevated pedestrian walkway) only opened in 2008. It is also because they are not particularly iconic. Flyovers in Mumbai are, with some important exceptions, not expressways; they are perhaps better described as "hop-overs" across one or sometimes two road junctions, while skywalks are extensions of railway footbridges along roads leading to station entrances. They are largely not from the *Big, Bigger, Biggest* school of infrastructural development beloved by the *National Geographic* television channel. Nor do they tend to offer a distinctive design or striking vista, such as the new Bandra-Worli Sealink in Mumbai, which was featured on the cover of the June 2011 edition of *Wallpaper* magazine. This seeming lack of spectacle and architectural merit means flyovers and skywalks in Mumbai are treated more as technocratic structures and as the preserve of engineers and transport consultants. Yet, elevated highways and walkways have often played a prominent role in cultural and architectural visions of the modern city. The vertical separation of cars and people was a key facet of the influential 1963 *Traffic in Towns* report in the UK, the "Streets in the Sky" brutalist architecture of 1960s and 1970s Britain, and the futuristic urban landscapes of Fritz Lang's 1927 film *Metropolis*.[2] However, this emphasis on elevation in urban transport planning has acquired an increasingly historic veneer in many Western cities. A proposed box grid of urban motorways in London was abandoned in 1973, expressways in central Boston in the US have been dismantled and replaced by tunnels in a project known as the "Big Dig," while several raised walkways known as "highwalks" in the City of London have been removed over the last ten years.[3] Contrary to recent developments in Mumbai, pedestrianisation, public transport, and car management schemes seem more *de rigueur* in contemporary transport thinking than sending people skywards.

The construction of elevated highways has also played a central role in analyses of the dramatic and often brutal restructuring of modern cities, a process that Marshall Berman identifies as a process of "urbicide." From the demolition and displacement of neighbourhoods in New York through the building of the Cross-Bronx Expressway in the 1950s and 1960s to socio-spatial divisions inscribed by Paris's *Périphérique* and the vertical geopolitics of Israeli roads over settlements in occupied Palestine, urban highways have often loomed large in stories of urban creative destruction and political control.[4] In contrast, the construction of flyovers and skywalks in Mumbai has rarely led to large-scale processes of eviction. They have generally been built directly over existing roads, while their construction can be understood as being shaped by the messy realities of Indian democratic politics rather than notions of a new military urbanism.[5]

Yet despite the comparatively mundane and seemingly "belated" architectural and political characteristics of flyovers and skywalks in Mumbai, investigating their planning, construction, and maintenance can help identify several interrelated dimensions to the dynamics of

2

contemporary urbanisation in mega-cities of the global South. Firstly, flyovers and skywalks can be understood as a key component in aspirations of forging Mumbai as a global city by emphasising efficiency, predictability and linearity over the fluid choreography and il-legibility of Mumbai's urban spaces.[6] With almost seventy flyovers and skywalks built since 1998 across a sprawling Mumbai metropolitan region, these structures have acted to stitch together and connect a new polycentric landscape of suburban business districts, shopping malls, and residential colonies. These projects have assembled materials, ideas, techniques and people not only from across the region but further afield; from Singaporean master plans to Canadian transport consultants and Italian piling rigs. Mumbai's "world-class" ambitions and status have been shaped as much through urban infrastructure as through financial services, cultural industries, and slum rehabilitation.

Secondly, flyover and skywalks in Mumbai have played a significant performative role in the city's politics, challenging understandings of urban infrastructure as increasingly hidden and politically inert.[7] Many politicians have been keen proponents and lobbyists for these schemes. The Shiv Sena-BJP coalition, who won power in Maharashtra for the first time in 1995, instigated what was dubbed the "55 flyover" project. The Minister of Public Works responsible, Nitin Gadkari, currently national President of the BJP, became labelled in the

2   Flyover on Santa Cruz Chembur link road, Mumbai (2009) Source: Photo by Andrew Harris

media as "Mr Flyover." The flurry of skywalk construction across the metropolitan region since 2008 has similarly been closely associated with the Indian Congress Party. There are several reasons politicians have displayed this keen enthusiasm for flyovers and skywalks. It may stem from how their main experience of the city tends to be from chauffeur-driven car windows driving through congested roads to the State Parliament building, *Mantralaya*, at the southern tip of Mumbai's main peninsular. Flyover and skywalks are also capital-intensive ventures, and allegations have been made about the lack of transparency in their planning, tendering, and construction.[8] But politicians also support these projects due to their highly visible presence in the city and close association with ideals of free-flowing, modern urbanism. As symbols of "take off" developmentalism, flyovers and skywalks are much more electorally persuasive than more cost effective but largely invisible traffic management schemes, and train-line widening projects that often involve significant displacement of residential communities.

Thirdly, the construction and maintenance of flyovers and skywalks is a clear example of new three-dimensional relations of power in a city such as Mumbai. Most notably, only the approximately 8.5 per cent of Mumbai's population with access to private vehicles are able to use flyovers, as access to pedestrians, bicycles, pushcarts, and buses is prohibited.[9] Skywalks are seemingly more accessible (at least to those able to climb stairs) but activities such as hawking are often forbidden or closely regulated, and their construction has allowed a greater number of vehicles to use the roads and pavements below. Compared to the frequently shoddy exteriors of Mumbai's rent-controlled buildings, and the bumpy surfaces of non-arterial roads, flyovers and skywalks can be understood, to use Stephen Graham's phrase, as "premium network spaces."[10] They not only favour car-owning classes but, unlike many structures in the city, are regularly cleaned and repaired. Even the residual spaces underneath flyovers have become increasingly shut off through barriers, security guards, and carefully landscaped gardens. Flyover and skywalk projects in Mumbai are not only specific examples of "splintering urbanism" but act to mark out and spatialise categories of informal/formal and citizen/non-citizen, creating both a literal and metaphorical underclass.

The recent construction of flyovers and skywalks in Mumbai demonstrates how the appeal of elevated transport projects remains undiminished. Within the context of a rapidly growing city region, flyovers and skywalks have offered a prime vehicle for the urban elite not only to assert Mumbai's global status but to demonstrate their role in attempts at making Mumbai "world class." Yet the financing, regulation, and maintenance of these car-centric structures have largely acted to reinforce social inequalities and produce new vertical relations of power. Rather than being viewed as technocratic solutions to increased urban congestion, flyovers and skywalks in Mumbai need to be conceived as clear indicators and charismatic components of a new three-dimensional fracturing of urban space.

Endnotes

1 This essay draws from a research project entitled "Vertical urbanism: geographies of the Mumbai Flyover" funded by the Economic and Social Research Council. For further flyover and skywalk material from Mumbai please visit www.verticalurbanism.com

2 See *Traffic in towns: a study of the long term problems of traffic in urban areas* (1963), reports of the Steering Group and Working Group appointed by the UK Minister of Transport; Reyner Banham, *The new brutalism: ethic or aesthetic?* (London: Architectural Press, 1966); Susan Robertson, "Visions of urban mobility: the Westway, London, England," in *Cultural Geographies* 14/1 (2007), 74–91; Eugene Hénard, *The cities of the future*. Royal Institute of British Architects, Town Planning Conference London, 10–15 October 1910, Transactions (RIBA, 1911), 345–367.

3 See Peter Hall, "London's motorways," in *Great Planning Disasters* (Harmondsworth: Penguin, 1981); Bob Stanley, "Taking a walk in the clouds," *The Times*, 24 August 2004.

4 See Marshall Berman, *All That Is Solid Melts into Air: The Experience of Modernity* (London: Verso, 1983); Kristin Ross (1995) *Fast cars, clean bodies: decolonization and the reordering of French culture* (London: MIT Press, 1995);

Eyal Weizman *Hollow land: Israel's architecture of occupation*. (London: Verso, 2007).

5 Stephen Graham, *Cities Under Siege: The New Military Urbanism* (London: Verso, 2010).

6 Nikhil Anand, "Disconnecting experience: making world-class roads in Mumbai," in *Economic and Political Weekly* 41/31 (2006), 3422–3429.

7 Maria Kaika and Erik Swyngedouw, "Fetishizing the modern city: the phantasmagoria of urban technological networks," in *International Journal of Urban and Regional Research*, 24/1 (2000), 120–138.

8 Darryl D'Monte, "Driving to nowhere," *The Hindu*, 12 August 2001.

9 MMRDA Basic Transport and Communications Statistics for Mumbai Metropolitan Region, August 2008.

10 Stephen Graham, "Constructing premium network spaces: reflections on infrastructure networks and contemporary urban development," in *International Journal of Urban and Regional Research* 24/1 (2000), 183–200.

CHENNAI AS "CUT-OUT" CITY

Pushpa Arabindoo

In a context where Mumbai and Delhi provide much of the empirical fodder for contemporary urban development discourses in metropolitan India, it is not often that southern counterparts such as Chennai, Bangalore, or Hyderabad make the headlines. It was thus intriguing when, in April 2008, a considerable amount of buzz was generated around a minute-and-a-half commercial, *A day in the life of Chennai,* released as part of a vast multimedia campaign to promote the Chennai launch of India's oldest and largest circulating English daily *The Times of India.*[1] Over the years, the Mumbai-based national newspaper had made forays with local editions into several Indian cities, but had stayed clear of Chennai, purportedly due to this Tamil/Dravidian city's rather conservative, orthodox image. The reorganisation of Indian states along linguistic identities in the 1950s had resulted in the reinscription of metropolitan cities such as Mumbai, Chennai and Kolkata with regional identities mainly framed by the local language—Marathi for Mumbai, Tamil for Chennai, and Bengali for Kolkata. In Chennai, this was further enhanced by the strong force of Dravidian politics, which emphasised a distinctive ethno-linguistic Tamil cultural subnationalism.[2]

Thus, when *The Times of India* decided to make a late entry into the Dravidian state, its marketing strategy recognised the need to highlight its understanding of the local culture to capture Chennai's citizens as consumers. Accordingly, the soundtrack was set to an addictive folk beat (popularly known as *kuthu*), and the title phrase *nakka mukka* was recovered from the underbelly of the city (primarily the slums) to prove that it can capture every aspect of the daily life of Chennai. Literally meaning tongue/nose, in colloquial dialect it is also an expression for letting your hair down and dancing like it is your last dance. It is not uncommon for Indian advertisements to look for populist references drawn from local cultural landscapes to build their lexical repertoire, and hence, it was not surprising when the song became an instant hit, turning into an anthem of sorts. The attention seemed well deserved when the commercial won several prestigious advertising awards including two golds at the Cannes Lions 2009, with juries highlighting the use of local culture in fresh and inspiring ways. The narrative of the advertisement is unmistakably strong as it singles out the key aspect of the city's quotidian life, a characteristic duality evident not just in its name Madras/Chennai, but also in its fascination for cinema and politics.[3] The film is conceptualised as a short satire on the life of a double-sided, giant "cut-out" character switching between the roles of an actor and politician, and navigating the ups and downs of cinema and politics through the course of one day in Chennai. This use of the icon of the cut-out is understandable given Chennai's informal claim as the cut-out capital of the world. Cut-outs emerged in the twentieth century as gigantic effigies hand-painted on plywood as part of political campaigns or outdoor advertisements (mainly promoting cinema), and evolved into an integral element of the cityscape.[4] However, even though the images in this film capture some of the essential elements of the city such as its exuberant fan clubs for movie stars and a politics dominated by endless rallies and effigy burning, they offer only a fragmented, and more worryingly, distorted peek into the city's urban kaleidoscope.

Advertisements that set up a dialogue with urban spaces do so in generally impressionistic terms taking only bits of the local landscape and placing them within a wider order of aestheticised intelligibility. Capturing Chennai's local frenzy through a rapidly cut, fragmented collage of shots, the selection of images are not meant to be extrapolated to the whole of the city but to create a specific visual representation of the city. At the same time, one cannot but question its understanding and portrayal of Chennai's spatiality. For, the urban route carved by the central cut-out character is confined mostly to stereotypical snapshots of the city. Commencing with *Kasimedu*, the quintessential fishing harbour in the northern part of the city, the cut-out as a rising movie star journeys down the landmark colonial trail from Esplanade (Parry's Corner) to Mount Road, switching sides (literally) into a politician whose fluctuating fortunes trigger chaos and violence on the streets, only to meet a mythical end in *the* public space of the city, Marina Beach, and is eventually exiled to peri-urban wilderness at the city's fringes. The visual shorthand employed in tracing this circulatory logic raises some anxieties about whether this is indeed Chennai. The unfolding scenes focus on particular kinds of spaces epitomising the local culture through which it can communicate with the citizens of the city. But somewhere this connection is not fully made as it ends up satirising rather than celebrating the local. A worrying aspect is the way the camera pans across a multitude of exchanges, each associating Chennai's public culture with the lifeline of the cut-out. In trying to suffuse a new urban consciousness, a specific kind of public is constituted in the process where hyper-real images present exaggerated tensions within this

1

realm. Marked by visible displays of chaos and disorder, there is a suggestion of a subaltern public sphere as elaborated by Nancy Fraser, which is clearly undermined through a stereotypical representation of a counter-public that is dominated by the irrationality of a violent crowd.[5]

More importantly, the populist commercial overlaps with a particularly bourgeois moment in the city when an officially sanctioned drive was launched to remove all "unauthorised" hoardings in the city. In the post-independence period, hand-painted plywood cut-outs had come to relay specific messages about film, politics, and religion—one that was specific to Dravidian urban culture.[6] Organising the city's spaces in less mundane and more spectacular ways, the surreal landscape of cut-outs served as makeshift mimicries of the real, integrating images of popular culture into the conventional paradigm of urban landscape. For years, Chennai's "urbanscape" was dominated by the text and images of cut-outs of all sizes, which rarely read coherently as text but nevertheless offered a fascinating commentary about the city. However, since the 1990s with the launch of neoliberalisation policies, a yearning for a bourgeois urbanism of orderly, regulated spaces has triggered an aversion to what is now considered not local culture but urban graffiti. Thus, located in the fuzzy boundaries of public/private spaces, this landscape involving a lucrative enterprise of rentals and taxes is condemned as an urban scourge that has recklessly mushroomed across the cityscape.[7] In 2008, coinciding with the release of *A day in the life of Chennai* was a Supreme Court verdict

1 Changing geography of cut-outs in Chennai (aerial view of Anna Flyover Junction) (2007)
Source: *Dinamalar*, Chennai

2

banning unauthorised hoardings in the city, after which more than half of the cut-outs in the city were promptly removed.

Anchored in the *Times of India* film is a phantasmic understanding of Chennai's socio-political geography, which brushes aside much of the emerging challenges associated with the Dravidian city's efforts to juggle the tensions of the local, the national, and the global. Instead, a rhetorical reimagination of the cityscape is produced where the interpretation of the local is mired in a parochial understanding of the city. Thus, at one level there is an urge to reject the advertisement's patronising fervour amidst a concern that more than stereotyping, these images stigmatise the city. While it is easy to dismiss the images as perhaps a north Indian newspaper's clichéd imagination of Chennai as a Tamil/Dravidian city, their visual aesthetics are however useful in furthering a discussion about the essence of contemporary Chennai that extends beyond the imagined into the real world. At a time when a new identity of a globalising city is being carefully constructed and staged with the city's public spaces projected as ideal circuits for the flow of global capital, the film's exorcism of a violent subaltern Other from the underbelly of these spaces is not gratifying. Nevertheless, it reveals in unexpected ways the disjuncture between Chennai's image and reality as a Dravidian capital, and hence is useful in challenging some of the recent development aspirations based on an agenda of sanitised aestheticisation that ironically involve the removal of cut-outs from the cityscape.

2 Changing geography of cut-outs in Chennai (aerial view of Anna Flyover Junction) (2010)   Source: The Hindu Photo Archives

Endnotes

1   The film is available online: http://www.youtube.com/watch?v=fEU_qyiQmYQ

2   This included a vehement opposition of Hindi as India's official language, and extended to a general dislike of political and economic dominance from a Brahmin dominated, supposedly Indo-Aryan culture prevalent in North India. However, a changing equation between regional and national parties based on coalition politics has muted the aggression of Dravidian politics. Even though Dravidian parties in one form or the other have been in power since the 1960s, Chennai falls woefully short of displaying a true Dravidian identity, with a forced "Tamil geography" that is visible only in bits and pieces. In 2004, the Delhi-based *Seminar* magazine in its special edition on *Changing Chennai* described it not just as a city but as an idea: conservative if not orthodox.

3   Madras was renamed as Chennai in 1996 in a move to vernacularise the city by rejecting the colonial toponym. While reassertion of a nativist agenda by a regional government played a critical role in this decision, the implications of this name change extended geographically, with both the names (Madras and Chennai) serving to spatially order an increasingly divided city. Thus, Chennai and Madras have come to exemplify the tale of two cities, where the former exhibits an elegant and ordered globalising landscape largely in the south, while the northern half portrays filth and decay associated with mal-development. Cinema has played an important role in Tamil politics, serving as a serious vehicle of political mobilisation for the Dravidian parties, with many leaders beginning their career in films, either as writers or actors. For discussions on Tamil cinema and politics see, for instance, S. Velayutham, (ed.), *Tamil cinema: The cultural politics of India's other film industry* (Abingdon: Routledge, 2008).

4   Cut-outs involved the materialisation of a film star or politician with a brusque, energetic touch, turning them instantly into an object of adoration. In recent years, this traditional form of cut-outs have been increasingly replaced by billboards that are computer-printed on vinyl fabric. See, O. Note, "Imagining the politics of the senses in public spaces," in *South Asian Popular Culture*, 5/1 (2007), 129–143.

5   Nancy Fraser, "Rethinking the public sphere: A contribution to the critique of actually existing democracy," in *Social Text*, 25/26 (1990), 56–80.

6   Note, O. *op. cit.*

7   See for instance, A. Srivathsan, M. S. S. Pandian, and M. Radhakrishnan (2005). "City in/as graffiti. Chennai's many cities," *Inter-Asia Cultural Studies*, 6/3 (2005), 422–427.

QUEER NOSTALGIA

Johan Andersson

1

1   The corner of West Fourth Street and Christopher Street, New York, cn the evening of   2 July 1969, five nights after the Stonewall riot.   Photograph by Larry Morris. Courtesy of The New York Times.

Retro-paraphernalia, remixes, re-evaluations, and a much publicised string of new documentaries and autobiographies celebrating the period between Stonewall and AIDS, all suggest that New York's gay community is currently undergoing a period of nostalgia. Recent attempts to list the East Village's Pyramid Club may even suggest that it is at a stage where it can be seen as a wing of the conservationist heritage movement. Yet what does it mean to hark back to and celebrate an era so closely associated with imminent death? Half of New York's gay men born between 1945 and 1960 are estimated to have contracted HIV and many of the men on the pictures now circulated as objects of nostalgia died young.

To think of this fascination as *morbid* would only reinforce the homophobic discourses that have historically linked homosexuality with death.[1] Rather, it must be seen in the context of a wider interest in this particular moment in the city's history, when in the cracks of the rapidly deindustrialising metropolis, a reconfigured public sphere opened up new possibilities for sexual experimentation (whether in the Meatpacking District's abattoirs or on the abandoned piers along the nearby waterfront). It is hardly surprising then, that so much of the current reminiscing for the 1970s and early 1980s is expressed through a post-industrial iconography of urban decay and faux-dereliction. The interior design of Industry, the latest addition to Hell's Kitchen's bar scene, is all about exposed brick, while the dilapidated exteriors of Brooklyn's hipster venue Sugarland look very much like the grainy black-and-white photos of the entrances to the Anvil or the Mineshaft in the 1970s. If the return of these aesthetic themes can indeed be read as a form of nostalgia, it should not be mistaken for a masochistic longing for the oppressions of the past, but rather as recognition that the now lost position on the margins was one from where alternative visions of intimacy could be formulated.

All this changed, of course, with AIDS. When, in the 1990s, urban gay culture recovered after the initial trauma of the health crisis, it did so through the deployment of new aesthetic themes that emphasised cleanliness and health. The *New York Times* reported on "A new generation of gay bars" and described how these had "all but jettisoned dark and dingy interior designs for cleaner, airier, more creative spaces … There is no end of difference between the clean, well-lighted places flourishing in New York and their sometimes notorious predecessors."[2] Physical ideals were also reshaped with a new emphasis on youth and smooth toned bodies, nowhere as perfectly encapsulated as in Bruce Weber's Calvin Klein adverts, which were placed on huge billboards in Manhattan. The ultimate symbol of the new sanitised gay culture was the go-go boy, an erotic dancer and obligatory form of aesthetic labour on New York's gay scene since the late 1980s. While New York City's Department of Health was shutting down sex clubs, the go-go boy kept the sexual economy alive and secured the circulation of capital. Perfect for the era of safe sex, you could touch— but only touch—with one hand for exactly as long as the other hand kept attaching dollar bills to his G-string. With gay culture contained in quarantine-like bars—and confined to this parody of sex—society at large was protected, not only from the virus, but also from the much anticipated "homosexualization of America."[3]

In the end, as the current emphasis on adoption rights and same-sex marriage suggests, the gay movement was instead incorporated into heterosexual society. Much of this alignment has come through the closer engagement with the state that AIDS necessitated, and significant legal advances have followed. Yet to look back on the queer culture of the 1970s and early 1980s is to acknowledge a recent past that did not merely aspire to assimilation. Such recognition is all the more important at a moment when queer history is being rewritten to better fit with the political agendas of the present. Take the response to Gus Van Sant's Oscar-winning film *Milk* (2008), in which Harvey Milk's campaign against Proposition 6 (which would have banned gays from working as teachers) has tended to be presented as analogical to the contemporary fight against California's Proposition 8 (which successfully banned gay marriage).[4] This historical parallel conveniently ignores how basic employment rights are a separate issue from marriage, which gay liberation in the 1970s, actually defined itself against. "Rather than a lifestyle, being gay seemed an entry point to remaking society," queer historian John D'Emilio recently wrote in a personal reflection: "By definition, we thought, queer life was subversive of marriage and the family."[5]

Moreover, the analogy between employment rights and marriage falsely suggests that we have "moved on" from those political battles, although the hypocrisy of *Milk* inadvertently reveals that the opposite is true. This is a film about gay politics and the importance of being out in the workplace, which is played by a straight cast in an industry that does not employ openly gay actors or actresses. In its revisionist take on "gay history," the sexual ethos of the 1970s (the piers, clubs, cruising grounds, and bathhouses) has been eradicated and replaced with saccharin dialogue for an era of reproductive aspirations ("Can two men reproduce? No, but God knows we're trying!"). The parallel real-life eradication of public sex from cities such as New York[6] does not mean that contemporary queer culture has been desexualised; only that liaisons arranged online or with GPS technology on smart phone applications are now more likely to take place in the private sphere of the home. While this reprivatisation of queer sexuality has opened up possibilities for those who never wanted or could be part of an open "gay community," it has simultaneously created problems for the targeting and distribution of safer-sex information. Often the groups with the least contact with the "scene" are the most difficult to reach and currently HIV-infection rates among African-American men who have sex with men are significantly higher than among their white and Latino counterparts.[7] In this context, the recent closure of Manhattan's only remaining African-American gay bar (Chi-Chiz on Christopher Street), after a campaign by local residents, should provide a moment of critical self-examination for the largely white residential community. While gay liberation in the 1970s held the promise of a different kind of city—one in which transient users had equal rights to the city as local residents—the gentrification processes, which initially were seen as emancipatory (not least through the bloc-voting that elected Milk) also set other trends in motion. Exchange value took priority over use value and the city of transience and play succumbed to the city of property and propriety.

Endnotes

1 Judith Butler, *Bodies That Matter: On the Discursive Limits of "Sex"* (New York and London: Routledge, 1993), 266; Lee Edelman, *No Future: Queer Theory and the Death Drive* (Durham: Duke University Press, 2004).

2 David Colman, "Dives no longer, new gay bars let in the light," *The New York Times*, 1 February 1998.

3 Dennis Altman, *The Homosexualization of America, The Americanization of the Homosexual* (New York: St. Martin's Press, 1982).

4 Both actor Sean Penn and scriptwriter Dustin Lance made references to the same-sex marriage debate in their Oscar acceptance speeches and several reviews of *Milk* drew parallels between Propositions 6 and 8.

5 John D'Emilio, "Will the courts set us free? Reflections on the campaign for same-sex marriage," in C. A. Rimmerman and C. Wilcox (eds.), *The Politics of Same-Sex Marriage*, (Chicago: University of Chicago Press, 2007) 40.

6 While New York City under Mayor Giuliani in the 1990s became a text book example of the sexual purification of urban space, regulatory and rhetorical responses to public sex have varied significantly between urban contexts. In London, for example, public sex has been commodified rather than marginalised in the last decade. See Johan Andersson "Vauxhall's post-industrial pleasure gardens: 'death wish' and hedonism in 21st century London," *Urban Studies*, 48/1 (2011), 85–100.

7 New York City HIV/AIDS Annual Surveillance Statistics 2009, http://www.nyc.gov/html/doh/html/dires/hivepi.shtml

LONDON'S TRELLICK TOWER AND THE PASTORAL EYE

Maren Harnack

1

1 Trellick Tower seen from
Golborne Road (2006)
Source: Photo by Maren
Harnack

"Trellick Tower's been calling
I know she'll leave me in the morning
Yeah yeah"
Blur, *Best Days*, 1995

Trellick Tower's distinctive thirty-one-storey silhouette is visible through much of West London and was designed by Ernö Goldfinger between 1968 and 1971. Shortly after it opened, this high-rise council block became known as one of the most notorious examples of public housing in London and experienced extensive vandalism and crime. Despite this difficult legacy, the flats are now highly sought after and have been counted among the "most fashionable addresses in London" [1]—although only 18 per cent of them have actually been sold off [2] in the wake of the 1980 "Right to Buy" legislation introduced by the Thatcher administration as part of their attempt to create a "property owning democracy."[3] Consequently, the majority of the neighbours a new owner will encounter are and will remain council tenants, often associated with a working-class background, and in some cases bearing the brunt of multiple forms of social and economic deprivation. Nevertheless, only relatively well-to-do professionals can afford to buy into this particular example of mass housing, and it is now generally and somewhat erroneously perceived to be a highly gentrified location.

The purported gentrification of Trellick Tower is a phenomenon that has provoked much public interest but little in the way of detailed analysis. This may be because there is no urgent need to add yet another type of gentrification to the somewhat jaded debate about this increasingly nebulous urban phenomenon. It appears that the long-standing supply-side versus demand-side arguments lack a sufficiently well developed cultural dimension indispensable for understanding the full complexity of urban phenomena and class-specific cultural connotations of urban change. Yet, the unexpected and thus far little explored popularity of ex-council flats can lead to some interesting insights into shifts in urban culture and the wider dynamics of contemporary urban change.

One concept worth considering in this context is that of the "pastoral," introduced by the literary critic William Empson, in his 1935 book *Some versions of pastoral*, as a way of understanding the class dynamics of modern culture. According to Empson, a classic pastoral is a narrative, which describes rural life in an idealised and strongly aestheticised way.[4] This requires a clear difference between the described object and the observer,[5] with the latter being socially superior but pretending to prefer the "simple" truths of the object's life. The "urban pastoral" can be read as a specific kind of cultural milieu in which a "simple but honest" working-class population forms the background for a middle-class imagination of "real" urban life, which is nonetheless idealised and has its "roughness" softened for wealthier residents by their affluence and social separation.[6]

The art historian Julian Stallabrass has linked William Empson's writings about the pastoral aspects of working-class literature to contemporary British Art. For Stallabrass, many of the so-called YBAs (Young British Artists) of the 1990s represent working-class culture and environments in their art works in a similar fashion to the "proletarian literature" described by Empson. The artists and onlookers apply a pastoral view to the subjects of the art, whose social background and physical environment they would only share voluntarily and not out of a lack of choice.

The wealthy owner-occupiers of flats in Trellick Tower have in a similar way chosen to set themselves up in a context that is dominated by and associated with people of a lower occupational status than themselves.[7] In return for their investment, they receive not only a comparatively well-designed flat, but also uncontrollable liabilities for potentially very substantial future repair bills and a greater exposure to a range of social problems such as noise and vandalism.

But, returning to the urban pastoral, there also is a cultural cachet of living in edgy, socially mixed urban neighbourhoods that seem to offset the undeniable disadvantages. In a similar vein to the observer of contemporary pastoral art in a central London gallery, the middle-class resident of Trellick Tower looks onto his working-class neighbours with a "pastoral eye," appreciating their supposedly superior honesty, simplicity, and authenticity, whilst their own participation in the simplicities of working-class life is bolstered with significant affluence. The modern council tenant has replaced the shepherds, nymphs, and peasants of the past.

Contemplating the implications of the pastoral eye we can understand why there is tension between council tenants and newcomers, although none of them is under direct threat of displacement through further privatisation—unless the entire block is divested of public ownership. Despite the professed admiration for working-class culture, the pastoral eye exudes a certain kind of social and intellectual superiority. It reduces the council tenant to a kind of social wallpaper, adding some degree of "authenticity" to the owner-occupiers' lives. Yet, however well meaning the newcomers might be, their pastoral eye cannot be appreciated by the incumbent council tenants and the underlying class differences remain largely intact.

Another important implication of the pastoral eye is the resentment the middle-class pioneers show towards the further upgrading of the picturesquely degraded, previously untouched neighbourhoods they once settled in. The authentic urbanity they have been seeking would inevitably disappear as further upgrading takes place, especially if this is combined with the influx of more middle-class residents like themselves. Thus the intangible benefits of having access to an authentic working-class community and its potential for conferring some kind of cultural distinction is directly under threat, if gentrification gains momentum. Edginess and authenticity are scarce commodities in modern western metropolises and they are worth fighting for.

2

3

2 High quality bone china with Trellick Tower decoration. Other social housing projects available include the Brunswick Centre and Keeling House. Source: peoplewilllalwaysneedplates

3 *Skirt with Trellick Tower façade pattern* Source: Peoplewilllalwaysneedplates/ Clothkits

In this context, living in Trellick Tower offers three potential advantages: in the current legislative and regulatory context, it is unlikely that further privatisation will occur because sitting tenants cannot afford to buy their rented apartments even if they wanted to. The newcomers have bought into a building stock in an eternal pioneer phase and are relieved of fighting against too much gentrification. Secondly, Trellick Tower's architecture is often described as "brutalist" and the façade of the building quite literally mirrors the roughness associated with working-class council housing, whilst at the same time bearing the hallmark of grade II* architectural listing as a component of modernist cultural heritage.[8] Most importantly though, Trellick Tower has become a pop icon over recent years. It has made appearances on T-shirts, skirts, crockery, book rests, and in various music videos. As such, it still embodies the "edginess" of its former state and communicates it to a wider public. Its fame extends far beyond its immediate surroundings and offers the rare opportunity to live in a building that might be recognised by design-conscious, avant-garde urbanites all over the world as sufficiently cool and authentic to ornament their homes or even themselves.

This brief foray into the cultural significance of Trellick Tower shows how we can better understand processes of urban change if we look beyond the level of the individual's necessity or the composite demand and supply structures of the economy. Rather than diluting the concept of gentrification by applying it to increasingly varied modes of urban change, we should work towards a theory of space that is able to explain gentrification as well as other urban phenomena. Processes within the world of art and pop culture are potentially as illuminating as those in economics, geography, and urban sociology.

Endnotes

1 Rory Caroll, "How did this become the height of fashion," in *Guardian G2*, 11 March 1999. See also Maren Harnack *Rückkehr der Wohnmaschinen. Gentrifizierung und sozialer Wohnungsbau in London* (Bielefeld, Transcript, 2011)

2 Data obtained from the Land Registry, www.landregistry.gov.uk (2007)

3 The Right to Buy was introduced by the conservative government under Margaret Thatcher in 1980 and forced local authorities to sell their housing stock at highly discounted prices to their tenants. Some councils such as Norwich tried to legally oppose this legislation but finally lost their case. The discount tenants would be granted through the Right to Buy was initially 45 per cent after three years of renting and was increased by another 2 per cent for every extra year in the flat up to a maximum of 70 per cent (1980 Housing Act). It was first reduced to a lump sum of £50,000 in 1989 (1989 Housing Order) by the Thatcher government, then to a lump sum of £38,000 in 1999 under New Labour (1999 Housing Order), and again to between £9,000 and £16,000 pounds in 2001 (2001 Housing Order). Under the conservative government, councils were only allowed to invest 25 per cent of the profit they made through the Right to Buy into maintenance or new housing, 75 per cent had to go towards the reduction of debts, which partly explains why many council houses are still in a relatively bad state of repair.

4 See William Empson (1935 / 1974): Some versions of pastoral p. 6 ff.

5 Ibid., 13.

6 Ibid., 19 f.

7 Prospective buyers do have other choices to make, as £500,000 would buy a Victorian terrace house in Kensal Green, just very slightly north of the Golborne area (data from 2007).

8 British listing categories work as follows
grade I—building of exceptional interest
grade II*—particularly important buildings of special interest
grade II—buildings of special interest
Only 1.4 per cent of all listed buildings are in the category grade I, and only 4.1 per cent In the category grade II*, which leaves the majority of 94.5 per cent of all listed buildings in the lowest category grade II.

A CONFIGURATION PREGNANT WITH TENSIONS

Jane Rendell

A constellation is a spatio-temporal configuration, it provides both a map and calendar of the individual stars and planets and their place in the overall pattern of the sky. Each star occupies a discrete position in relation to the others; it also has its own unique life span or time. Each star has a different duration, and what we see of a star today is not simply a function of what is physically present right now, but it is also a trace of what has occurred, which even as we look at it now is no longer present.[1]

On a visit to a ruined arts and crafts house in London's green belt ten years ago, I salvaged a few items—notably one book, *New Architecture of London: A Selection of Buildings since 1930*,[2] along with a selection of black and white photographs, some of which are reproduced here. Recently, I have become fascinated with tracking down the buildings imaged in the photographs. As well as the architectural qualities of the structures, I have had five text-based clues to work with: a board in front of one block of flats with the name, Ernest Knifton Ltd.; a car parked outside another with the registration plate, SLX 956; a street sign reading Westmoreland Terrace; and letters over the entrances to two other buildings with the words 1-24 Edmund Street and Witl-.

The "reassertion of space in critical social theory," the subtitle of geographer Edward Soja's Postmodern Geographies *of 1989, refers to one of the main projects for cultural geographers in the 1970s.[3] A number of Marxist geographers in that period took issue with the dialectical processes of historical materialism, where history was taken to be the active entity in shaping social production; and space was considered merely as the site in which social relations took place. Instead, geographers argued for the importance of space in producing social relationships.[4,5]*

In working between *New Architecture of London*, as well as web searches for the various clues, I have managed to track down most of the structures—it turns out that the majority we now regard as modernist icons. These include The Elmington Estate (1957), Picton Street, London SE5, designed by the London County Council Architects' Department, now largely demolished; The Hallfield Estate (1952–1955), Bishops Bridge Road, W2, designed by Tecton, Drake and Lasdun for Paddington Borough Council; The Alton East Estate (1952–1955), Portsmouth Road, SW15, designed by the LCC Architects' Department; The Alton West Estate (1955–1959), Roehampton Lane, SW15, designed by the LCC Architects' Department; and Churchill Gardens (1950–1962), Grosvenor Road, Lupus Street, SW1, designed by Powell and Moya for Westminster City Council.

The "turn" to spatial theory in the late 1980s and early 1990s highlighted the importance of space rather than time in the post-modern period. Academics from all kinds of disciplines turned to geography for a rigourous and theoretically informed analysis of the relationship between spatial and social relations. Interrogating the reciprocity of the relation between the social and the spatial highlighted an interest in "unfixing" place,[6] stressing the importance of understanding the specifics of particular places as parts of larger networks, systems and processes, physically and ideologically.

At the same time, I was searching for a new flat of my own in London to live in and buy. So I took the opportunity to view these buildings via *primelocation.com*. The search revealed their "value" in economic terms, as property. From an estate agent's perspective, these flats are described as ideal investments, not as places where the purchaser might choose to live, but rather as buy-to-let opportunities, real estate to be rented out to students and others. The images of fully occupied domestic settings on the property website provides an interesting counterbalance to the just completed exteriors photographed from the outside, positioning the architecture as a commodity to be purchased by individuals as well as (or instead of?) social entities to be lived in by communities.

While the geographers were unfixing place, those in the art world were specifying "site," developing an understanding of site beyond an indication of the physical location of a work and instead making strong arguments for site as a performed place and positioning site within an ethnographic perspective that included the research processes of fieldwork.[7] Sounding a warning of "undifferentiated serialisation," Miwon Kwon pointed to the dangers associated with taking one site after another without examining the differences between them.[8] Kwon pointed to Homi Bhabha's concept of "relational specificity" as a way of emphasising site as mobile, located between fixed points.[9]

In these decaying photographs, taken sometime in the late 1950s, and left out for years to weather the rain on the Weald, the buildings are new, they all look ahead. Returning to examine them now, it is not only the photographs that have deteriorated over the years, but the buildings too. However, what becomes apparent when investigating their exterior fabric, as well as the views of the interiors presented on *primelocation.com*, is that they have decayed differently depending on their position in London's economic geography; this is not simply a factor of rain and wind, but of the ways in which different boroughs have had the capacity—and will—to invest in their social housing stock.

Walter Benjamin notes in his study of Baroque allegory "an appreciation of the transience of things."[10] An important aspect of the allegorical method, according to Benjamin, is its focus on the image as an "amorphous fragment" instead of an "organic totality". In this sense, rather than a singularity, an ambiguity or multiplicity of meanings is produced.[11] Yet the ruin that features in baroque dramas in terms of decay and disintegration, and as a site for a melancholic reflection on the transience of human and material existence, as a dialectical image in Benjamin's unfinished Passagen-Werk *or* The Arcades Project, *becomes politically instructive.*

Some of the modern movement's public housing projects have become oases of cool property in the London postcodes associated with the rich, have often been well maintained, sometimes privatised and provided with concierge schemes, while those in the poorer boroughs have declined materially, frequently not included in the large-scale council repair and maintenance cycles. Those in areas of regeneration have been connected with the aspirations of up and coming neighbourhoods and demolished because the original construction is viewed to be too expensive to overhaul.

Composed of fragments, quotes collected by Benjamin, and words written by him between 1927 and 1939, The Arcades Project *focused on a particular ruin—the Parisian arcade,[12] arguing for its role as dialectical image, and describing it as a "residue[s] of a dream-world."[13] If the arcade is a dialectical image—an image of dialectics at a standstill— a moment where the past is recognised in the present as a ruin that was once desired, then for Benjamin, its key quality is its ability to create a moment when the usual patterns of thinking stop and new ones are given the chance to emerge: "Thinking involves," he writes, "not only the flow of thoughts, but their arrest as well. Where thinking suddenly stops in a configuration pregnant with tensions, it gives that configuration a shock."[14]*

But the seemingly pragmatic solution an economic perspective offers is perhaps better understood as a symptom of a particular attitude to the principles of modernism. The brutalist aesthetic of some modern architecture is often believed to be directly connected to social deprivation—to produce it—and this has forced the designers of certain regeneration schemes, the Elmington, for example, to adopt a new architectural language, one which is not so obviously "utopian" and therefore capable of suggesting better standards of living in a different way. In England at least, successive governments keen to promote an ideology of home-ownership, are driving out the aspirations for public ownership and social community that post-war modernism embodies. If everyone is weighed down by a hefty mortgage, the capacity for dissent is drastically reduced.

Emergent themes in spatial thinking, such as experience and travel, trace and deferral, mobility, practice, and performance,[15] have come to define what has become known as the "performative turn": a turn I am describing as the "reassertion of time" into the spatial. Thinking time in relation to space is not of course new, it is an activity at the heart of philosophical enquiry, yet what we might consider here is how this particular reacknowledgement of time in today's urban theory might lead us to explore new ways of writing the patterns of specific time-space interactions—configurations, cartographies, topographies of flow, flux, duration, ephemerality—and event constellations perhaps.[16]

There is a lot at stake when the social housing of the modernist project is sold off as "a good opportunity for investment" on *primelocation.com*; it is perhaps not overstating the case to suggest it has created a disaster for the Left, not only because the number of homes available to let by local government are reduced for those who need them, but also because those who buy them become part of the propertied class and all that entails. I know this because I am part of the problem.[17]

Page 136 (top)
Churchill Gardens (1950-1962), Grosvenor Road, Lupus Street, SW1, designed by Powell and Moya for Westminster City Council.
Page 136 (bottom)
The Alton East Estate (1952-1955), Portsmouth Road, SW15, designed by the LCC Architects' Department.

Page 137 (top)
The Hallfield Estate (1952-1955), Bishops Bridge Road, W2, designed by Tecton, Drake and Lasdun for Paddington Borough Council.
Page 137 (bottom)
The Elmington Estate (1957), Picton Street, London SE5, designed by the LCC Architects' Department.

All photographs were found at a derelict house, MayMorn, Gracious Lane, Sevenoaks, England in March 2001.

Endnotes

1   In popular parlance we use the term constellation to refer to "a group of celestial bodies (usually stars) that appear to form a pattern in the sky or appear visibly related to each other." This is actually something astronomers would call an asterism, and in astronomy the term constellation refers to the stars and other celestial bodies that are present in a particular area of the night sky. See http://en.wikipedia.org/wiki/Constellation#Definitions (accessed 9 June 2011).

2   Sam Lambert (ed.), *New Architecture of London: A Selection of Buildings since 1930* (The British Travel and Holidays Association in collaboration with the Architectural Association, 1963).

3   Edward Soja, *Postmodern Geographies: The Reassertion of Space in Social Theory* (London: Verso, 1989).

4   See David Harvey, *The Condition of Postmodernity* (Oxford: Blackwell, 1989); and Doreen Massey, *Space, Place and Gender* (Cambridge: Polity Press, 1994).

5   In so doing they turned to the work of Henri Lefebvre and his understanding of the two-way relation between the spatial and the social: "Space and the political organisation of space," he argues, "express social relationships but also react back upon them." See Henri Lefebvre, *The Production of Space* (Oxford: Basil Blackwell, 1991), 8. This quote from Henri Lefebvre, emphasised by David Harvey, is discussed in Soja, *Postmodern Geographies*, 81. See footnote 4.

6   Michael Keith and Steve Pile (eds.), *Place and the Politics of Identity* (London: Routledge, 1993), 5.

7   See Nick Kaye, *Site-Specific Art: Performance, Place and Documentation* (London: Routledge, 2000); and Alex Coles (ed.) *Site Specificity: The Ethnographic Turn* (London: Black Dog Publishing, 2000).

8   Miwon Kwon, *One Place After Another: Site-Specific Art and Locational Identity* (Cambridge, MA: MIT Press, 2002) 1, 166.

9   James Clifford, "An Ethnographer in the Field," interview by Alex Coles, in Alex Coles (ed.), *Site Specificity: The Ethnographic Turn* (London: Black Dog Publishing, 2000), 52–73.

10 Walter Benjamin, *The Origin of German Tragic Drama*, [1925] trans John Osborne (London: Verso, 1977), 223.

11 Ibid., 176–7.

12 See Walter Benjamin, *The Arcades Project (1927–39)*, trans Howard Eiland and Kevin McLaughlin (Cambridge, MA: Harvard University Press, 1999).

13 Walter Benjamin, "Paris: the Capital of the Nineteenth Century" [1935] trans Quintin Hoare, *Charles Baudelaire: A Lyric Poet in the Era of High Capitalism*, trans Harry Zohn (London: New Left Books, 1997) 176.

14 Walter Benjamin, "Theses on the Philosophy of History" [1940] trans. Harry Zohn, *Illuminations* (London: Fontana, 1992) 245–55, here 254.

15 Mike Crang and Nigel Thrift (eds.), *Thinking Space* (London: Routledge, 2000). See Crang and Thrift's "Introduction" to *Thinking Space*, 1–30, especially 19–24.

16 Part 2 of Jane Rendell, *Art and Architecture* (London: IB Tauris, 2006), explores the temporality of "critical spatial practice" using Walter Benjamin's work on montage and allegory to consider the time-based modes of experiencing site-specific artworks. More recently I organised Jane Rendell, *Site-Writing: The Architecture of Art Criticism* (London: IB Tauris, 2010) around five configurations, where each one attempts to perform the site of an particular encounter with an artwork through the space of writing itself.

17 In *Site-Writing*, I argue that a critic's relation to her object of study is a spatial relation and that this positionality needs to be made explicit through the critical spatial practice of writing itself, producing an architecture of criticism between critic and work, page and reader.

TERROR BY NIGHT: BEDBUG INFESTATIONS IN LONDON

Ben Campkin

Bedbugs were already a feature of life in medieval London, but their detection, extermination, and management emerged as an increasingly complex industry in the modern metropolis.[1] Armed with gases and chemical solutions, in the late-nineteenth and early-twentieth centuries modernising reformers sought to control these insects as part of a wider "civilising" process focused on public health and housing. By the mid-twentieth century, the bedbug, *Cimex lectularius*, was considered virtually eliminated through chemical treatments, slum demolition programmes, and effective educational campaigns. Yet, according to pest controllers, scientists, and journalists, the 1990s saw a dramatic return of these persistent insects.[2] There is now an increasingly fragmented but flourishing pest control industry associated with their success. They have "returned" as a material presence and cause of physiological and psychological distress, and as a spectral presence in urban discourse.[3] What might we learn through historicising contemporary discussions of bedbugs, as a consistently problematic feature of urban nature?

In 1730, Southwark "bugg destroyer," John Southall, published his elaborate tract, *A Treatise of Buggs*.[4] No doubt with his own professional interests in mind he declares that "every season

[bedbugs are] increasing upon us, as to become terrible to almost every Inhabitant in and about this Metropolis."[5] This text conveys the sense of a city overrun by bedbugs, the spread of which is linked to international trade, and to the condition, materiality, decoration, furnishing, maintenance, and orderliness of housing stock. Reassuringly for his wealthy clients, Southall makes it clear that although all can suffer from bites, those "healthy of body" will suffer less, and servants' clothes and possessions should be checked carefully. Southall's practice as "bugg destroyer" is described as "design"—a purposeful and artful act—and is reliant on the purported discovery and importation of a natural compound learned from an ex-slave in Jamaica. In this narrative bedbugs link the bodies, domestic interiors, and furnishings of Londoners to the global politics of colonialism.

In *London Labour and the London Poor* (1861) Henry Mayhew traces the English and Celtic etymology of the bedbug, the "terror by night" of the Psalms, respectively to "wall-louse"

1 "The Devil's Architecture. A typical crumbling and vermin-ridden staircase," *House*

Happenings 7, London, St Pancras House Improvement Society, Christmas, 1930.

Reproduced courtesy of Camden Local Studies and Archives Centre.

and "ghost or goblin," indicating their curious occupation of a space between material ar-chitecture and uncanny nature.[6] He refers to transitory street traders making a precarious income selling treatments for this "abundant" problem, and to more established specialists.[7] Mayhew's account is substantiated through his inclusion of a testimony from an expert wit-ness, a Mr Tiffin of Tiffin and Sons, "Bug-destroyers to her majesty," located on The Strand. Tiffin describes the history of the company, emphasising its longevity, having been estab-lished in 1695, and its basis in a tradition of scientific expertise and cleaning techniques passed down through the generations. The firm had an exclusive business model comprising a list of a hundred wealthy clients, with available spaces auctioned in bidding wars via the newspapers.[8] Their success was down to the development of a compound that got rid of the bugs, or at least appeared to. They were contracted to visit houses annually and advise on the cleansing of furniture, woodwork, and ceilings.

Tiffin's clients were from the wealthiest classes. Poorer Londoners had instead to develop their own tactics for living with the bugs, their bites, and the disruption they caused to sleep. In resonance with wider modernist hygiene discourses and their class- and race-based prejudices, foreign and poorer others were also blamed as vectors.[9] Both Southall and Tiffin also attributed infestations to the use of North American pine—foreign wood—in the re-building of London after the Great Fire.

Strangely, after a remarkably long lifespan, Tiffin and Sons ceased trading in the 1930s,[10] when bedbugs were a particularly high-profile public health concern.[11] Perhaps this was because of increased competition and the range of new products on the market. During this period, new institutions and state apparatuses for public health improvement were intro-duced, including the Ministry of Health in 1919, and the London School of Hygiene and Tropical Medicine in 1922. A new building for the latter, completed in 1929, to a design by Morley Horder and Verner Rees Architects, featured decorative gilded bedbugs amongst a selection of disease transmitting pests.

In the 1920s and 1930s, bedbug infestations occupied a prominent place in the work of reformers focused on the problem of London's slum housing, both because of the extent of infestations, and because of their power to convey a spectrum of problems. In the Somers Town district poorly constructed, degraded, and overcrowded houses were infested with rats, fleas, cockroaches, and other pests, as reinforced by the local and national press. Bedbugs featured as "the most difficult problem" identified by the reformers,[12] the St. Pancras House Improvement Society, prompting them to build new rather than recondition existing build-ings.[13] They documented infested walls and furniture in photographs, and included close-up footage of living bugs in films used to promote their work.[14] Chartered Surveyor Irene Barclay vividly evoked the pests at length in the Society's pamphlets, and later in her mem-oirs, describing how "they feed on blood, and attack the soft bodies of children unmerci-fully."[15] Barclay drew on a literary heritage of using bedbugs to powerfully represent the suffering of the abject poor,[16] as did her contemporary, George Orwell, who describes how

2

they are embedded in the degraded fabric and peeling wallpaper of poorly constructed and maintained dwellings, in which they were easily transmitted due to overcrowding.[17] Orwell anthropomorphises the bugs as soldiers on the march to comedic effect, so that they contribute to the "spectacle of the slum," to borrow Keith Gandal's term.[18]

In Barclay's writing, the pests are depicted through religious and spectral imagery and as a cause of repulsion, while they, like the slum inhabitants, are also considered with quasi-scientific interest.[19] The society's elaborate exhibition displays, and super-sized models of common pests, functioned in a similar way, as both spectacle and learning tool. Rather than admonishing the poor for their unhygienic behaviour, for these reformers, the pests indicated the landlords' neglect. Here, and in other parts of London, they gave voice to slum residents, interviewed in their homes talking about the impact of insects on their daily lives.[20] Documentary photographs, also in the "slum spectacle" mode of those of the late-nineteenth century, show residents' bagged possessions hanging from the ceiling to prevent transmission.

The Somers Town case demonstrates how, at this time, a range of built environment experts concerned themselves with bedbugs—from surveyors, such as Barclay, to architects, such as the Society's own, Ian Hamilton, who experimented with new lime plasters as a deterrent to invasions of the flats the Society was busy constructing. The bedbugs became a pretext for the reformers' innovative actions, while in their accounts of slum life these manifestations of "bad" nature were mobilised as a general metaphor for the conditions of the slums, conceived as irrevocably infested—degraded and degrading in both physical and moral terms.

2 "Mrs. Fry and her baby in her old house in Gee Street," c. 1920s.

Reproduced courtesy of Camden Local Studies and Archives Centre.

The insects were also a primary concern of state-employed Medical Officers of Health, as we see in *The Bed Bug* (1936), a health education film focused on west London. In this film, the narrator points out that bedbugs can invade any kind of house, but that they take advantage of cracks in floors and walls, and peeling wallpaper. So again there is an association with deterioration through neglect. In addition, infestations are blamed on furniture removal, through second-hand furniture or new furniture transported in contaminated vans. The pests are even suggested to spread during the course of demolitions, as timber from demolition sites is stolen by poverty stricken children to use as firewood. This film therefore emphasises the bedbugs' relationship to all stages within the cycle of the production and demolition of the built environment. Like earlier sources, it stresses that the houses of both poor and wealthy are vulnerable. However, lack of access to the resources to fight infestations, and the overcrowding of slum houses, clearly made the problem more difficult for the poor to overcome, just as it does today.

Like other species categorized as urban pests, bedbugs force us to think of the city as more than an agglomeration of architectural objects with clearly defined limits. In the contemporary city, development and design have been largely decoupled from the grand public health agendas associated with modernism. However, historical discourses about these insects, and the responses to them, have surprising parallels with contemporary debates. Now, as in the past, bedbugs complicate our understanding of nature as a benign presence. We place them in a category of undesirable transgressive species; yet they both reflect and actively influence the production of the built environment, patterns of inhabitation, divisions of responsibility for its management, and socio-economic inequalities. When we look closely at these minute insects they connect the urban fabric, and its occupants, their hosts, to a wider set of political, environmental, social, and technological processes.

Endnotes

1   Henry Mayhew refers to a 1503 report of the insects in Mortlake. Henry Mayhew, *London Labour and the London Poor*, Vol. 3 (New York: Dover Publications Inc., 1968; first published 1861) 34.

2   For scientific accounts of the return of the bedbug see A. Romero, M. F. Potter, D. A. Potter, and K. F. Haynes, "Insecticide resistance in the bed bug: a factor in the pest's sudden resurgence?" in *Journal of Medical Entomology*, 44/2 (2007), 175–178; M. C. Ter Poorten and N. S. Prose, "The return of the common Bedbug" in *Pediatric Dermatology*, 22 (2005), 183–187. For media and pest controllers' accounts see, for example, "Don't let the bedbugs bite," *BBC News Magazine*, 3 September 2010 http://www.bbc.co.uk/news/magazine-11165108 (accessed 21/6/11), which refers to expert reports of a "worldwide bedbug pandemic"; and "Don't let the bedbugs bite," *The Guardian*, Monday 9 February 2009, http://www.guardian.co.uk/lifeandstyle/2009/feb/09/bed-bug-extermination (accessed 21/6/11).

3   In New York City, media discourses around infestations have reached levels of hysteria, with outbreaks in high-profile stores, hotels, tourist attractions, multi-national headquarters and homes, all threatening economic consequences through affecting corporate reputations, property and rental values, and tourist industry profits. For example, see: "Time Warner centre succumbs to New York bedbug epidemic" http://www.guardian.co.uk/world/2010/aug/16/new-york-bedbugs-time-warner (accessed 21/6/11). However, some experts such as Renee

Corea, campaigner and author of the blog "Bedbugs vs. New York," have critiqued the idea of a return, arguing instead that bedbugs never actually went away. Corea proposes, instead, that the myth of a return forms part of a narrative that places the blame on foreigners from the developing world bringing infestations with them as they migrate. Interview with Renee Corea, 10 September 2010, New York City.

4   John Southall, *A Treatise of Buggs shewing when and how they were brought into England* (2nd edn. 1730, London: J. Roberts.) I have been unable to source the original edition of this text, so the date it was written is unclear. According to Harry Weiss, the publisher had a reputation for inaccuracy and bringing out new editions of previously unpublished works. Harry B. Weiss, "John Southall's 'Treatise of Buggs,'" in *Journal of the New York Entomological Society*, 39/2 (June 1931).

5   Ibid., 1.

6   Mayhew, op. cit., 34.

7   Ibid., 36.

8   Interview with David Cain, Bed Bugs Limited, London, 25 February 2011.

9   Tiffin in Mayhew, op. cit., 37–38.

10 Interview with David Cain, 2011.

11 See, for example: I. Hamilton, I. T. Barclay, and E. E. Perry, "The truth about bugs," in K.M. England (ed.), *Housing: a citizen's guide to the problem* (London: Chatto and Windus, 1931) 73–77; C. G. Johnson,

"The ecology of the bedbug, cimex lectularius L., in Britain: report on research, 1935-40," in *Epidemiology and Infection* 41/4 (1941), 345–461; Medical Research Council, *Report of the Committee on Bed-Bug Infestation: 1935-1940,* Medical Research Council Special Report Series No. 245 (1942); Ministry of Health, "Memorandum on the bed-bug and how to deal with it," London, H.M.S.O. (1935).

12 Barclay in Hamilton et al, op. cit., 75.

13 E. Darling, *Re-forming Britain: narratives of modernity before reconstruction* (London and New York: Routledge, 2007), 21.

14 Excerpts can be seen in the documentary, *Somers Town* (1984) (dirs. Sue Crockford and Richard Broad).

15 I. Barclay, *People need roots: the story of the St Pancras Housing Association* (London: Bedford Square Press, National Council of Social Science and the St. Pancras Housing Association, 1976) 23; Barclay in Hamilton, op. cit.

16 For example, in *The Cherry Orchard*, which opened in 1904, Anton Chekov's character Trofimov describes how "the workers eat abominably, sleep without pillows, thirty or forty to a room, and everywhere there are bedbugs, stench, dampness, and immorality." See Bernard

Beck, "Bedbugs, Stench, Dampness, and Immorality: A Review Essay on Recent Literature about Poverty," in *Social Problems* 15/1 (Summer, 1967), 101–114.

17 George Orwell, *Down and out in Paris and London* (London: Penguin Books, 1933; repr. 2003).

18 Keith Gandal, *The Virtues of the Vicious: Jacob Riis, Stephen Crane and the Spectacle of the Slum* (New York: Oxford University Press, 1997).

19 Orwell's depiction of bed bugs as soldiers on the march in *Down and out in London and Paris,* published in 1933, mobilises the military and sacrificial metaphors commonly deployed by modernising hygiene reformers. In New York City, radical left-wing journalist, Itzok Isaac Granich's fictionalised autobiography, under the pseudonym of Michael Gold, *Jews without money* (New York, Carroll and Graf, 1996 [1930]), provides a parallel to Barclay's description in its evocation of the smell of bedbugs as a signifier of conditions in the slum tenements of the Lower East Side in the 1920s.

20 Bedbugs or descriptions of them feature in films such as *Housing Problems* (1935) (dirs. Edgar Anstey and Arthur Elton, British Commercial Gas Association); *Kensington Calling!* (1930), Kensington Housing Trust; *Land of Promise* (1945) (dir. Paul Rotha), Films of Fact.

DICTATORS, DOGS, AND SURVIVAL IN A POST-TOTALITARIAN CITY

Ger Duijzings

The inhabitants of Bucharest blame former communist leader Nicolae Ceauşescu and his wife Elena for certain issues that have troubled the Romanian capital since the pair's drastic and megalomaniac urban interventions of the 1980s. The couple's most concrete legacy is *Casa Poporului* (the People's House), now renamed Palace of the Parliament, one of the largest and most grotesque buildings in the world. It is impossible to overlook or tear down, as some Bucureşteni would wish, because of its immense size. The couple demolished around a quarter of the historical core of the city in order to build it, together with the Avenue of the Victory of Socialism—the three-and-a-half-kilometre-long boulevard that leads up to it—lined by luxury apartment blocks for the elite. It was part of a plan to modernise the city's centre after the 1977 earthquake, which provided Ceauşescu with a pretext to create a tabula rasa and build a monumental Civic Centre that would help to undergird his growing personality cult. Ceauşescu was impressed and inspired by the North Korean example of Kim Il Sung, whom he much admired after visiting the country in 1971. For most of the 1980s, the five-kilometre-long strip of land stretching from the Uranus Hill in the west to Piaţa Alba Iulia in the east of Bucharest was a heavily secured building site and no-go zone for the city's inhabitants, who got used to navigating their ways around it while traversing the city. In spite of its grandeur, it still is an area that people tend to avoid.

Hundreds of Romanian architects were involved in the design process of this building, which begs the question to what extent this project was only "authored" by the dictator himself and whether many others should not be seen as complicit in his monstrous "achievement."[1] In any case, while the dictator and his wife—with the help of an army of architects and engineers—were building the palace and avenue, 40,000 people who had been driven out of their homes, often at very short notice, were housed in newly designed socialist apartment blocks in neighbourhoods on the outskirts of the city. The story goes that this is the cause of the huge stray dog population of Bucharest, one of the most protracted and unsolvable problems of the city. People were forced to put their dogs, which were usually kept in courtyards to guard the typical one-storey family homes in Bucharest, on the streets because there was no space and no use for them in the new socialist apartment blocks.

Numbers are hard to establish but at some point after the 1989 revolution the number of stray dogs surpassed 200,000 compared with a human population of around two million. Now the number is down again, but sources suggest that it may still be around one hundred thousand, in spite of the campaigns of mass extermination at the beginning of the 2000s.[2] The stray dogs have become a standard feature in streets, parks, and public squares in the Romanian capital. They form part and parcel of the social fabric, since they are often taken care of by individuals in a neighbourhood. As they are territorially based and linked to a particular neighbourhood, they are also called *câini comunitari* or community dogs. One

1 *Indirect Bucharest* (1992)
Source: Iosif Király

gets to know them, and they get to know you, when living in a neighbourhood: humans and stray dogs share the same space and develop a relationship based on everyday proximity. However, the canine co-inhabitants of the city can also become aggressive, crossing the boundary between community dog and predator. In January 2006, a Japanese businessman died after a dog attacked him close to Victoria Square where the Romanian government headquarters is located, causing an outburst of moral panic in Romanian public opinion. Cyclists also know that dogs can become dodgy. The peril for cyclists is not necessarily other road users as one may expect in the unruly traffic of Bucharest but stray dogs. They bark and run after passing cyclists. They attack much more ferociously when it gets dark, one of the most fascinating aspects of the urban night in Bucharest and an interesting inversion of the usual (daytime) patterns. Although dogs are normally diurnal animals, stray dogs come alive especially during the evening and at night. Whereas during the day they are often cautious about people and other dogs, taking a nap in a park or street gutter, when it gets dark they bark and start fights with other dogs, while looking for food in packs of half a dozen or so.

2   *Indirect Bucharest* (1996)
Source: Iosif Király

It is then that they feel unhindered and unthreatened by people. The night is when the day turns black and this is the moment they feel they can strike back.

In *The Ecology of Stray Dogs: A Study of Free-Ranging Urban Animals* (1973), the ethologist Alan Beck suggests that stray dogs "provide insight into the effects of urbanisation on man. Once their ecology is understood, urban dogs may serve as indicators of stress, pollution, and environmental deterioration, and as models for behavioural adaptations to urban life."[3] There are indeed apparent parallels between the human and canine inhabitants of Bucharest, as has been explored in the work of documentary filmmaker Alexandru Solomon. Referring to the situation in Bucharest at the end of the 1990s, Solomon's film *A Dog's Life* (1998) tells how "man and dog are two species intimately mingled into one another like the damned souls of Dante's inferno. Here, the human-eyed dog daily confronts the dog-eyed human. Our city has a population of over 200,000 dogs. There are rich and poor dogs, dogs of the street and dogs that go to the hairdresser. This film documents the life of this parallel society, which is a mirror of the human society in Bucharest."[4] Recently, artist Călin Dan explored the parallel and similar destinies of humans and dogs in the Romanian context in his play *Ca(r)ne: This is Our City* (2007) and film *Wings for Dogs* (2009), where he exposes in a potent manner the legacies of Ceaușescu's palace, the waste of ordinary lives, and the injustices it has produced and still engenders.[5]

The erasure of the historical parts of the city has entered a new stage with the demolition of *Hala Matache*, one of the oldest Bucharest market halls, which stands in the way of a new thoroughfare and boulevard being developed into the new business district of Bucharest; it connects Victoria Square (the government headquarters) with Ceaușescu's palace (the seat of parliament). The process has been accompanied by evictions of Roma and other urban poor from the dilapidated houses that were left to decay over the last two decades. Most of them are homeless again, building improvised shacks on wastelands in other parts of Bucharest or on the city's periphery. In another random part of Bucharest, people are reported to have poisoned the stray dogs that were living in front of their apartment blocks. The dogs have disappeared.

Endnotes

1   Maria Raluca Popa, "Understanding the urban past: the transformation of Bucharest in the late socialist period," in: Richard Rodger and Joanna Herbert (eds.), *Testimonies of the city: identity, community and change in a contemporary urban world* (Aldershot: Ashgate, 2007), 159–186.

2   Adriana Mica, "Moral panic, risk or hazard society—the relevance of a theoretical model and framings of *maidan* dogs in Chișinău and Bu-

charest," in *Polish Sociological Review*, 1/169 (2010), 41–56, here 48.

3   Alan M. Beck, *The ecology of stray dogs: A study of free-ranging urban animals* (West Lafayette, IN: Purdue University Press e-books, 1973), viii.

4   www.alexandrusolomon.ro/a-dog%E2%80%99s-life-1998/ [accessed 10.04.2011].

5   Călin Dan, *Emotional Architecture 3*. (Bucharest: MNAC, 2011).

INTERSTITIAL LANDSCAPES: REFLECTIONS ON A BERLIN CORNER

Matthew Gandy

1

1 The Chausseestrasse site in July 2009. Photo: Matthew Gandy

It is a warm July evening in Berlin. The aromatic white flowers of yarrow *Achillea millefolium* stand out strikingly against the gloomy undergrowth of a patch of waste ground where the busy Chausseestrasse, running north-south, meets the quieter Liesenstrasse from the east. Unnoticed to most of the people walking past, this site is teeming with life as nocturnal insects dart about amidst the flowers and bats swoop occasionally from the trees. Among the interesting species found on this site is a subtly marked moth, *Cucullia fraudatrix*, an Eastern European species associated with steppes and dry grasslands, that is near the western edge of its range in Berlin. This rare species has colonised the site in part through the abundance of its larval foodplant, mugwort *Artemisia vulgaris* (known as Beifuß in German), which is closely associated with urban wastelands.[1]

This five-hectare ecological paradise marks a boundary between the district of Mitte, the centre of the former East Berlin, and "Red Wedding," the traditional bastion of working-class Berlin and one of the poorest districts of the former West Berlin. On a site where the Berlin Wall once stood, a vibrant meadow has developed full of birds, butterflies, and wild flowers dominated by brilliant blue patches of *Echium vulgare*, which goes by the extraordinary English name of Viper's Bugloss (it is also known in German as Snake's Head or *Natternkopf*).

The site is aesthetically and scientifically much more interesting than the closely managed municipal park to the north side of the street with its short turf and widely spaced trees. This urban meadow is an example of what the urban ecologist Ingo Kowarik terms "fourth nature" that has developed without any human design or interference to produce a "new wilderness." This once grim space, where East German border guards and their dogs had patrolled, has been transformed through a process of ecological alchemy into something completely different. And at the edges of this meadow, young trees have appeared—principally silver birch (*Betula pendula*) and grey alder (*Alnus incana*)—marking the first stages of a "wild urban woodland" developing in the heart of the city.[2] Parts of Berlin are returning to nature, the distinctions between nature and culture becoming progressively more indistinct, as remnants of human activity such as rubble, rusting metal, and other objects become gradually absorbed into a new kind of socio-ecological synthesis.

In the 1960s, the island city of West Berlin emerged as an international centre for the study of urban nature. Berlin, along with a number of other German cities extensively damaged by war, presented an array of so-called ruderal spaces—this botanical term is derived from the Latin word *rudus* meaning rubble—that had produced a series of novel ecological formations. In West Berlin, however, botanists looked inwards rather than to the *terrae incognitae* of the surrounding GDR and produced a series of extraordinarily detailed accounts of their city's biodiversity.[3] Artists also became fascinated by the ecology of West Berlin, including poignant works such as Paul Armand-Gette's *Exoticism as banality* (1980), which details the presence of adventitious tree species that had become naturalised in a subtle riposte to "nativist" conceptions of urban landscape: North America, for example, is represented by

2

the maple species, *Acer negundo*, whilst China's presence is indicated by *Ailanthus altissima*, known also as the tree-of-heaven.[4]

With the unification of Berlin, a new array of anomalous spaces became gradually integrated into the city's unique urban ecology, which ranged from former security zones to abandoned industrial facilities. Ecological surveys have revealed that levels of biotic diversity within Berlin now exceed that of the surrounding agricultural or peri-urban landscapes. At the latest count, Berlin has some 2,179 species of wild plants of which 52 per cent can be considered part of the original flora of the region before extensive human influence.[5] Botanical studies of these unusual combinations of species in Berlin and elsewhere have challenged the analytical strictures of landscape ecology. For the geographer Gerhard Hard, the study of such marginal spaces forms part of a wider intellectual assault on the conservative idea of landscape as a holistic unity that denies difference.[6] The growing recognition of the aesthetic and scientific value of spaces hitherto regarded as "wastelands" has also introduced a much greater awareness of the independent agency of nature into urban design discourses.[7] The age of labour-intensive municipal landscapes is now fading for a mix of reasons—cultural, ecological, and fiscal—so that the idea of "wild spaces" or at least "wilder" urban spaces has begun to connect with a series of environmental concepts such as "ecological floodplains" and new approaches to urban hydrology; the creation of ecological ribbons to produce a connective lattice of "green infrastructure"; and an upsurge in vernacular interest in urban nature exemplified by Berlin's now annual festival entitled "Der lange Tag der StadtNatur" [The long day of urban nature]. Over the last twenty years, an array of alternative spaces has

2 *Cucullia fraudatrix* (Eversmann, 1837). Chausseestrasse, Berlin, 17 July 2009. Photo: Matthew Gandy.

become an emblematic feature of post-unification Berlin, encompassing not just new forms of environmental awareness but also vibrant developments in art and culture.[8]

The concept of the "green city"—a theme explored extensively in the writings and projects of the Weimar-era Berlin planner Martin Wagner—is being radically reworked in a contemporary context, yet latent tensions between biodiversity, ecology, and capitalist urbanisation remain: just as Wagner and others struggled to expand public access to Berlin's lakes and other natural features in the 1920s, there are recurrent tensions between conceptions of the city as an ecologically enriched public realm or a mere speculative arena.

Since 2009, however, this particular urban meadow has been fast disappearing: about one-third has become a petrol station, another third a parking lot, and the refuse-scattered remainder has been fenced off completely, marking a moment of enclosure before its final erasure. Across the street there are now billboards advertising luxury apartments. Computer-generated images show faux-Wilhelmine façades—the favoured retro look for wealthy newcomers to Berlin—along with modern blocks little different from the latest developments in London, Buenos Aires, or elsewhere.

When the GDR collapsed in 1989, there were brief hopes that an alternative and truly democratic German state might emerge, but the remnants of East Germany were quickly subsumed within the capitalist behemoth of West Germany. In the hollow imprint of the absent GDR, however, a unique medley of spontaneous landscapes has emerged over the last twenty years that provide a poignant symbol of urban possibilities. They reveal a city within a city that is not stage-managed for tourism or consumption, but open to multiple alternatives; a network of unregulated spaces within which both ecological and socio-cultural diversity can flourish. Although many of these spaces have now been lost there are still many interstitial landscapes that remain. Indeed, their eradication is not inevitable, as successful recent efforts to protect other sites across the city such as the meadows between the former runways of Tempelhof airport or the remarkable Südgelände nature reserve along an abandoned railway line attest.

Endnotes

1   See, Gabor Ronkay and László Ronkay, *Noctuidae Europea. Cuculliinae i* (Stenstrup: Apollo Books, 1994). *Cucullia fraudatrix* has been placed in category V (threatened) on the German Red List of endangered species. See *Gesamtartenliste und Rote Liste der Schmetterlinge ("Macrolepidoptera") des Landes Brandenburg* (Brandenburg: Landesumweltamt, 2001).

2   See Ingo Kowarik, "Wild urban woodlands: towards a conceptual framework," in Ingo Kowarik and Stefan Körner (eds.), *Wild urban woodlands* (Berlin: Springer, 2005), 1–32.

3   On the emergence of urban ecology as a distinctive field of study in Berlin, see: Jens Lachmund, "Exploring the city of rubble: botanical fieldwork in bombed cities in Germany after World War II," in *Osiris* 18 (2003), 234–254; Herbert Sukopp, H. P. Blume, and W. Kunick, "The soil, flora and vegetation of Berlin's wastelands," in I. C. Laurie (ed.), *Nature in cities* (Chichester: John Wiley, 1979); and Herbert Sukopp, *Stadtökologie: Das Beispiel Berlin* (Berlin: Dietrich Reimer, 1990).

4   Paul-Armand Gette, *Exotik als Banalität / De l'exotisme en tant que banalite* (Berlin: DAAD, 1980).

5   On urban biodiversity in Berlin and elsewhere see, for example: Ingolf Kühn, Roland Brand, and Stefan Klotz, "The flora of German cities is naturally species rich," in *Evolutionary Ecology Research* 6 (2004), 749–764; Stefan Zerbe, Ute Maurer, Solveig Schmitz, and Herbert Sukopp, "Biodiversity in Berlin and its potential for nature conservation," in *Landscape and Urban Planning* 62 (2003), 139–48. For further details on Berlin's flora see:
http://www.stadtentwicklung.berlin.de/natur_gruen/naturschutz/artenschutz/de/freiland/wildpflanzen.shtml (accessed 3 July 2011).

6   See, for example, Gerhard Hard, *Ruderalvegetation: Ökologie und Ethnoökologie, Ästhetik und "Schutz"* (Kassel: Arbeitsgemeinschaft Freiraum und Vegetation, Notizbuch der Kasseler Schule, 1998).

7   See, for example, Gilles Clément, *Le jardin en mouvement: de La Vallée au parc André-Citroën* (Paris: Sens & Tonka, 1994).

8   See Senatsverwaltung für Stadtentwicklung, *Urban Pioneers. Berlin: Stadtentwicklung durch Zwischennutzung / Temporary use and urban development in Berlin* (Berlin: Jovis, 2007); *Skulpturenpark Berlin_Zentrum* (Köln: Walther König, 2007).

PHANTOM LIMBS: ENCOUNTERING THE HIDDEN SPACES OF WEST BERLIN

Sandra Jasper

Behind an ordinary metal door at Berlin's underground station Rathaus-Steglitz lies a hidden world of public transport infrastructure that was never completed, Berlin's U10 underground line. Stepping into the station's carcass, one's gaze follows a tunnel hitting the dead end of a brick wall. Every once in a while, underground carriages rumble as the U9 line passes below, yet sounds are difficult to locate. A few graffiti and cigarette stubs provide hints of recent human presence in an otherwise sterile utilitarian sub-terrain. In surprisingly good condition, these "blind" tracks seem to be connectable any day. A whole collection of Berlin's residual transport structures is hidden behind doors at Rathaus-Steglitz, Potsdamer Platz, and Alexanderplatz stations, amongst others. Why, then, was the U10 line never finished or only partially constructed in the first place?[1]

The U10 line is not the only infrastructural project that was abandoned for political reasons in a city that experienced multiple ruptures from the mid-twentieth century onwards. In fact, Berlin's subterranean landscape is littered with technological relics. While the most controversial relics of Berlin's twentieth-century history were quickly removed in the 1990s, thus leaving behind spatial voids,[2] the incomplete U10 line has survived to this day. It is a technological relic of Berlin's geopolitical division and resulting cycles of politically driven investment and disinvestment in the city's infrastructural networks above and beneath the surface.

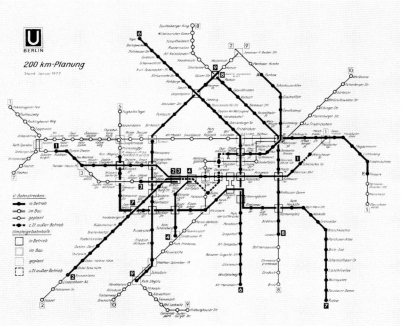

Looking at the city through its hidden infrastructure opens up new perspectives on its spatial history. Berlin's municipal supply systems—gas, water, electricity, and wastewater—and the city's public transport infrastructure played a key role during the Cold War. Pipes, cables, ducts, the physical infrastructure that links human bodies to infrastructural networks,[3] became the subject of intense political negotiations during and after the blockade of West Berlin in 1948–1949.[4] Berlin's transport networks were newly entrenched in ideology only four days after the Berlin Wall was built when the *DeutscherGewerkschaftsbund* (DGB, Confederation of German Trade Unions) and West Berlin's mayor Willy Brandt called for a boycott of the *S-Bahn*.[5] S-Bahn lines, Berlin's fastest public transport network, were still running through West Berlin despite being under the operational management of the *Deutsche Reichsbahn*[6] owned by the German Democratic Republic. Subsequently, passenger numbers dropped and the Reichsbahn abandoned almost half of its West Berlin track system. In the late 1960s, West Berlin received enough funding from the federal government and the international donor community to begin the costly construction of the new U10 underground line,[7] which was to run from Steglitz in south-west Berlin to Alexanderplatz, only a few hundred metres parallel to the existing S-Bahn. However, in 1985, the construction of the U10 in West Berlin came to a halt after the West Berlin senate negotiated the

1 200-kilometre plan of the Berlin underground including U10 line (January 1977) Source: Landesarchiv Berlin

2

right to the S-Bahn in the Western part of the city. Thereafter, all public transport funding was invested into the repair of this dilapidated network. Whereas many Western cities have been faced with the decreasing investment in urban infrastructure since the 1970s, Berlin's derelict S-Bahn network was reconstructed after 1985, and, after reunification, modernised on a large scale alongside all municipal supply networks.[8]

This interconnected history of the divided city's subterranean infrastructure sheds new light on metaphors deployed to examine the city. West Berlin is often referred to as an "island city"—a cohesive entity demarcated by Cold War politics and ideology. However, despite the fact that "the notion of infrastructure as a force for spatial cohesion … was retained"[9] on both sides of the city's geopolitical divide, important flows of gas, water, sewage, and electricity continued across the Iron Curtain. In fact, representing West Berlin as a self-contained "island" overlooks those important instances of infrastructural management when functional requirements of technical networks superseded political ideologies. Moreover, much of the vocabulary currently employed to account for the marginal spaces of the post-industrial city is concerned with how to utilise these "leftover" or "waste" spaces in the future. Such metaphors are linked to organicist notions of the city as an integrated body with clearly identifiable organs that have clearly discernible functions. Unlike these anatomical

2   "Entfernte Züge" by Bill Fon-   Sound" Musik-Texte 6: 60.
tana, Anhalter Bahnhof, Berlin
(1984) Source: Barthelmes,
B. (1984): "Photographer of

analogies based on a clear separation between body and mind "that enabled the city … to be acted upon, disciplined, regulated, and shaped according to human will,"[10] the *phantom limb* metaphor speaks to those spaces that are invisible in different ways. In a medical sense, "phantom limbs" are sensations we experience after the traumatic loss of a limb or an organ. In scientific accounts, patients' spatial perceptions of "sensory ghosts" that extend the physical boundaries of their bodies were for a long time relegated to the non-cognitive sphere because of culturally prevalent notions of a clear separation of body and mind.[11] The phantom limb phenomenon can extend our understanding of the body-city nexus to encompass aspects of cultural memory in relation to Berlin's marginal spaces hidden above or beneath the surface of a city.

Moreover, a closer investigation of Berlin's "phantom limbs" also opens up ways of charting the corporeal experience of space and those sensory aspects of the body's spatial experience that go beyond the visual realm. In the 1980s, West Berlin's derelict transport infrastructures and the interstitial spaces alongside these structures became a focus for a wave of sound art practice. Over the years, the city's disconnected rail-tracks turned into "biotopes" that caught the imagination of a growing number of photographers, artists, and urban ecologists.[12] Sound artist Rolf Julius explored West Berlin's hidden spaces in his installation piece "Musik für die Erde" (music for the earth) set up on 21 March 1982. He placed ten loudspeakers in a circle on a gravel path overgrown by plants near the abandoned train tracks of the Anhalter Bahnhof station. The tape that Julius played was composed of field recordings of nature sounds to give these hidden objects and creatures next to the tracks "a voice."[13] While Julius's piece drew attention to the present conditions of the tracks, in 1984, Berlin's International Building Exhibition, *Internationale Bauausstellung* (IBA) commissioned American sound artist Bill Fontana to create an acoustic landscape at the same station that recalled a world that had been lost in the wake of Berlin's division. Fontana's sound sculpture "Entfernte Züge" (distant trains) was comprised of loudspeakers that were buried in the large derelict field behind the station's ruin so that they remained invisible. With field recordings collected at Germany's busiest station—Cologne—where Fontana had placed live microphones in different locations, he reconstructed the station's acoustic space.[14] For a month, visitors could wander through the open field around the derelict station and listen to an acoustic landscape that conjured up memories of a bustling past—voices, signals, sounds of people in motion, announcements, and arriving and departing trains. Fontana sought to alter the acoustic meaning of the sound source radically by relocating it to what used to be Berlin's busiest station and an icon of modern mobility.

Scholars have argued that landscape and infrastructure are closely related, especially "if we extend our understanding of landscape to encompass the interconnectedness of space and of infrastructure to encompass the experience of space."[15]

Revisiting sound art projects of the early 1980s draws our attention not only to the aesthetic qualities of hidden spaces in the former West Berlin, but opens up reflections on the wider historical, political, and cultural contexts in which these urban landscapes were experienced. Moreover, it is crucial to develop a critical vocabulary that can help to analyse these marginal spaces. Incorporating the phenomenon of phantom limbs into our understanding of the body-city nexus, enables us to explore questions of cultural memory and sensory experience in relation to those invisible spaces that—in the case of West Berlin—emerged through intersecting processes of geopolitical division and cycles of investment and disinvestment in urban infrastructures.

Endnotes

1 The U10 has become accessible to the public through the recent engagement of a group of artists commissioned by the *Neue Gesellschaft für Bildende Kunst* (New Society for Visual Arts). The aim is to engage the public in discussions on past and future transport planning decisions.

2 A. Huyssen, "The Voids of Berlin," in *Critical Inquiry*, 24/1 (1997), 57–81.

3 M. Gandy, "Cyborg urbanization: complexity and monstrosity in the contemporary city," in *International Journal of Urban and Regional Research*, 29/1 (2005), 28.

4 T. Moss, "Divided City, Divided Infrastructures: Securing Energy and Water Services in Postwar Berlin," in *Journal of Urban History* 35/7 (2009), 923–942.

5 The S-Bahn is Berlin's rapid transit railway system. The history of the S-Bahn is documented in *5 Jahre S-Bahn bei der BVG – eine Dokumentation*, Berliner Verkehrs-Betriebe (Eigenverlag), 1989.

6 Deutsche Reichsbahn was the operating name of the state-owned railway in the German Democratic Republic.

7 For details on the costs of municipal infrastructure reconstruction in West Berlin, see Merritt in Moss, op. cit., 932.

8 On the large infrastructural investment programmes in the former Eastern part of the city in the 1990s, see Moss, op. cit., 937–938.

9 Moss, op. cit., 935. Moss points out that engineers and network managers on both sides followed their professional conduct rather than political ideologies and were focussed on developing practical solutions.

10 Gandy, 29.

11 P. Halligan, "Phantom limbs: The body in mind," in *Cognitive Neuropsychiatry* 7/3 (2002), 255.

12 See for example photographer Ingeborg Ullrich's projects "S-Bahn Biotop" (1981/1982) and "Wo die Gleise enden" documented in K. Hickethier, E. Schachinger, and E. Knödler-Bunte, *Die Berliner S- Bahn. Gesellschaftsgeschichte eines industriellen Verkehrsmittels* (Fachbibliothek Verlag, 1990). Derelict urban infrastructures and rubble sites became field sites for urban ecologists in post-war Germany, see J. Lachmund, "Exploring the City of Rubble: Botanical Fieldwork in Bombed Cities in Germany after World War II," in Osiris 18/2 (2003), 34–254; and in H. Sukopp and R. Wittig, Stadtökologie (Spektrum Akademischer Verlag, 1998).

13 Rolf Julius sound installation was part of a larger project "Berliner Konzert Reihe (1981/82), documented in H. De la Motte-Haber (ed.), *Klangkunst- Tönende Objekte und klingende Räume* (Laaber-Verlag, 1999).

14 The project "Entfernte Züge" is documented in B. Barthelmes, "Photographer of Sound—'Entfernte Züge'—Bill Fontanas Klangskulptur auf dem Gelände des Anhalter Bahnhofs," in *Musik Texte* 6, Oct. 1984, 59–60. It can be listened to at: www.resoundings.org/Pages/Distant Trains.html

15 M. Gandy, "Landscape and Infrastructure in the Late-Modern Metropolis," G. Bridge and S. Watson (eds.), *The New Blackwell Companion to the City* (Wiley-Blackwell, 2011), 57.

EVICTIONS: THE EXPERIENCE OF LIEBIG 14

Lucrezia Lennert

On the morning of 2 February 2011, twenty-three people were evicted from their home at Liebigstrasse 14 in Berlin's Friedrichshain district. As part of the post-unification urban renewal of former East Berlin, this once dilapidated area has seen rapid transformation since the 1990s as a result of a growing tourism, retail, and nightlife-based economy and waves of property redevelopment. The forced removal of lower-income residents to allow for profit-maximisation on property is an all too common story in gentrifying inner-city neighbourhoods such as Friedrichshain. What was unusual in the case of Liebigstrasse 14, however, was the refusal of the inhabitants to leave their home, the 2,500 police mobilised for the eviction, the thousands who took to the streets in protest, and the subsequent re-prisal actions by protesters targeting the local economy through street blockades and dam-age to banks, shopping centres, and government offices throughout Berlin. "Liebig 14" was a "*Hausprojekt*" (house project), a collective living and alternative cultural project that had existed for over twenty years. For many in Berlin, the eviction of Liebig 14 came to represent the damage wreaked by uncontrolled gentrification as it displaces lower-income residents and forces the closure of alternative subcultural spaces.

1

The eviction of Liebig 14 also resonated internationally as a loss in the struggle for autonomous spaces. As with the "nomadic war machines" described by Gilles Deleuze and Félix Guattari in *A Thousand Plateaus: Capitalism and Schizophrenia*,[1] these spaces develop through anarchic multiplicity: their horizontal collective structures and consensus-based organisation ward off hierarchies within the group, while practices of self-reduction of costs and non-commercial production resist further capture into flows of value production and extraction. Living in Liebig 14 in its last year of existence, I joined an eclectic constellation of people: an international mix including musicians, students, carpenters, social workers, and the unemployed. Politics was deeply engrained in everyday life and the house was a meeting space for a spectrum of left activists, from antifascist to queer, community gardeners to anarcho-syndicalists. The project organised itself through consensus decision-making and a weekly house meeting, while materials, skills, and knowledge were shared and one could learn how to play an instrument, speak a language, organise a demonstration, or repair a toilet from any given housemate. Liebig 14 formed part of an alternative infrastructure in Berlin made up of legalised squats, bookshops, info-shops, and non-commercial bars and event spaces. In Berlin, these spaces are becoming islands of resistance to the logic of capital accumulation as their relative withdrawal from the urban economy grows increasingly incompatible with the intensified economic exploitation of the surrounding areas.

Liebig 14 was originally squatted in 1990 and was the product of a second wave of the German squatters movement, when—seizing a moment of political vacuum after the fall of

1 Liebig 14 in 2009. Source:
Christian Hetey.

the Wall and responding to a crisis in housing supply—over 120 abandoned buildings were occupied in the former East of the city.[2] Most of these squats were evicted within a year as West Berlin's hard-line policy towards squatting was applied to the entire city,[3] while the houses that survived did so through the negotiation of rental contracts with the state. Faced with the choice of legalisation or eviction, the squatters' movement, a social movement based on radical claims and practices towards ownership of urban space, was forced into the legal and political straightjacket of rental contracts in a privatising city. Some squats managed to secure self-ownership as house co-operatives, but many continue to be engaged in struggles against landlords, often speculative investors biding their time until they can evict. The case of Liebig 14 is exemplary of this trajectory: in 1993 the squatters at Liebig 14 negotiated rental contracts with the state property-holding company *Wohnungsbaugesellschaft Friedrichshain*[4] (WBF), which subsequently sold the building to private property developers in 1999. The conflict over the building then entered a new dynamic: from squatters against the state to renters against private landlords. The new landlords were hostile to the collective and sought ways to evict the project. In 2009, after a four-year legal battle with the tenants, a judge granted the building's owners the right to cancel the contracts on the grounds that the tenants had built an "illegal" second front door to the house.[5]

2

2 Inhabitants of Liebig 14 on the roof of the house during the filming of an anti-eviction "solidarity video" in January 2011.

Source: Alexandra Fransson.

After the loss of the rental contracts, the house survived another year with the ever-present threat of eviction and of the project and community suddenly coming to an end.[6] Somewhere between planning for the future of the collective and being unable to do so, we got on with the everyday life of the house; the uncertainty playing out in our decisions about whether to stock up on coal to last the winter, whether to repaint the living room, or whether to barricade the front door daily. While this state of contingency brought limitations to the life and work of the project, it also created openings in the experience of collective life. AbdouMaliq Simone has examined how contingency is negotiated by residents of cities in the global South where a state of emergency brought about by pervasive crisis in governance and infrastructure leads to a "rupture in the organisation of the present."[7] Simone suggests that "emergency connotes both the end of a certain flexibility of interpretation, of the ability to put off until another day a reckoning of commitment and conviction now found to have been the wrong way to go. At the same time, this state of emergence enables, however fleetingly, a community to experience its life, its experiences and realities, in their own terms: this is our life, nothing more, nothing less."[8] In Liebig 14, the emergency of eviction created a similar dynamic: thus while impending eviction demanded action to secure the future of the house, to reach consensus on strategy and tactics, it also afforded, even necessitated, an immediacy in the present life of the collective.

The eviction notice arrived on 10 January 2011. After years of court cases, campaigning, political actions, and roundtable meetings with local politicians, the house now had three weeks until it would be evicted and we threw ourselves into a final struggle. A flurry of activity unfolded and every waking hour was spent working against the eviction: demonstrations were organised, a publicity campaign built, we assessed our strategy options daily and devised plans for the physical defence of the building. We felt empowered by the 4,000 who demonstrated in support of Liebig 14 in Berlin and by the solidarity actions carried out across the world[9]; despair when a final legal attempt at preventing the eviction failed; and pangs of defeat as we dismantled our beloved kitchens, so full of the history of the many people who had, over twenty years, been a part of these spaces. Two days before eviction, barricade construction began and the house underwent its final transformation as Liebig 14: from home to fortress.

The dawn of eviction day was accompanied by the sounds of the hammering and welding of barricades. An eerie atmosphere filled the air as this desperate chorus was added to by the sound of a lone violinist, a former inhabitant of the house, who played in the street until the arrival of the police at 5 a.m. The neighbourhood then turned into a militarised zone as riot police, intent on keeping the gathering crowds of protesters away, blocked all entry to Liebigstrasse. Neighbours went to their windows and began banging on pots in a show of anger that persisted into the afternoon. Shortly before 8 a.m., without the legally required presence of the bailiff and refusing to let the house lawyer past the police barriers, the eviction began. After entering through the roof, the police found one impenetrable barricade after another in their path and resorted to breaking holes through walls until, five hours later, they reached the third floor kitchen where the remaining inhabitants were sitting with their arms locked together.

Evictions of autonomous spaces—the eradication of resistant territories and their collectives—confront us with the nihilism of capital accumulation and the accompanying state repression of radical grassroots alternatives in urban living. When the life and production of these spaces cannot be captured and integrated into the capitalist market, the spaces are instead destroyed. War machines are dislocated, while the practices and knowledges that form and grow out of projects such as Liebig 14 are dissolved until they can be reconcentrated again at opportune moments. In a context where "for too long we have been losing, perhaps to the extent that we have forgotten what it would mean to win,"[10] it becomes necessary to rescue from situations of seeming defeat our senses of political agency and collective empowerment, to deepen our determination and strengthen our practices.

Endnotes

1 G. Deleuze and F. Guattari, *Mille Plateaux: Capitalisme et schizophrénie* (Paris: Les Éditions de Minuit, 1980).
2 A. Holm and A. Kuhn, "Squatting and Urban Renewal: The Interaction of Squatter Movements and Strategies of Urban Restructuring in Berlin," in *International Journal of Urban and Regional Research*, 35 (2011), 644–658, here 650.
3 G. Katsiaficas, *The Subversion of Politics: European Autonomous Social Movements and the Decolonization of Everyday Life* (1997; 2nd edn., Edinburgh: AK Press, 2006,),154.
4 Post-Wall, the WBF took ownership of unowned building in the East of the city. The WBF is now merged with the *Wohnungsbaugesellschaft Mitte* (WBM).
5 The door had been built to prevent the landlord from entering the building as well as to separate the ground floor event area from the living area of the house. For a full history of Liebig 14 see http://liebig14.blogsport.de/das-haus/chronik/ (in German).
6 Although it is legally required to send an eviction notice informing the tenants of an eviction date, this is not always the case. In 2009, another Berlin *Hausprojekt* at Brunnenstrasse 183 was evicted without notice.
7 A. M. Simone, *For the City Yet to Come: Changing African Life in Four Cities* (London: Duke University Press, 2004), 4.
8 Ibid, 5.
9 Protests and solidarity actions in support of Liebig 14 took place in Denmark, Japan, Peru, the UK, Moldova, France, and the United States.
10 Escalate Collective, "Marching for Whose Alternative?" http://escalatecollective.net (2011)

A ROUGH AND CHARMLESS PLACE: OTHER SPACES OF HISTORY IN TEL AVIV

Noam Leshem

1 Salama Mosque, view from the north (2009).
Source: Photo by Noam Leshem.

By the time Jewish armed forces entered the Arab village of Salama on the outskirts of Tel Aviv in late April 1948, all of its inhabitants had fled. The following day, when Israel's first prime minister David Ben-Gurion visited the village, he encountered "only one old blind woman."[1] Despite its depopulation, most of Salama's houses stood unharmed. Two weeks later, Israeli authorities began settling Jewish immigrants and war refugees in the village, partly to alleviate the severe housing shortage of the time and to physically block the return of Palestinian Arab refugees to their homes. In 1949, Salama was incorporated into Tel Aviv's municipal boundaries, and three years later the Israeli Government Names Committee assigned it a new, Hebrew name—Kefar Shalem.

Prevailing historiographical conventions view such extreme transformation as a watershed moment, marking the abrupt end of an Arab village and the beginning of the Jewish-Israeli neighbourhood. "Erasure" or "spatial annihilation" are common tropes in the critical corpus analysing the radical transformation of the Arab landscape in Israel, spaces that were subjected to policies of physical ruination as well as historical and cultural "de-signification."[2] Widespread destruction, depopulation, and cultural chauvinism are crucial to the understanding of Israel's spatial history, but do they simply wipe the spatial slate clean? What other histories continue to claim their place in the Israeli space?

On the night of 9 October 2000, shortly after the violence of the second Palestinian uprising (*Intifada*) engulfed Israel, the West Bank, and the Gaza Strip, a little known incident took place in Kefar Shalem. Armed with metal bars and hammers, hundreds of Jewish residents began tearing down one of the walls of the derelict Salama Mosque. A squad of twenty police officers armed with clubs was sent to surround the structure to shield it from the crowd.

What could trigger such a severe onslaught against a building that had not been used for Muslim religious purposes since 1948 and sealed shut since the early 1980s? The attack on the mosque suggests that despite being fenced off, locked, and isolated, Salama Mosque was not empty. For those who set out to bring the building down, the Arab village of Salama was neither erased nor forgotten. While the building may have stood abandoned and disused, the time that passed did not erode its identification as a container of symbolic meaning; in the eyes of the Jewish protesters there was no doubt that the building was "Arab" or "Muslim," and as such, a worthy target of anger, aggression, and fear. The unsettled presence of a vacant building that attracts such fierce and violent emotions illustrates the deceptive nature of seemingly empty spaces and challenges some of the conventions that govern spatial and historical research: what are the criteria according to which we select and categorise phenomena and observations, deeming some worthy and other irrelevant? How do we measure degrees of presence and absence that direct our attention to certain objects but not others?

Israeli authorities have sought numerous "ways of forgetting"[3] the Arab past of Palestine, and the alteration of spaces played a key role in this regard, both through planned demolition and through the creation of a new symbolic geography of Hebrew names and Jewish historical narratives. But while maps can be redrawn and names replaced, former Arab spaces in Israel are not merely mute traces, devoid of context or contemporary consequence. For example, Salama Mosque was turned into a youth club in 1949, catering to the region's socio-economically disadvantaged population for over three decades, but this significant change of function did not blur the historical meaning of the place. Archival material shows that the building's identification as "the mosque" continues to appear decades after it ceased serving this purpose. These traces in the archive may be prosaic, anecdotal examples. They do not constitute an official acknowledgement of the Arab past of Salama or commemoration of the loss suffered in 1948. Yet official practices of commemoration are not the only sources through which "empty space" becomes historically intelligible.

Greater attention to the complex historical, political, and social processes lodged in so-called empty spaces highlights facets of "situated knowledge of colonial practice and power relations"[4] that are embedded in, rather than marginalised by processes of emptying and ruination. Even in extreme spaces of ruination, it is possible to identify creative expressions of defiant memory, as in the case of Yalo, Amwas, and Beit Nuba, three villages that were demolished in the 1967 War. After the war, a national park was planted over the ruins, a practice often cited as part of the Israeli authorities' efforts to obscure Arab presence. Various signs placed around the park mention the area's rich history—from Roman and early Jewish periods, to Ottoman rule—yet remain silent about the Palestinian history of the site. But destruction did not mean that the villages simply vanish from sight and memory. On weekends, whole families of former Arab residents arrive in the park for seemingly innocuous picnics, but ones that nonetheless express a structure of feeling between people and place, an intimate relationship that has otherwise been severed. Although these are powerful spatial practices and social instruments that maintain a community's relation to its past, they are easily overlooked. Yet these are precisely the forms of "haunting" that highlight the social and cultural meaning of ruins, explicating "how that which appears not to be there is often a seething presence, acting on and often meddling with taken-for-granted realities."[5]

The analytical effort to "repopulate the emptiness" requires attention to seemingly mundane, even banal, places and practices. "What we have to do with banal facts," Michel Foucault reminds us, "is to discover—or try to discover—which specific and perhaps original problems are connected with them."[6] Ordinary places like Salama/Kefar Shalem, a working-class neighbourhood on the edge of the metropolis, provide insights into the actual negotiations that take place between people and the spaces in which they live, work, seek leisure, or simply pass by. Such places are rarely monumental or extreme in their appearance: they are old and decrepit, hidden in the peripheral neighbourhoods; they are encrypted in the contradictions and ambiguity of official documents and texts; they aggravate officials seeking urban "order," and frustrate planning authorities. The ambiguity of empty space, the recurring sense that it is never wholly devoid of "things" that continue to carry an unsettling meaning, suggests that the rich archive of emptiness, as it were, bears evidence to more than just the brute force of ethno-national chauvinism. At times, it emerges in the subtle form of mundane picnics, while at others it bluntly reappears in a violent attack against a mosque after sixty years of disuse.

Endnotes

1   David Ben-Gurion, *The War Diary: The War of Independence, 1947–1948 [Yoman ha-Milhamah: Milhemet ha-'atsma'ut, 708–709]*, Vol. II, ed. Gershon Rivlin and Elhannan Orren (Tel Aviv: David Ben-Gurion Heritage Centre; Israel Ministry of Defence Press, 1982), 377.

2   See for example, Ghazi Falah, "The 1948 Israeli-Palestinian War and Its Aftermath: The Transformation and De-Signification of Palestine's Cultural Landscape," *Annals of the Association of American Geographers* 86/2 (June 1996), 256–285; Meron Benvenisti, *Sacred Landscape: The Buried History of the Holy Land since 1948* (Berkeley: University of California Press, 2000).

3   Uri Ram, "Ways of Forgetting: Israel and the Obliterated Memory of the Palestinian Nakba," in *Journal of Historical Sociology* 22/3 (September, 2009), 366–395.

4   Cole Harris, "How Did Colonialism Dispossess? Comments from an Edge of Empire," in Annals of the Association of American Geographers 94/1 (March 2004), 166.

5   Avery Gordon, *Ghostly Matters: Haunting and the Sociological Imagination* (Minneapolis, MN: University of Minnesota Press, 1997), 8.

6   Michel Foucault, ed. Lawrence D. Kritzman, *Politics, Philosophy, Culture: Interviews and Other Writings, 1977–1984* (New York: Routledge, 1988), 58–59.

"A FOOTPRINT AMONG THE RUINS"[1]

Karen E. Till

"The community's stories were a substantive part of the architecture of the neighbourhood's memory. A form of resistance in the face of oblivion, a potential footprint among the ruins." [2]
Rolf Abderhalden Cortés, *Mapa Teatro Laboratorio de Artistas*

December 2003 and 2004. Project Prometeo: Acts I & II. An outdoor 'stage' in downtown Bogotá.
A clown becomes a magician. From the torch held by his assistant, he lights a paper and performs his interpretation of Heiner Müller's *The Liberation of Prometheus*: tapping his empty magic box with a wand, he pulls two white doves out of nowhere. It is night. Along with hundreds of candles in the surrounding open-air fields, two large screens, three to six storeys high, illuminate his actions and simultaneously project live images of his performance and previously recorded footage of the elderly man's personal story. We learn that he joined the circus at the age of nine and we watch images of him and his grandson dressing up as clowns. They are in temporary housing and a pale green wall of their single room is adorned with their belongings carefully organised according to their function: a frying pan, a pair of scissors, a material bag, a framed picture. In other clips, we see them looking out of the windows of a city bus across fields in which buildings are under different phases of demolition. Upon these razed fields, we the audience, now sit. The magician throws the flapping doves up to the night sky. They are free. Amidst our applause, with bolero music beginning to play, the magician invites us, the audience, to come join him and the other performers on stage and dance atop the ruins of the Santa Inés-El Cartucho neighbourhood, their former homes.

As a literal and metaphorical "footstep in the ruins" of a city neighbourhood, *Project Prometeo* documented, celebrated, and reimagined the densely settled communities, lived spaces and peoples known locally as El Cartucho.³ In contrast to the official story of "sustainable" urban renewal, which designated the area as in need of "cleaning up"—thereby rendering existing routines and spaces of everyday dwelling and the residents themselves (often referred to as "disposables" by city officials⁴) as invisible or non-existent—the stories of *Prometeo* honoured residents' "right to the city" according to an ethics of mutual witnessing and place-based care.⁵ Residents of Santa Inés-El Cartucho invited city residents, urban professionals, and guests to attend to their embodied stories of displacement on the very twenty hectares (200,000 square metres) of razed earth from which they were removed. Within two years, this historic neighbourhood would be unveiled as the "Public Park of the Third Millennium" (Parque Tercer Milenio) as part of one mayor's attempt to "green the city."⁶ Working with residents to create two performances of the *Project Prometeo*, the artistic collaborative Mapa Teatro raised ethical questions about the politics of placemaking in the name of progress at the same time that they called attention to the possibilities of art, memory, and imagination in their city.

> …displacement is the problem the twenty-first century must solve. Africans and aborigines, rural peasants and city dwellers have been shunted from one place to another as progress has demanded, "Land here!" or "People there!" In cutting the roots of so many people, we have destroyed language, culture, dietary traditions, and social bonds. We have lined the oceans with bones, and filled the garbage dumps with bricks.
> —Mindy Fullilove⁷

As recorded and projected on the large screens of the *Prometeo* performances, the Santa Inés-El Cartucho residents reflected upon the emotive and material gaps created by their forced removals, as well upon the trauma of having been already forgotten by other city residents and public authorities even before they were evicted. Their performances might be considered what medical anthropologists Arthur and Joan Kleinman call "enacted assemblages" of body-social memory.⁸ A person's "interconnected cognitive, affective, and transpersonal processes" shape the body, just as bodies shape social and material spaces through the local interpersonal world, or place. One's emotional ecosystem includes social and embodied memories, as well as the places a person (re)makes, cares for, and to which he or she is connected. The everyday routines, social institutions, material landscapes (textures, tastes, sounds, scents), stories, and legends of place become a part of a person at the same time they are socially shared.

When a person experiences "the destruction of all or part of one's emotional ecosystem," he or she may experience a "traumatic stress reaction" that social psychiatrist Mindy Fullilove calls "root shock."⁹ The root shock resulting from the demolition of and displacement from

1

2

1 Mapa Teatro, Bogota
2 Mapa Teatro, Bogota.
Prometheus Project: Daniel and
Johrnell Carpintero interpret

Heiner Müller's *Prometheus*
atop the ruins of their former
neighbourhood.

Source: © Mapa Teatro Laboratorio de Artistas. Photographs
courtesy of Mapa Teatro

any historic neighbourhood will always exceed existing hegemonic narratives (and narrative structures) of modern urbanisation and public memory. One way to attend to root shock might be through an ethics of caring for place, such as through imaginative and physical processes of return that enact a form of memory- and mourning-work. One practice of memory-work would be to follow the open-ended pathways of body-social-place memory, and in this way both remember possible pasts and imagine possible futures.

> The remainders [of remembering] do not consist in depositions laid down—as is assumed in theories preoccupied with leaving marks and traces in an unchanging material base—but in pathways that branch off ever more diversely into a multiple future.... An open future helps to keep the remembered past alive.... the thick autonomy of remembering dismantles ... the temporal determinancy of the past.
> —Edward Casey[10]

The projected images, sounds, props, and bodies in motion of *Project Prometeo* depicted stories in the imagination (interpretations of the Prometheus myth) and experience (enactments and recorded images). Former streets and walls of buildings, marked with candles in white paper bags, framed the "stage"; images, stories, and maps of what was once the landscapes of El Cartucho were projected behind resident-actors just at the place being represented on screen. Residents' stories were enacted, retranscribed (in a Freudian sense) and rediscovered.[11] As the performance unfolded and recorded stories revealed, each moment, each possible combination of bodies, images, sounds, stories, and environments was different.

This belatedness is a quality of what Edward Casey describes as the "unresolved remainders of memory," whereby the past is continually reshaped in the present, not so much in terms of deferred events or as records of events, but in the sense of the *possibilities of memory*.[12] The concept of unresolved remainders assumes that remembering is a process of ongoing "remanence" defined by open-ended pasts and futures. Unlike Derrida's "restance", which is an unresolved remainder of the imagination, the intensified "remanence" of remembrance signifies, for Casey, "a perduring remainder or residuum", similar to the remanent magnetization left behind in matter after an external magnetic field is removed.[13] Casey suggests that unresolved remainders of memory inhabit the body, place and social rituals (such as through story-telling and myth) and consist "in pathways that branch off every more diversely into a multiple futurity".

In contrast to the "cartographic anxiety" of city planners and officials, *Project Prometeo* was a multi-sensual mixed art form sensitive to the multiple rhythms of time and to shared becomings.[14] The performances by the former residents of El Cartucho thus had the potential to transform memories of violence into shared stories of relevance through the collective witnessing of these unresolved remainders of memory.[15] Rather than mere spectators, residents and guests were invited to move between realms of the real and symbolic, the material and the metaphorical, the perceived and remembered, and the experienced and imagined. According to Mapa Teatro, the creative process leading up to the performances—meeting Santa Inés residents amidst demolition or in temporary housing; documenting their life histories and experiences; engaging in body work and social activities with residents; readings, interpretations, rewritings of the Prometheus myth; the practices, performances and subsequent artistic productions—became "a poetic reconstruction of once inhabited places."[16] In related artistic projects, the textures of El Cartucho were made visible through city mappings and walks, domestic installations; video projections on exterior walls of buildings and in public squares; street, body, and landscape ethnographies; and post-demolition archaeologies.

Mapa Teatro understood their artistic work with residents as engaging El Cartucho as place not so much in terms of loss, but as a living eyewitness to the process of urban change. Mapa noted that their work with the residents of Santa Inés changed how they worked and believe it also affected many individuals with whom they collaborated, some with whom they still work: "its unique resonance was due to its particular qualities and implications, which were not only aesthetic but ethnographic, anthropological, sociological and above all human and *relational*."[17] During the four or so years of collaborations, residents worked with each other and the artists to access voices, inheritances, and resources that might provide them with a language of belonging.

Endnotes

1 In memory of Daniel Carpintero.

2 Rolf Abderhalden Cortés, "The Artist as Witness: An Artist's Testimony," talk delivered at the *Academia Superior de Artes de Bogotá in 2006*, available at: http://www.hemisphericinstitute.org/journal/4.2/eng/artist_presentation/mapateatro/mapa_artist.html (last accessed 20 March 2011).

3 The artistic collaborative Mapa Teatro Laboratory of Artists (based in Colombia) worked with residents of El Cartucho from roughly 2001–2005 on five related large-scale urban projects. The actors/participants of *Project Prometeo: Acts I & II* (in 2003 and 2004) included: Luis Carolos Arango, Jairo Alfredo Cárdenas, Daniel Carpintero, Johrnell Carpintero, Carolos Alberto Carrillo, Jorge Enrique Gaitán, Giovanni García, Clara Emilia González, Édison López, Hilda Zoraida López, Claudia Moreno, Luz Ángela Moreno, Margarita Palacic, Luis Ernesto Parado, Camilo Rengifo Tangarife, Sandra Milena Tangarfe. See: Mapa Teatro Laboratorio des Artes webpage, "Arte, memoria y ciudad," http://www.mapateatro.org/artememoria.html, last accessed 21 March 2011); Rolf Abderhalden and Juanita Cristina Aristizábal (eds). translated by Curtis Glick and Tony Hastings, *Catalogue and Multi-Media: Project Cúndua, Years 2001-2003* (Bogotá: La Silueta ediciones Ltd., multimedia: CD SYSTEMS, n.d.); and Karen E. Till, "'Art, Memory, and the City' in Bogotá: Mapa Teatro's artistic encounters with once inhabited place," *Buildings and Landscapes* (under review).

4 Personal interview with Rolf Abderhalden Cortés by the author, Berlin, 2008.

5 On the "right to the city," see: Henri Lefebvre, "The Right to the City," partial reprinting in *Writings on Cities: Henri Lefebvre*, Transl. and Ed. Eleonore Kofman and Elizabeth Lebas (1st edn. 1968; Oxford: Blackwell, 1996), 147–159. On a "place-based ethics of care," see: Karen E. Till, "Resilient Politics and Memory-Work in Wounded Cities: Rethinking the City through the District Six in Cape Town, South Africa," Bruce E. Goldstein (ed.) *Collaborative Resilience: Moving from crisis to opportunity* (Cambridge, MA: MIT Press, 2011), 283–307.

6 For a discussion of the park project see: Karen E. Till, "'Greening' the City? Artistic Re-Visions of Sustainability in Bogotá," in *e-misferica* 7/1 (2010): http://hemisphericinstitute.org/hemi/en/e-misferica-71/till.

7 Mindy Thompson Fullilove, *Rootshock: How tearing up city neighborhoods hurts America, and what we can do about it* (New York: One World/Ballatine Press, 2004), 5.

8 Arthur Kleinman and Joan Kleinman, "How Bodies Remember: Social Memory and Bodily Experience of Criticism, Resistance, and Delegitimation following China's Cultural Revolution," in *New Literary History* 25/3 (1994), 707–723; quotes this and next sentence, on page 719.

9 Fullilove, 11.

10 Edward Casey, *Remembering: A Phenomenological Study* (Bloomington IN: Indiana University Press, 2000; 2nd edn.) 277–278.

11 Freud discusses how the "retranscription" (*Umschrift*) of memory-traces occurs in the material present through evolving circumstances. For Casey, memories can gain a new psychical efficacy through the belatedness associated with retranscription (274).

12 Ibid; quote at end of paragraph, 277.

13 According to Casey, mourning, as a slow process of working-through in the psychical sphere, transforms remanence into remnants, a process that both exorcizes "the ghosts of their external haunting power" and aids "us in identifying with what is left" (Ibid), 273.

14 On cartographic anxiety, see: Derek Gregory, *Geographical Imaginations* (Oxford, Blackwell, 1994); Leonie Sandercock, *Cosmopolis II: Mongrel Cities of the 21st Century* (New York: Routledge, 2003).

15 On witnessing as an active political and aesthetic practice, see: Jane Blocker, "A Cemetery of Images: Meditations on the burial of photographs," in *Visual Resources* 21/2 (2005), 181–191; Jacques Ranciére, *The Emancipated Spectator* (New York: Verso, 2009); Diana Taylor, *Disappearing Acts: Spectacles of Gender and Nationalism in Argentina's "Dirty War"* (Duke University Press, 1997).

16 Mapa Teatro webpage.

17 Abderhalden Cortés, "Artist as Witness."

5

PROJECTIONS

TRACES AND SURFACES

Stephen Barber

Many forms of creative media intersect with the work of scanning, interrogating, and incising urban surfaces as a method of cultural and historical analysis. Film, visual art, photography, and digital-image generation—among other media—all possess a range of intricate (and often intersecting) dynamics in their relationship to the perception of urban surfaces: walls, hoardings, screens, façades and other exterior "projections" into space. In analysing the residues of urban explorations, as with those of densely layered surfaces in cities such as Berlin, the eye of an urban "spectator," on foot and moving through the city, may juxtapose what is seen with memories of those surfaces' rendering in film, art, or digital images, intentionally or involuntarily, through the infiltration of film and art images into the perception of urban architecture. In his short, fragmentary essays of the early 1930s, from transits through the space of Berlin and Paris, Siegfried Kracauer's seminal urban writing conjures an amalgam of oscillations between the immediate instant of what he is viewing, and that act of viewing's inflections from film and visual-arts cultures, along with equally irresistible historical insights and premonitions.[1] Similarly, in his 1982 film *Sans Soleil,* Chris Marker's traversals of Tokyo's space—exacting a vertical archaeology of its surfaces—are always intercut with the abrupt intrusions of memories, of other films, and media images, which then determine the film's future course.

The medium of cinema attached itself to urban space, and to interrogating its surfaces, from the first film images, such as Louis le Prince's film of Leeds Bridge and its adjacent warehouses in 1888, and the Skladanowsky Brothers' panorama of northern Berlin's brewery chimneys and tenements, in the originating film images of Berlin, shot from the roof of a building in 1894; such experimental sequences, often fragmentary in form, were almost invariably shot from vantage points, so that they appeared simultaneously omniscient and vertiginous. Around the end of the 1920s, at the zenith of the "city-film" genre of urban film-making, exemplified by such works as Dziga Vertov's *Man with a Movie Camera* (1929), the filming of urban surfaces often probed the division between aimlessness and intentionality, which is implicit in all urban methodologies. A specific element of urban space must be sought, but it may often reveal itself unexpectedly, in defiance of the method used, in an underhand and aberrant way. One of the great urban city-walk films, through Prague, Alexander Hammid's *An Aimless Walk* (1930), probes this issue: in order to seize pivotal urban traces, a rigourous structure must be set up, but may then productively be dissolved—in the process of moving through that urban arena—through the lapsing or erasure of intention.

The juxtaposition of a human figure against an urban surface always formed a dynamic filmic preoccupation, from the Skladanowsky Brothers' dancing figure filmed against a panorama of Berlin, to figures in extreme crisis, as in the urban-maddened figures in Andrzej Zulawski's film *Possession* (1981), set against the surfaces of emptied-out West Berlin avenues and subway-passageways that become imbued and marked with corporeal convulsions and internal psychoses, which threaten to make those surfaces erupt. In visual art, such as painting, the relationship between corporeality and urban surface necessarily produces volatile concoctions of traces that may either be conjoined or inassimilable. Urban

1

1 *Alexanderplatz*, 1895, dir.
Max and Emil Skladanowsky
Deutsche Kinemathek Berlin.

painting, divested of any human presence, may transmit a melancholic aura, as in Gustav Wunderwald's 1920s paintings of vast, windowless Berlin firewalls, as though denying the gestural and exclamatory imperatives that always made such surfaces the privileged site for direct inscriptions, such as tea-painted advertising hoardings and graffiti.

Photography and painting—notably, the overpainting of urban photographs—forms a further conjoined medium that has absorbed contemporary artists, and often intimates an oncoming catastrophe or abandonment, as in Anselm Kiefer's book of overpainted photographs, *Grass will grow over your cities* (1999), in which the photographic traces of an anonymised megalopolis (viewed from a tower or overflying aeroplane) may either be eroded or accentuated by the paint that screens away those traces. Even in the early decades of urban photography, as in Eadweard Muybridge's innovative San Francisco panoramas of 1877–78, the photographic image's juncture with painting formed a vital and sensitised one in establishing and recasting urban "auras"; Muybridge would manually paint moons onto his negatives to transform his sun-lit cityscapes into nocturnal ones, alongside an extensive array of other manipulations of urban surfaces that fragmented and overhauled the spectatorial perception of urban space, which was often cast into intentional disorientation

2 *Possession*, 1981, dir. Andrzej Żuławski Image from film.

3 *San Francisco Panorama* (panel 8 of 13), 1877–78, by Eadweard Muybridge

Kingston Museum and Heritage Service.

by those strategies. Muybridge's distortions of urban space formed tactile, artisanal ones, achieved though multiple exposures, but contemporary digital photography allows a new limitlessness of such ocular manoeuvres, in which urban surfaces and components may be dislocated and seamlessly reintegrated at will, and uprooted from city to city; as in the work of the Berlin-based photographer Beate Gütschow, which scrambles contemporary and obsolete façades into borderless urban configurations that, like Kiefer's images, appear to project the traces of near-abandoned, forgotten, or depopulated cities.

That preoccupation with urban surfaces that undergo a seeping of memory, to the point of dereliction and effacement, is also one that haunts Japanese digital art—such as the work of Takao Minami—and counterpoints the experience of urban environments and façades that initially appear to be saturated, over-inscribed ones, constellated by image-screens that project relentlessly looped corporate animations, but also integrally transmit their own capacity for imminent extinguishment, through an all-engulfing digital crash, or a self-regulated shutdown such as that enacted in Tokyo in March 2011 during the aftermath of the Tohoku earthquake. Japanese performance-art and dance, from the work of influential collectives such as dumb type and Gekidan Kaitaisha in the 1980s and 1990s through to contemporary work, frequently employs projections of digital sequences of densely inscribed urban façades and surfaces across the bodies of the performers, in the form of an intensive probing of corporeal and urban boundaries, in which the body (often viewed as "surpassed" and "anachronistic" in digital art and its theoretical context) may transmutate to the extent that it simultaneously emits both new urban elements and new organs. Digital art is often closely integrated with the material forms of urban architecture and the spectatorial perception of it (since many digital art works are built into the ground-level display-facades of buildings, or projected from large-scale screens on the summits of towers, in cities such as Los Angeles, Bangkok, and Tokyo), and as a result, it may infuse its preoccupations—with vanishing corporeal traces and imminent ecological, political and structural calamity—directly into, and through, those surfaces.

Contemporary cities, in the context of urban research, form experimental laboratories in which the future manifestations of perception and media—and urban life itself—are in the process of being formulated in ways that require disciplinary amalgams and infinite flexibility, since such ongoing experiments are never linear ones, and prove elusive to fixed methodologies. Similarly, the intersection of art and film with urban surfaces, over a century or more, has amassed a multiplicitous sequence of contacts and traces, so that contemporary digital projections invariably hold, embedded within them, an intricate and often colliding history of filmic, photographic, and other visual engagements with urban space.

Endnote

1   Siegfried Kracauer, *Strassen in Berlin und anderswo* (Berlin: Das Arsenal, 1987).

FACES, STRUCTURES, WORDS, AND COLOURS: COLLAGES AND DÉCOLLAGES OF BERLIN AND OTHER CITIES IN THE WORK OF POLA BRÄNDLE

Joachim Schlör

The idea that the big city is, in some ways, a *palimpsest*—a collection of different layers of historical meaning, a means of memory storage—may already have become a cliché. But stereotypes do contain occasional glimpses of truth. Contemporary archaeological diggings in Berlin's central district, brought about by the building of a new underground line from Alexanderplatz to Brandenburg Gate—a project related to the future and the technological and ecological development of a twenty-first-century city—revealed Berlin's medieval street grid, the earliest matrix that has been built over time and again and long been deemed completely vanished. But there it is for all to see, and so strong in the manifestation of its importance for local memory that the new underground station "Rotes Rathaus" (the name is in memory of Kaiser Wilhelm's dislike of democratic institutions so close to his palace, which itself is another vanished building that will soon re-emerge in a different form) will

1 Pola Brändle: *Wiener Blut*, Collage/Decollage, 40 x 95 cm, 2008 Source: Courtesy of the artist.

2 Pola Brändle: *Caught in my Dreams*, Collage/Decollage, 100 x 55 cm, 2010 Source: Courtesy of the artist.

have to move; and make place for historical awareness. We see tourists stroll through the city in search of "traces" of the Berlin Wall, and at some places the wall itself, together with its very specific infrastructure of lamp-posts and minefields—so thoroughly removed in the euphoria of November 1989—had to be partly rebuilt as part of a memorial device on Bernauer Strasse. And where we do still have remnants of the wall, as in Niederkirchner Strasse opposite the Berlin parliament, a very forceful urban contingency—and constellation—enables us to view them in relation to the ruins of the former Gestapo headquarters, the *Topographie des Terrors* (Topography of Terror).

It takes an effort to make the historical layers visible and accessible. For many years now, I have been trying to capture this ever-changing wave of disappearance and reappearance in photographs. Especially posters (advertisements, public announcements, concert or theatre notices, political propaganda in different languages) on the many empty and unused spaces "in-between" show fragments of words and letters, half-torn faces or other body parts, but also colours and structures that—overlapping and criss-crossing each other—create new "images" and illustrate the fragmentary and collage-like character of the urban experience. When I moved from Gneisenaustraße, just around the corner from Kreuzberg's slowly gentrifying district "61," to a new flat on Mehringdamm and Googled our future neighbours, it turned out that one of them was Pola Brändle, an artist whose work reflects and edits exactly such visual elements of our daily ambience. In Brighton in 2003, as William Hess writes in the introduction to her book *Plakatief*, "Pola discovered weeks, months, perhaps years of local cultural history reduced to a single image slowly interweaved via the hands of nature and happenstance."[1] During the following six years she travelled (as part of a juggling duo) around the world and "discovered that with careful study the walls of every city told their own original story." Next to documentary photography (where she doesn't disturb or change walls before the photo is taken), Pola also takes off such posters from their "habitat" and, in a process of collage and décollage, reframes them as individual works of art, as expressions of her own interpretation of the lines, colours and figures that had been created by accident. Obviously, Pola is not the first artist to use such posters, Mimmo Rotella and Jacques Villeglé, among others, have worked with this material. But she seems to me unique in her consequence and in her outreach: from Berlin to Lisbon, from London to Prague or Athens, and even from Montevideo to Buenos Aires, she has performed an urban foray, the results of which provide us with visual information about both the similarities between the cities and the very significant local singularities.

Urban studies have often profited and learned from literary and visual artistic interventions and interpretations of the city, and this might be another occasion to integrate works of art into the framework of our research. The faces of politicians, singers, Kurdish freedom fighters or smiling (but only half-smiling since the poster is torn) consumers of advertised products, remind me of Kurt Tucholsky's poem "Augen in der Großstadt," which expresses the experiences of quick glances, on a street or in an underground train, between busy city-dwellers (who might well never meet again) but for a short moment manage to suspend the feelings of loneliness and isolation of the individual among the crowd.[2] Words and letters, fragments of former meaningful sentences and urgent messages, "talk" to us and form part of the daily discourse—sequences of signs or "enouncements," to use Foucault's terminology—that surrounds us and challenges us to try and "read" the city. I have never completely understood, or accepted, the notion of "city as text" and sometimes felt that such an approach would take us too far away from the realities of our built surroundings: the houses we live in, the streets we walk through, the infrastructure we need to use, the differences in social and cultural contexts that we research. But indeed there is a lot of "text" in the city, words and sentences written down or printed for a context that has since vanished and is now free to move around and find other ways to associate or enter into a dialogue with the passer-by.

In many cases, and this is especially true for Berlin, the places where we can find such images, are on the margins or at least in more remote areas of the city. The posters and some of their producers—street artists who intervene with their own décollages or commentaries—can therefore serve as guides on an urban pioneering trail far away from the main tourist attractions. Following their traces, we venture into more obscure parts of our cities, empty former factories or hospital grounds, abandoned railway tracks, building sites, or other "Geisterstätten" and forgotten spaces (and again Berlin more than anywhere else is full of them) or discover new routes through the places we thought we knew, and construct new connections between them. Maybe this is the most important aspect of the work I have presented here—the search for, and documentation of, such "artefacts hidden in plain sight"[3] forces us out of our offices and invites us to use our feet again for long and instructive "walks on the wild side."[4] This is an element of urban research that has been, it seems to me, neglected for too long and left to (very good) literary authors such as Iain Sinclair and Will Self in England or Wolfgang Büscher in Germany. The *dérive* thus initiated is not at all aimless, nor is it related to immediate political action in the situationist sense. It rather serves to capture surprising (sometimes quite funny, sometimes also saddening, in any case *moving*) constellations in the ongoing dialogue between the cities and us, artists *and* scholars, who have made them the focus of their loving attention. This is very romantic, I know. But it is the love affair with the city in Pola Brändle's work that makes it so inspiring for academic urban studies.[5]

Endnotes

1 William M. Hess, "Introduction," in *Plakatief. A World in Layers.Photographs by Pola Brändle* (Bielefeld, Leipzig, Berlin: Kerber Photo Art, 2011), 8.
2 Kurt Tucholsky, "Augen in der Großstact," in *Gesammelte Werke in zehn Bänden. Band 8* (Reinbek bei Hamburg: Rowohlt Verlag, 1975), 69–70.
3 Hess, 8.
4 Cf. Rolf Lindner, *Walks on the wild Side. Eine Geschichte der Stadtforschung* (Frankfurt am Main: Campus Verlag, 2004); for a celebration of the work of this most original urban researcher, also see the *Festschrift*, Beate Binder, Moritz Ege, Anja Schwanhäußer, and Jens Wietschorke (eds.), *Orte. Situationen. Atmosphären. Kulturanalytische Skizzen für Rolf Lindner* (Frankfurt am Main: Campus Verlag, 2010).
5 See her website http://www.polabraendle.com/ and the weblog (in English) http://polabraendle.wordpress.com/ (both accessed June 3, 2011).

WONDERFUL LONDON: SILENT-ERA TRAVELOGUES AND THE WALKING TOUR

Karolina Kendall-Bush

The 1924 travelogue film *The Sidelights of London* opens with a shot of a man walking along a tightly enclosed alley toward the camera. This shot is emblematic of how the travelogue takes viewers around the capital: on their feet. *The Sidelights of London* is one of twenty-two travelogue films that make up Harry B. Parkinson's series *Wonderful London*. Unlike most travelogues of the 1910s and and 1920s, the *Wonderful London* series offers more than picture-postcard views of well-known landmarks. The films reveal features of the city only appreciable to pedestrians and frequently invoke the act of walking through their cinematography, onscreen inter-titles, and recurrent shots of passers-by. The series recalls the intricate paths taken by walking tours that criss-cross the capital daily.

1

Multi-shot travelogue films of the 1910s and 1920s often did little more than expand upon the single-shot actualities included in travel lectures and variety programmes in the early and transitional period of silent cinema. The Pathé Frère's *Londres* (1908), for instance, presents viewers with a series of exterior shots of well-known tourist landmarks cut together with shots of iconic individuals. The film's disjunctive editing between landscapes, inter-titles, and people follows what film historian Jennifer Lyn Peterson calls a "logic of collection," in which the film "preserves the integrity of each shot rather than making connections between."[1] The films of the *Wonderful London* series, however, organise their shots in a logical spatial progression. Furthermore, whether the story revolved around the haunts and homes of Dickens and his characters in *Dickens's London*, the weekend habits of Londoners in *London's Sundays*, or the progress of a barge from Limehouse to the Paddington Basin in *Barging Through London*, the inter-titles explained the narrative progression between shots as a walking guide might moving between sites.

The travelogue films tour the *Wonders of Westminster*, as well as the more intriguing *Unknown London*. The films' titles recall those of walking tours named "The Famous Square Mile" or "Secret London." Each tour, like each film, shows walkers a different "version" of the city

1 *Wonderful London: Cosmopolitan London* (Harry B. Parkinson, UK, 1924). Source: Courtesy of the BFI archive.

governed by thematic and geographical concerns. Creating a thematised London, both indulge in a form of urban editing. A walking tour of "Legal and Illegal London," for instance, constructs a route that moves between the courtyards and gardens of the Inns of Court, ignoring busy thoroughfares that might interfere with this specific vision of the capital. Likewise, *Dickens's London* moves between the authentic settings of Dickens's novels, and cuts out the contemporary spaces that lie between. Films and walking tours create routes through the city by editing together places and cutting out the interim spaces.

The *Wonderful London* series does more than evoke walking tours through the structure and subjects of its films. The films frequently frame pedestrian-eye-views, shoot walkers strolling past the camera, and include inter-titles that invite viewers to "cross" the street. When the inter-titles of *London Off the Track* declare that it is "but a step," from the Old Cheshire Cheese on Fleet Street to the Thames Embankment "*via* Essex Stairs," they give a route that actual tourists could follow. Furthermore, the film presents viewers with an eye-level shot at the top of the stairs, before cutting to the bottom of the stairway. Spectators watch people descend, as if they had skipped down the steps to await their arrival. In *Dickens's London*, a figure dressed as David Copperfield strides towards the camera through the dark arches of the Adelphi, pedestrians walk before the camera through Clifford's Inn, while another pedestrian emerges from a walkway to cross the footbridge at Charing Cross. Each of these shots is framed by dark archways that in themselves imply a "passing through." These films summon the views experienced by wandering tourists, and so put film viewers in the position of actual walkers.

If the montage of *Wonderful London* mimics the walking tour, and the camera's framing puts spectators in the shoes of urban pedestrians, then the fundamentally sensual act of walking becomes central to understanding how spectators apprehend these films. In their study of "Fieldwork on Foot," anthropologists Tim Ingold and Jo Lee describe how walking enacts a series of shifting interactions between people and their environment.[2] Walking offers more than vision: its evocation in the *Wonderful London* series is indicative of how the films' images offer viewers more than visual stimuli.

Walter Benjamin argues that cinema spectators apprehend film in a state of "distraction" much as individuals apprehend buildings. People appropriate their architectural surroundings by touch as well as sight, so that architectural apprehension is achieved through "tactile appropriation."[3] Drawing on Benjamin's thesis, film theorist Giuliana Bruno argues that filmic and architectural spaces are thus both "lived" and inhabited "tangibly."[4] Spectators moving through the filmic space of *Wonderful London*, thus not only encounter the same visual spectacles as actual walkers on the capital's streets, but phantasmically experience the city's other sensual pleasures.

Moving through architectural space one sees, smells, touches, and hears.[5] The senses are similarly alive when moving through the filmic space of *Wonderful London*. The language of the films' inter-titles appeals to the senses, reminding us of the "thunder" of traffic at Hyde

Park Corner in *London Off the Track*; the "fruity" language of market traders at Billingsgate fish market in *London By Night*; and the feel of the floor of Covent Garden Market "slippery" with banana skins and "fetid with decaying vegetation" in *Flowers of London*. These evocative inter-titles appear between street-level scenes of traffic and market traders rushing past the camera. Placed amidst the action, viewers supplement their visual experience with non-visual ones.

Flowers of London goes further. Its cinematography evokes the act of smelling. At a florist's shop by London Bridge, the inter-titles tell us: "the nostrils are assailed by the scent of the homely." There follows a close-up of some flowers against a black background. The film continues in a similar pattern, following medium shots of flowers in florists with their close-ups against black backdrops. The close-ups seemingly mimic the act of bringing the flowers close to smell their scent. The black backgrounds shut out other visual clutter and take viewers out of the diegetic space of the film. These close-up images of flowers become like those envisioned in the mind's eye as one shuts off vision in order to concentrate on smell. When walking, tourists are able to vary their pace and pause to sense the city.[6] The *Wonderful London* series mimics this walking, helping spectators to imagine the various tactile, aural, olfactory, and visual sensations London has to offer. The *Wonderful London* series thus avoids the pitfalls of travelogues that showed spectators well-known views of the capital and prefigures the more recent "alternative" travelogues, *The London Nobody Knows* (1967) and *London* (1994), which concentrate on the city's details—its bollards, lavatories, and lamp posts—to uncover alternative histories of the city. By putting viewers on the ground and making them walkers, travelogues can go on trips of urban exploration where, around every corner and beyond every cut, there is always a new and unexpected aspect of *Wonderful London*.

Endnotes

1   Jennifer Lyn Peterson, "Travelogues and Early Non-fiction Film: Education in the School of Dreams," Charlie Keil and Shelley Stamp (eds.), *American Cinema's Transition Era: Audiences, Institutions, Practices* Stamp (Berkeley: University of California Press, 2004), 197.

2   Jo Lee and Tim Ingold, "Fieldwork on Foot: Perceiving, Routing, Socialising," Simon Coleman and Peter Collins (eds.), *Locating the Field: Space, Place and Context in Anthropology* (Oxford: Berg, 2006), 68.

3   Walter Benjamin, "The Work of Art in the Age of Mechanical Repro-duction," in *Illuminations*, trans. H. Arendt (London: Cape, 1970), 233.

4   Giuliana Bruno, *Atlas of Emotion: Journeys in Art, Architecture, and Film* (New York: Verso, 2002), 65.

5   Sarah Pink, "Walking with Video," in *Visual Studies* 22/, 245.

6   In anthropologist Adam Reed's study of walking guides in London, he describes how guides claimed that by walking, they were able to pause and "sense the city." Adam Reed, "City of Details: Interpreting the Personality of London," in *The Journal of the Royal Anthropological Institute* 8/1 (March 2002), 129.

CHINATOWN, AUTOMOBILE DRIVING, AND THE UNKNOWABLE CITY

Iain Borden

1

1 Jake Gittes observes Hollis Mulwray in the mirror of his 1935 Ford V8 De Luxe Phaeton. Source: *Chinatown* (Roman Polanski, 1974. DVD edition, Paramount Pictures, 2007)

Roman Polanski's cinematic masterpiece, the latter-day film noir *Chinatown* (1974), has been fêted as a Los Angeles film par excellence—famed for its convoluted narrative and cinematographic sophistication, and subjected to substantial critical interpretation. Based in part on the land and water disputes of inter-war California, with clear references to William Mulholland, the chief engineer of the LA Department of Water and Power who helped secure water rights in the Owens Valley, *Chinatown* has been variously construed as exploring environmental injustice, moral corruption in the context of Plato's notions of justice, social and political hypocrisy, a state of mind and correlative psychic geography, the essential futility of human existence, sexism and racism in the context of Western male subjectivity, masculinist detachment, the tale of Oedipus, and metaphors for the process of film-making.[1]

Embedded within these many interpretations, however, and most germane here, is that of *Chinatown* as a reverse urban constellation, that is as an assemblage of apparently disparate elements (the various components of the film's plot and LA settings), which can perhaps be combined into some form of intelligible schema (through detective Gittes), but which nonetheless ultimately serves to represent only the essentially unknowable and unmappable nature of the modern city.

So how does this all unfold? In *Chinatown*, private detective J.J. "Jake" Gittes (Jack Nicholson) investigates what he initially believes to be a relatively simple case of adultery. However, after realising that his mark, Hollis Mulwray (Darrell Zwerling), is somehow caught up in a convoluted swindle involving cheap land purchases and water supply, Gittes quickly finds the scenario to be even further complicated by various emotional relationships, false identities, murder, incest, police corruption, water department politics, and so forth. In this kind of city, as Gittes neatly explains to Mulwray's wife Evelyn (Faye Dunaway) "you can't always tell what is going on."

Although the interweaving strands of Robert Towne's Oscar-winning original screenplay are in themselves complex if not bewildering, even more sophisticated is Polanski's filmic representation of this labyrinthine tale. In order to construct Towne's dark plot visually, the director deploys a highly complex arrangement of views, searches, and surfaces. This is a visual system that renders Los Angeles less as a coherent urban or architectural space and more as a set of mysterious internalised and sometimes external spaces interconnected in some kind of, as yet, indecipherable manner.

In particular, as one would expect in the setting of 1937 LA, Gittes' movements through the city predominantly take place in an automobile, and so it is that car driving here comes to play a primary role in knowing—or not knowing—the city, its spaces, events, and mysterious connections. In part, the task of the automobile drive is a process of discovery—a means of opening up the internalised and hidden spaces of the city. Gittes thus deploys his 1935 Ford V8 De Luxe Phaeton in order to track Mulwray across various sites in the valley, to investigate drought-ridden orange groves and their combative owners in the north-west San Fernando Valley, and to visit Noah Cross (John Huston), the murderous, incestuous, and manipulative mastermind whom we later discover lies behind the complex land scam. In part, this automobile-born investigation is a tactic of observations and reflections, as when Gittes surveys Mulwray in the side mirror of his Ford. Here, while Gittes slowly parks the car, this mirror gently vibrates as Mulwray starts to walk towards somewhere unknown, and then, as Gittes turns off the V8, the same mirror snaps into clear and still focus as Mulwray walks out of view, descending down a steep path in the centre of the mirror's circle of observation. But above all—and as the automobile mirror's subtly mannered behaviour suggests—most significant here is the matter of Polanski correlating the spatiality and movements of the car with the seemingly impenetrable complexity of the situation that Gittes is facing. For example, at one point Gittes follows Evelyn during a night-time journey across LA, during which journey the screen turns almost black as they make their way across unlit roads. However, Gittes is nonetheless aided here by his having already smashed the red tail-light cover of Evelyn's 1938 Packard Twelve, a tactic he deliberately deploys to make the Packard easier to recognise on the murky road.

Polanski's mastery of cinema as an analogue for cognitive possibilities and impossibilities is most apparent in a tense concluding scene. Here, Gittes drives Noah Cross and water department security chief Claude Mulvihill into Chinatown, en route to a meeting with Evelyn and Katherine, the latter being—through Evelyn's incest with her father Noah when aged 15—both Evelyn's sister and her daughter. In the few seconds of this highly sophisticated depiction of driving experience, city space is both viewed from inside of the car (where it is obscured through reflections and movement) and accompanied by the tense and silent intimacy of the car interior. Disturbingly, the camera sits in the rear alongside Noah Cross and behind Gittes and Mulvihill upfront, and in this position it simultaneously views the

2

2 Jake Gittes drives into Chinatown with Noah Cross and Claude Mulvihill.
Source: *Chinatown* (Roman

Polanski, 1974. DVD edition, Paramount Pictures, 2007).

face of Gittes in the driver's rear-view mirror and swivels to inspect the passing signs, traffic, and busy street life of Chinatown outside—and in doing so it places the audience among the action as an unannounced fourth participant. And yet, the camera also remains unacknowledged by the other occupants of the car, a position of distanced invisibility that is punctured only by the occasional and seeming direct eye contact from Gittes in the driver's mirror, and here the audience is posited as the contemplative analogue for Gittes himself. In short, we ride along with Gittes, Cross, and Mulvihill, not as a physical presence, but as a psychological intensifier, parallel, and supplement.

The result is a multi-layered and fractured space of suspension—a system of looks, glances, views, and reflections that briefly and intensively emerges as the car reaches its destination in Chinatown. City driving here is at once mobile and static, revelatory and confusing, internal and external, physical and immaterial. It renders the city at once known and unknown, intelligible and irrational, certain and fragmented. In this dense spatio-visual construction, the experience of driving in cities attains what is perhaps one of its most significant attributes, as a way of not just travelling around or of discovering new places, but of confronting the complexities of the city with all that it has to offer, and of trying—without ever quite succeeding – to accommodate oneself within that complexity physically, spatially and mentally. In this sense, one might even conclude that *Chinatown* is less an urban constellation in which all comes together or is made clear, but more of acting as its very opposite. Indeed, while driving is often interpreted as an act of deliberate movement towards a particular destination—and so is supposedly redolent with modernist connotations of certainty, clarity, determination, rationality, resolution, and transparency—in fact, the kind of driving that takes place in this film suggests that there is always an embedded tension within the cognitive landscape of our cities, a tension which discloses that such modernist qualities are at the very least uncertain and quite possibly unachievable. *Chinatown* thus serves as reminder that our cities ultimately resist representation, comprehension, and ordered understanding, and that, in turn, driving in them makes this essential condition even more apparent.

Endnotes

1 See, for example, Stephen Cooper, "Sex/Knowledge/Power in the Detective Genre," in *Film Quarterly*, 42/3 (Spring 1989), 23–31; Margaret Leslie Davis, *Rivers in the Desert: William Mulholland and the Inventing of Los Angeles*, (New York: Harper Collins, 1993); Mike Davis, "*Chinatown*, Part Two? The Internationalization of Downtown Los Angeles," in *New Left Review*, n 164 (July–August 1987), 65–86; Rosalyn Deutsche, "*Chinatown*, Part Four? What Jake Forgets about Downtown," in *Assemblage*, 20 (April 1993), 32–3; Michael Easton, *Chinatown*, (London: BFI, 1998); William Galperin, "Bad for the Glass: Representation and Filmic Deconstruction in *Chinatown* and *Chan Is Missing*," in *Modern Language Notes*, 102/5 (December 1987), 1151–70; Tony Fitzmaurice, "Chinatown and the End of Classical Hollywood," in *Irish Journal of American Studies*, 7 (1998), 149–161; Daniel J. Goulding (ed.), *Five Film-makers: Tarkovsky, Forman, Polanski, Szabo, Makavejev* (Bloomington: Indiana University Press, 1994); Deborah Linderman, "Oedipus in Chinatown," in *Enclitic*, 10–11 (Fall 1981–Spring 1982), 190–203; Phillip Novak, "The Chinatown Syndrome," in *Criticism*, 49/3 (Summer 2007) 255–83; Jeanne Schuler and Patrick Murray, "Anything Is Possible Here: Capitalism, Neo-Noir and *Chinatown*," Mark T. Conard (ed.), *The Philosophy of Neo-Noir* (Lexington: University Press of Kentucky, 2007), 167–82; Vernon Lionel Shetley, "Incest and Capital in Chinatown," in *Modern Language Notes*, 114/5 (December 1999), 1092–109; and Garrett Stewart, "*The Long Goodbye from Chinatown*," in *Film Quarterly*, 28/2 (Winter, 1974–1975), 25–32.

INTIMATIONS OF PAST AND FUTURE IN THE CINEMATIC CITY

Mark Tewdwr-Jones

"The eye does not see things, but images of things that mean other things." [1]
Italo Calvino

1 Rome (2011)
Source: Photo by Mark
Tewdwr-Jones

The urban has long been a feature of motion pictures and the use of urban landscapes for the setting of films has taken varied forms since the dawn of cinema more than one hundred years ago. There are the studio urban landscapes, recreating the real in a controlled and filmic managed setting, which offer filmmakers the opportunity of playing, rearranging, and collapsing space; Hitchcock achieved this feat with *Rear Window* (1954), building what was then the largest film set and sound studio in the world for his depiction of a Greenwich village courtyard. There are the location urban landscapes, where places are recognisable either because they serve to represent actual spaces or where they masquerade as other locations; Stanley Kubrick's *Full Metal Jacket* (1987) depicts war-torn Vietnam but actually filmed large parts of it in the derelict docklands of Beckton, East London. There are the mainstream depictions, and there are alternative counter perspectives, from big production on-location films, to hand-held Youtube videos, experimental, and animated films. The urban landscapes form part of the narrative text to these films that are necessary to convey a unified sense of space.

The eclecticism of the contemporary study of cities—associated with a growing body of theory on place identity, on "placeness," and spatial awareness; on the interrelations between place, space, people and politics, with a long-standing interest in urban form and city life; and with an understanding of the use of urban space and arrangement—provides an opportunity for an alternative critical perspective, gleaned from celluloid representation, which might explain the prevalence and significance of people's perceptions of places that social scientists often feel remote from or unable to discern. Similar to maps, films are just another way of looking at the world but evoke matters concerning power and contestation.

Globally, we may think of the way Gorky was captured by Vertov in *Man With a Movie Camera* (1929), Chicago masquerades as Gotham in the Batman films, New York City forms the backdrop to Woody Allen's *Manhattan* (1979), San Francisco is used in Hitchcock's *Vertigo* (1958), or revolutionary-era Havana infuses the atmosphere of Kalatozov's *I Am Cuba* (1964). Film generates emotion about the here and now, and on what has gone before. The ubiquitous city skyline, serving to represent progress and the future, of urban bridges, gateways between different communities, or living on the right or wrong side of the tracks, of car chases, and crime caper getaways. All these are employed in film narratives and the city as filmic location can be as important as the storyline itself. But film can also evoke a sense of history, of nostalgia for things past. Terence Davies's *Of Time and the City* (2008) is a remarkable homage to a long vanished Liverpool, one not only devastated by the collapse of manufacturing, but also by what the planners and architects did to the city in the name of progress between the 1950s and 1970s. But his narrative sometimes jars with the imagery: recollections of his personal experiences when he was young, not always happy, juxtaposed with other people's super 8 home cine movie footage of old Liverpool. Whose city are we talking about? And we sometimes forget in our rush to create modern places, with the best architecture and most rational solutions to urban form, that there is often a desire to look backwards in order to make sense of change. Marshall Berman describes this as a feature of modernity—the backward glance to a long vanished time as we sit on the edge of an uncertain abyss. And film is perfectly suited to portray this dynamism, "between recreated past and threatening future," to use Charles Barr's phrase.[2] Sometimes, this backward glance is for comfort, to familiar and cherished scenes that often awaken conservation and heritage sensibilities in attitudes toward real space. Blue heritage plaques attached to the outside of buildings in London, for example, are but one testament to this desire to remember what or who went before in very specific locations of the city; often they mark the birthplace of film actors, celebrities and politicians. Or the popularity of walking or photographic tours around cities to capture fragments of the past, or specific events that caused upheaval in our urban landscape.

In the films of Patrick Keiller—such as *London* (1994), *Robinson in Space* (1997), and *Robinson in Ruins* (2010)—we find an eye for detail at capturing conditions of places, through entertaining journeys and oblique perspectives of change. Echoing the literary works of J.G. Ballard and Iain Sinclair, and a fascination for psychogeography, the films evoke, to quote Sinclair, a "quiet provocation" to audiences, noting: "The truth of a city, divided against itself, can only be revealed, so Keiller believes, through a series of obscure pilgrimages, days spent crawling out on to the rim of things. The transcendent surrealism of airport perimeter roads, warehouses, and reservoirs."[3] Keiller's films provide an imaginative capture of the direct impacts of urban planning and of the places that planners have left behind or neglected. These images are not the stuff of picture postcards, of architects' and urban designers' glossy portrayals. Rather, they are images that capture fragments of place history and place memory—"liminal spaces," to use Andrew Higson's phraseology—and reveal places we might otherwise regard as routine or irrelevant. To those of us involved in urban planning and the analysis of place, these films are both familiar and baffling. Is Keiller presenting a critical perspective or an ironic one? And how does it challenge our own perspectives of the familiar in new and unnerving ways? A similar style can be found in films by Paul Kelly for the pop group Saint Etienne. *Finisterre* (2002), an imaginary twenty-four hours in London, owes some of its ideas to aspects of Keiller's work but is also guided by a previous London-centred documentary, *The London Nobody Knows* (1967, directed by Geoffrey Fletcher) and to Ian Nairn's work on London. Nairn, writing in his 1955 book *Outrage*, provided a forceful defence of the individuality of places, whilst castigating "the world of the universal low density mess ... a mean middle state, neither town or country," which he termed "Subtopia."[4]

The geographer Doreen Massey has argued persuasively for a relational politics of space-time based on the fullest conception of space as "the sphere of the existence of multiplicity." Here, "space is not stable, not a cross-section through time, it is disrupted, active and generative."[5] With space as the product of interrelations and the sphere of multiplicity, interventions in the urban will be temporal in nature and of course partial. But the perceptions of space, of theorisations and of imaginations, will be multiple, too. Film and photography provide a means by which those multiple identities and understandings can be revealed. These filmic images of space and place are selective too, but they can be viewed as a catalyst for less static forms of space and place perceptions. We recognise buildings instantly from filmic images, and where they are located, what they serve to represent, from what period of history, and how they are symbolic of changing times. Some of these notions are erroneous, whereas some are genuine forms of affection. As with Calvino's eye on the city, the camera lens may be used to depict the multiple meanings of places, to represent both difference and distinctiveness, and to challenge our existing perceptions of the urban.

Endnotes

1 Italo Calvino, *Invisible Cities* (New York: Harcourt Brace Jovanovich, 1974).

2 Charles Barr, *Ealing Studios* (2nd edn.; London: Studio Vista, 1993). See also A. Higson, "The instability of the national," in J. Ashby and A. Higson (eds.) *British cinema: Past and present* (London: Routledge, 2000) 35–47.

3 Iain Sinclair, "London: Necropolis of fretful ghosts," in *Sight and Sound*, reprinted in the booklet accompanying the DVD *London*; and Patrick Keiller, *Robinson in Space* (London: BFI, 1994).

4 Ian Nairn, *Outrage* (London: Architectural Press, 1955).

5 Doreen Massey, "Space-time, 'science' and the relationship between physical geography and human geography," in *Transaction of the Institute of British Geographers* 24 (1999), 261–76.

URBAN VISTAS AND THE CIVIC IMAGINATION

Rebecca Ross

"Three rooms were erected for us there on the roof where the draftsmen and every person who touched this plan could look out from the windows and see the problem laying right before him, the problem of the lake front and looking in the other direction the problem of the great city itself." [1]

So was described the small structure atop the seventeen-storey Railway Exchange from which the 1909 *Plan of Chicago* was prepared under the direction of Daniel Burnham and Edward Bennett.[2] The purpose-built addition to the north-east corner of the roof, paid for by the Commercial Club at Burnham's request, echoed that of a previous workspace shared by Burnham and Bennett in 1904 in San Francisco, "Willis Polk was putting up a shack at Mr. Burnham's request to be high up on Twin Peaks where it commanded a view of the entire city."[3] Polk had been commissioned by the Association for the Improvement and Adornment of San Francisco, a group of elite businessmen who had invited Burnham to develop a comprehensive plan for the city in an effort to, as in the later case of Chicago, "stimulate the sentiment of civic pride."[4]

These heightened vantage points cum workspaces, "selected to command the panorama of the city and to permit uninterrupted study,"[5] invited contemplation of and fascination with the unfathomability of the early twentieth-century American city. They engendered feelings of wonderment at the same time that they underscored anxieties about an ever complexify-

1

ing urban landscape and the desire to bring it to order. This experience of the view was am-
plified through its inscription in extravagant volumes dedicated not only to comprehensive
plans seeking to intervene in the future of each city but also to the establishment of city
planning itself as a new category of professional practice. These volumes featured sketches
and photographs taken from the specific perspective of the workspaces. The *Report on a
plan for San Francisco*, in particular, begins with an eighty-five-centimetre-wide fold-out
panoramic photograph taken from the exterior of the Twin Peaks bungalow. Mostly though,
the dramatic views served as backdrops to a variety of activities carried out by commercial
artists, draftsman, illustrators, and writers with occasional visits from members of the com-
missioning associations. Jules Guerin, perhaps the most notable of Burnham and Bennett's
hired craftsmen, was well known for his ability to create fully resolved and complete looking
bird's eye views whilst stripping away all but the most crucial details and rendering them
in muted tones.

Burnham's insistence on panoramic workspaces as a precondition for comprehensive
planning presumes seeing the "whole city" as an obvious prerequisite to interposing in
its future. It literalises, perhaps to the point of absurdity, a variety of metaphors invoking
views from above employed within many brilliant critical engagements with empiricism
and ideology.[6] However, rather than retrace the dangers and limitations of conflating
purportedly sweeping vision with presumed omniscience, here I will explore the role of
vantage points in facilitating a shared sense of what I will refer to as the "civic imagina-

1 Burnham at the Twin Peaks
Cabin likely to have been
taken by Edward Bennett, circa
1904. From Lake Forest College
Library Archives and Special
Collections, Marcia O. and Edward H. Bennett III Collection.

tion." In documents such as the *Plan of Chicago* this was enacted through a progression from vistas to images—from painted and photographic views designed to inspire a sense of possibility for a reorganised and beautified Chicago, to diagrams and mechanically drafted plans which substantiated planners' status as experts—in particular architects—ambitiously positioning themselves as capable of realising this now shared fantasy of a new kind of city.

In employing the specific term, "civic imagination," my intention is to draw explicitly upon the legacy of the civic art movement, as it was incorporated into the comprehensive city planning movement at the start of the twentieth century, in order to distinguish and value a productive thread of today's urban culture. The Civic Art movement was a call for the pursuit of urban beauty to the extent that cities would be considered as great works of art.[7] Civic imagination is partially an emotional or precognitive, perhaps conflicted, response to urban complexity and partially a quasi-fantastical and quasi-intellectual projection of what is observed as well as speculation beyond the limits of what is observed into a vision of a potential future. Neither entirely disconnected from the concrete city nor fully expressed as image, civic imagination is based primarily in an active response to looking at urban conditions. Would-be planners aspiring to apply the ideals of the civic art movement at the scale of the city—in their efforts to conscript the broader public into their own vision—articulated a vantage point that would focus the collective civic imagination on the future of the city. As an effort directly connected to the development of the planning profession, however, the need to engage the public at the centre of urban planning matters was de-emphasised with the profession's permanent installation as a function of local government subject to political and market forces.[8]

The artists employed by planners during the progressive era had begun, however, to feed the civic imagination by engaging with the complex experience of the city as seen from dramatic vantage points. Today, historic observation decks such as at the top of the Eiffel Tower or the Empire State Building, which themselves developed out of late nineteenth-century enthusiasm for captive balloons and Ferris wheels, remain an industry and new purpose-built high points are being commissioned all the time. The winning entry to a 2010 architectural competition to design a tower in Taichung to commemorate the centennial anniversary of the founding of Taiwan features eight large floating observatories supported by helium, and attached to tracks on the sides of the building via which they propose to transport groups of eighty 350 metres into the sky.[9] Such observatories provide occasion for millions of visitors each year to consider urban complexity from a staggering vantage point. While this particular viewpoint is, albeit for good reasons, no longer of special concern to city planning professionals who have moved on to other ways of seeing and knowing urban conditions, it does endure as an experience that interacts with a large-scale civic imagination. The question is how this can be brought into more active relation to contemporary urban conditions. What is at stake then for the future of a shared "civic imagination"? In recent years, cultural enthusiasm for urban vistas and high points has, of course, been complemented by the widespread availability of satellite photography and other spatial data incorporated into services such as Google Maps. Google, as part of their own corporate strategy, makes images and information accessible to individuals and governments on the same basis. The effect of this and other shifts in our media environment have been, to some extent, to close a gap between what for a hundred years have been distinct professional and public vantage points. As Burnham once brazenly hung large-scale watercolours of the Chicago of his dreams at the Art Institute in order to inspire Chicagoans to engage with his own aspirations, contemporary publics have new fields upon which to negotiate with specialists and experts. Designers and artists once charged with articulating the visions of would-be planners are themselves increasingly using such tools to break down technocratic boundaries and inspire new and alternate interventions.[10] However, in order for these activities to transcend niche creative experimentation and have a deep and meaningful impact on urban conditions, they will need to compel the civic imagination on a much larger scale.

Endnotes

1 Charles Norton to the Commercial Club of Chicago, 25 January 1908. Box 2, Commercial Club Record, Chicago Historical Society.

2 *The Railway Exchange* was designed by Frederick P. Dinkelberg on behalf of Burnham & Co. Construction was completed in 1904. It is now called the *Santa Fe Building*. The Commercial Club of Chicago, the association of elite Chicago businessmen who had commissioned Burnham and Bennett's *Plan of Chicago* (Chicago: Commercial Club, 1909), also financed the construction of the dedicated rooftop structure.

3 Edward Bennett, "Notes on Daniel Hudson Burnham 1917–18," Lake Forest College Library Archives and Special Collections, Marcia O. and Edward H. Bennett III Collection.

4 Daniel Burnham, *Report on a Plan for San Francisco* (San Francisco: Association for the Improvement and Adornment of San Francisco, 1905), 7.

5 Ibid, 8.

6 See Donna Haraway, "Situated Knowledges: The Science Question in Feminism and the Privilege of Partial Perspective," in *Feminist Studies* 14 (Autumn 1988), 575–599; Michel de Certeau, *The Practice of Everyday Life* (Berkeley: University of California Press, 1984), 91–93; Roland Barthes, *The Eiffel Tower and other mythologies* (New York: Hill and Wang, 1979), 3–18; and Henri Lefebvre, *The Urban Revolution* (Minneapolis: University of Minnesota Press, 2003), 182–183. Also see Patrick Joyce, *The Rule of Freedom* (London: Verso, 2003), 35–57 for an example from within discussions of governmentality.

7 For an example of the application of the principles of Civic Art to the comprehensive planning movement, see Charles Mulford Robinson, "Planning for City Beauty," in *Municipal Journal and Engineer* 21 (September 5, 1906), 230–231. This thinking drew upon the influence of Camillo Sitte as brought to the Americas by Werner Hegemann. See Werner Hegemann and Elbert Peets, *American Vitruvius: an architect's handbook of civic art* (New York: The Architectural Book Publishing Company, 1922).

8 Jon A. Peterson argues that the progressive ideals of early planners were abandoned in the face of political and economic pressure. *The birth of city planning in the United States, 1840–1917* (Baltimore: Johns Hopkins University Press, 2003). Also, see Christine Boyer, *Dreaming the Rational City* (Cambridge, MA: MIT Press, 1986), for a discursive account of the failure of the planning profession to live up to its social and aesthetic promise.

9 *Floating Observatories* by Dorin Stefan/DSBA, Mihai Carciun, and upgrade.studio won first prize in the 2010 Taiwan Conceptual Tower Competition.

10 Local citizen groups such as cycling coalitions or ad hoc campaigns against redevelopment programs have begun capitalising on the collective visual and technical skills of their membership to put forth their own detailed alternatives to government-favoured proposals. US-based examples include The Greenline station modeling workshop (Boston), Develop Don't Destroy (New York), and the San Francisco Bicycle Coalition's cycling infrastructure proposals. Other organisations stage small-scale interventions that seek to reinspire active engagement with places and neighbourhoods. The Center for Urban Pedagogy, for example, pairs graphic designers with advocacy groups to publish clear explanations of public policy. Laura Kurgan's 2001 project, *Around Ground Zero*, a series of independently published and widely distributed maps of lower Manhattan issued during the months following 11 September to promote and ease re-engagement with the site of a sudden and violent change to the city.

"THE SUN WILL SHINE ON THE HOMES OF THE FUTURE": DANISH WELFARE ARCHITECTURE ON A SCALE OF 1:1

C. Claire Thomson

"The panorama-city is a 'theoretical' (that is, visual) simulacrum, in short a picture, whose condition of possibility is an oblivion and a misunderstanding of practices." [1]

In 1947, a strategy for the development of the Greater Copenhagen area was officially codified and published under the leadership of Peter Bredsdorff.[2] The plan was instantly graspable and profoundly humanist: Copenhagen was to develop in the shape of a hand, represented by *Fingerplanen*, the Finger Plan. The aim was to prevent untrammelled urban development and to protect natural landscapes and recreational areas. Between each "finger" of the hand, green corridors would extend all the way in towards the "palm," central Copenhagen. Overground trains (the s-tog lines) would run through the middle of each finger, bringing commuters from the planned suburbs to the centre. As post-war Copenhagen developed, the plan assured a "uniquely cohesive" integration of the city's infrastructure,[3] with democratic access to fresh air, well-functioning living spaces, cultural experiences, transport, and utilities. The Finger Plan was never officially adopted by any forum or body, but its clarity and imagery are so powerful that local authorities have always obeyed its principles.

On the thumb of the Finger Plan, to the south-west of central Copenhagen, lies the suburb of Avedøre Stationsby, built between 1972 and 1982. The suburb is a prime example of a wave of super-planned new towns that sprang up in Denmark in the 1960s and 1970s—architectural translations of the principles of welfare and well-being. It encompassed 2,500 prefabricated homes, several schools, a church, a library, a shopping centre, a sports centre, community meeting places, and (as its name suggests) its own commuter train station. A population of around 5,000 was projected in an area of about a kilometre in diameter.[4] The planners also acknowledged the influence of medieval townscapes—Dubrovnik in particular—conceptualising these as an admixture of closure and enclosure. That is, the townscape's linear parameters give a sense of closure and continuity (for example, the city "wall" formed by the taller blocks around the outer edge of the development); but there is also a sense of privacy and spatial enclosure for the individual or nuclear family. Theoretically, residents would understand how the space of the town was to be used, how to move through it, and how to feel at home in it.[5] In evidence here is the principle of legibility, as laid out by the American town planner Kevin Lynch in the 1960s, whose work was an acknowledged influence on the planners of Avedøre Stationsby.[6] Lynch is well known for the typology of urban elements he identified as essential to a town's legibility: paths, nodes, edges, districts, and landmarks. All of these are clearly visible from the aerial projection of Avedøre.

This aerial projection, and the tensions between planned and lived space it evokes, is the centrepiece of the extraordinary opening sequence of *1:1*, directed by Annette K. Olesen. Premiering in 2006, *1:1* is one of the few Danish films to tackle thoughtfully the experience of living in intercultural Copenhagen. As can be deduced from its title, the film works with, through, and within architecture and planned space to evoke and to question the sensory, dynamic, relational experience of living in, moving through, and interacting with a given material and cultural environment.

The opening sequence of *1:1* cross-cuts between 2D and 3D models of the planned suburb, documentary footage of the construction process and of Avedøre's first few residents, and the multiethnic community of the present day (or, at least, its fictional counterpart). The voiceover is provided by the architect, whose commentary betrays the linearist progressivism of the Nordic Welfare era, waxing lyrical on the longer-term fate of his planned suburb: "Traffic noise will not blot out the birdsong, and the sun will shine on the homes of the future."

From the outset, then, 1:1 lays out its spatio-historical agenda using the visual arsenal of film. In spatial terms, it situates its characters firmly in a planned space that crystallises the now discredited social ideals of the period of its construction, a space in which, the film suggests, human dramas are experienced more acutely precisely because of the tension between the spatial plan and the social reality. In historical terms, the device of cross-cutting urges reflection on a Benjaminian, "constellar" understanding of history and architecture. Like Benjamin's "historical materialist,"[7] the filmmaker regards it as her task not to "tell the sequence of events like beads on a rosary," but to visualise her own era in constellation with the earlier idealism of the architects of Welfare.

The crucial final shot of this opening sequence features a perceptible digital morph from one form of projection to another: from aerial plan of the suburb, to aerial night-time view. The *segue* between title sequence and story is thus self-reflexive; in playing with the cartographer's scale, the film draws our attention to the same paradox of representation identified by Michel de Certeau in his essay "Walking in the City." The "condition of possibility" for the city is "an oblivion and misunderstanding of [planning] practices" on the part of its denizens; if the city is planned on a scale of 4000:1, it is lived at 1:1. But in revealing the blindness of planners to lived experience, the film also gestures to its own medium-specific limitations.

However, in defiance of these limitations, *1:1* explores the tension between planned and lived space by privileging the non-visual senses. Laura Marks writes of intercultural cinema that it "evoke[s] memories both individual and cultural, through an appeal to nonvisual knowledge, embodied knowledge, and experiences of the senses."[8] If we now return to Lynch's classic book, we see that despite his focus on the "imageability" of the city, he opens up a space in which the mastery of vision can be resisted. He frequently refers in his writing to the role of the other senses, and to alternative systems of orientation in ethnographic

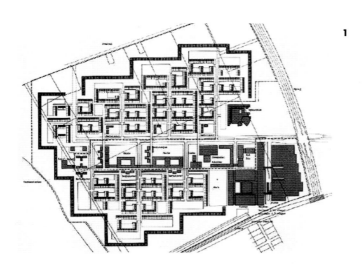

1 Aerial Plan of Avedøre
Stationsby, 1970
Source: Danish Suburban
Museum, Forstadsmuseet

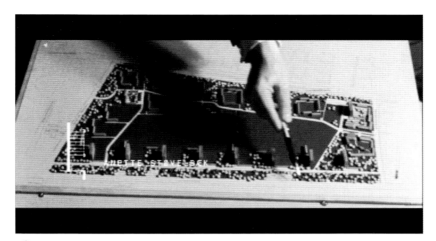

2

records, in navigating the environment, and in producing, as he puts it, "the emotional satisfaction, the framework for communication or conceptual organisation, the new depths that it may bring to everyday experience."[9] Environmental objects, he thinks, should not only be visible, but "presented sharply and intensely to the senses."[10] He lists the orientation cues used across species: the visual sensations of colour, shape, motion, or polarisation of light, as well as other senses such as smell, sound, touch, kinesthesia, sense of gravity, and perhaps of electric or magnetic fields.[11]

The sensory and proprioceptive interaction of residents with the environment are transposed into the film's interaction with its location, in two ways. Firstly, *1:1* is very concerned with the bodies of its protagonists. The plot centres on the beaten body of an attacked teenager, hovering between life and death in hospital. In the encounter of the prosthetic "body" of the intrusive handheld camera with the bodies of the main characters (our Romeo and Juliet), Mie and Shadi, we participate in a corporeal arena in which the physical, sensory, and occasionally violent intercultural encounter is thrashed out.

Secondly, much is made of orientation. With the handheld camera, we patrol the area alongside a guard and his dog, on foot and in his cramped car; walking with groups of teenagers from one place to the next; traversing the park in the dark; waiting at the train station; but we never learn how to navigate the space as continuous or *known*. As spectators, we are put in the position of an incomer or immigrant (in Danish *indvandrer*, literally "in-wanderer"). Odd, perhaps, considering the time devoted to mapping the town at the

2 The opening sequence of *1:1* incorporates documentary footage of the planning process (*1:1*, dir. Annette K. Olesen,

Denmark, 2006)
Source: Danish Film Institute

beginning, but not so paradoxical when we remember De Certeau's tension between planning the city and walking the city. The visual cues designed by the planners turn out not to be so "legible" on the ground. What the film seems to evoke here is proprioception, which is, as Brian Massumi puts it, "a sixth sense directly attuned to the movement of the body" and to "displacements of the parts of the body relative to one another." Moving through a known space, explains Massumi, involves not "visible form" but "a bodily memory" of "contortion and rhythm."[12] The film *1:1* lingers on the cartographers' town plan all the better to disorientate us when we encounter the same space at ground level, with neither a map nor bodily memory of the townscape.

1:1 ends unhappily, *in medias res*, with an escalation of interracial gang violence. The film dissects the dynamics of intercultural living in a space planned for the progressivism of another era, and finds a chain of "misunderstanding of practices": in the Avedøre of *1:1*, the ideals of the architects and planners are as incomprehensible as the cultural practices of neighbours. As the titles roll, one realises that, in defiance of the architect's vision, not once have we seen the sun shine on these homes of the future.

Endnotes

1 Michel De Certeau, "Walking in the City," in *The Practice of Everyday Life* (London: Vintage, 1984), 92.
2 See http://kulturkanon.kum.dk/en/Architecture/The-Finger-Plan/. This entry in the government-sponsored *Danish Cultural Canon* (2006) is an expression of the Finger Plan's hold on the collective imagination, as is the adoption of the term "The New Finger Plan" for the Ministry of the Environment's 2007 ten-year plan for Copenhagen.
3 *Fingerplan 2007: Landsplandirektiv for hovedstadsområdets planlægning* (Miljøministeriet, 2007) p12.
4 Forstadsmuseet, 'Avedøre Stationsby: Historien om en plan.' http://www.forstadsmuseet.dk/Default.aspx?ID=212. A detailed history of the project is available (in Danish) from Forstadsmuseet's website: http://www.forstadsmuseet.dk/Default.aspx?ID=2322.
5 Dansk Arkitekturcenter, 'Værkleksikon: Avedøre Stationsby, 1982.' http://www.dac.dk/visKanonVaerk.asp?artikelID=2653.
6 Dansk Forstadsmuseet, 'Avedøre Stationsby: Ideerne bag planen.' http://www.forstadsmuseet.dk/Default.aspx?ID=2324.
7 Walter Benjamin, "Theses on the Philosophy of History," in *Illuminations* (London: Verso, 1999), 255.
8 Laura U. Marks, *The Skin of the Film* (London and Durham: Duke University Press, 2000) 1–2
9 Kevin Lynch, *The Image of the City* (Cambridge, Mass.: MIT Press, 1992; orig. pub. 1960), 5.
10 Ibid., 10.
11 Ibid., 3.
12 Brian Massumi, *Parables for the Virtual: Movement, Affect, Sensation* (London and Durham: Duke University Press, 2002), 178–9.

CONTRIBUTORS

LARA ALMARCEGUI is a Spanish artist whose work often explores neglected or overlooked sites, carefully cataloguing and highlighting each location's tendency towards entropy. Her projects have ranged from a guide to the wastelands of Amsterdam, to the display —in their raw form—of the materials used to construct the galleries in which she exhibits. Recent group exhibitions include: *Radical Nature,* Barbican Art Centre London (2009); Athens Biennale (2009); Gwuangyu Biennale (2008); Sharjah Biennale (2007); São Paulo Biennial (2006); Seville Biennial (2006); *Public Act,* Lunds Konsthal 2005. Solo exhibitions include: Secession, Vienna (2010); *Ruins in the Netherlands,* Gallery Ellen de Bruijne Projects, Amsterdam (2008); the FRAC Bourgogne, Dijon (2004); and INDEX, Stockholm (2003).

JOHAN ANDERSSON is a Research Fellow in the School of Geography at Leeds University and completed his PhD in the Bartlett School at UCL. He has published on a wide range of topics relating to minority sexual identity and urban culture in journals such as *Antipode*, *Urban Studies*, *Environment and Planning A* and *The London Journal*. Whilst completing his PhD he co-authored a book on planning in England's urban fringe and also worked for the UCL Urban Laboratory.

PUSHPA ARABINDOO is Lecturer in Geography and Urban Design at University College London. She trained as an architect and urban designer in India and the USA and completed her PhD in planning at the London School of Economics. Her research investigates several aspects of India urbanisation including aesthetic dimensions to planning, emerging forms of middle-class militancy, and the political impact of environmental disasters such as the 2004 tsunami and the 2005 floods. She has published articles in various journals including *City, Development and Change* and *International Journal of Urban and Regional Research*.

KAREN BAKKER is Professor of Geography, Canada Research Chair in Political Ecology, and founding Director of the Program on Water Governance at the University of British Columbia. Her work on urban political ecology has been published in journals ranging across several disciplines (development studies, environmental studies, geography, urban studies) including *World Development, The International Journal of Urban and Regional Research*, and *Environment and Planning*. She is author of *Privatizing Water: Governance Failure and the World's Urban Water Crisis* (Cornell University Press, 2010); *Eau Canada* (UBC, 2007); and *An Uncooperative Commodity* (Oxford University Press, 2004).

STEPHEN BARBER is Professor of Film and Visual Culture in the School of Art and Design History, Kingston University, London. He is the author of several books on urban and film cultures including: *Fragments of the European City* (Reaktion, 1995); *Projected Cities: Cinema and Urban Space* (Reaktion, 2002); *The Vanishing Map: A Journey from LA to Tokyo to the Heart of Europe* (Berg, 2006); *Abandoned Images: Film and Film's End* (Reaktion, 2010); and *The Walls of Berlin. Urban Surfaces: Art: Film* (Solar, 2010).

SARAH BELL began her career as a process and environmental engineer at an aluminium smelter in Australia before completing her PhD in Sustainability and Technology Policy at Murdoch University. She taught sustainable agriculture and land management at the University of Sydney before moving to UCL where she teaches engineering history, environmental systems engineering, and an introduction to engineering for liberal arts students. Her research focuses on the interactions between society and technology as they impact on sustainability, with particular focus on urban water systems.

IAIN BORDEN is Professor of Architecture and Urban Culture at the Bartlett School of Architecture, UCL, where he is also Vice Dean for Communications for the Faculty of the Built Environment. His authored and co-edited books include: *Bartlett Designs: Speculating With Architecture* (Wiley, 2009); *Skateboarding Space and the City* (Berg, 2001); *The Unknown City: Contesting Architecture and Social Space* (The MIT Press, 2001); and *InterSections: Architectural Histories and Critical Theories* (Routledge, 2000). He is currently working on a history of automobile driving, urban experience, and cinema, to be published by Reaktion Books as *Drive: Automobile Journeys through Cities, Architecture & Film.*

NEIL BRENNER is Professor of Urban Theory at the Harvard Graduate School of Design. He formerly taught Sociology and Metropolitan Studies at New York University. He is the author of *New State Spaces: Urban Governance and the Rescaling of Statehood* (Oxford, 2004); co-editor of *Spaces of Neoliberalism* (with Nik Theodore; Blackwell, 2002), *The Global Cities Reader* (with Roger Keil; Routledge, 2006), and *Cities for People, Not for Profit* (with Margit Mayer and Peter Marcuse; Routledge, 2011). His research interests include critical urban theory, socio-spatial theory, state theory, and comparative geopolitical economy.

BEN CAMPKIN is Lecturer in Architectural History and Theory at the Bartlett School of Architecture, University College London and has been a Co-Director of the UCL Urban Laboratory since 2008, becoming Director in 2011. He is co-editor of *Dirt: New Geographies of Cleanliness and Contamination* (IB Tauris, 2007) and has published articles in *The Journal of Architecture* and *Architectural Design*. He is currently writing a cultural history of decline and renewal in London.

MUSTAFA DIKEÇ is Reader in Human Geography at Royal Holloway, University of London. His research is focused around three themes: the politics of space, the politics of alterity, and the politics of time. On the first two, he has published *Badlands of the Republic: Space, Politics and Urban Policy* (Blackwell, 2007) and co-edited *Extending Hospitality: Giving Space, Taking Time* (with Nigel Clark and Clive Barnett; Edinburgh University Press, 2009). On the politics of time, he is embarking on a new project entitled *Pumping Time: Geographies of Temporal Infrastructure in Fin-de-siècle Paris* funded by Arts and Humanities Research Council.

GER DUIJZINGS is Reader in Anthropology of Eastern Europe at the School of Slavonic and East European Studies, Director of the Centre for South-East European Studies, and Co-Director of the Urban Laboratory at University College London. He published widely on the conflicts and wars in the former Yugoslavia, and is currently doing research on post-socialist urban transformations, social inequality, and the nouveaux riches in Bucharest. He also developed the idea for *CitiesMethodologies*, an exhibition with talks and workshops showcasing innovative methods in urban research, which has been held three times at UCL and once in Bucharest.

MICHAEL EDWARDS is an economist and planner at the Bartlett School, UCL. He works on rent and property markets and on supporting challenges to the dominance of landed interests over workers' and citizens' interests in England and especially in London planning. He was a founding member of INURA, the International Network for Urban Research and Action, and of the Planners Network UK. He is semi-retired and blogs at michaeledwards.org.uk

MATTHEW GANDY is Professor of Geography at University College London and was Director of the UCL Urban Laboratory from 2005–11. His publications include *Concrete and Clay: Reworking Nature in New York City* (MIT Press, 2002); *The Return of the White Plague* (co-edited with Ali Zumla; Verso, 2003); *Hydropolis* (co-edited with Susanne Frank; Campus, 2006) along with articles in *Architectural Design, New Left Review, International Journal of Urban and Regional and Research, Society and Space* and many other journals. He is currently researching cultural histories of urban infrastructure, cinematic landscapes, and urban biodiversity.

DAVID GISSEN is a historian and theorist of architecture and urbanism. He is Associate Professor of Architecture and Visual Studies at the California College of the Arts. His recent work focuses on developing a novel concept of nature in architectural thought, and the parameters for an experimental form of practice in architectural history. He is currently preparing a manuscript on architectural environments that emerged during New York City's crisis years.

STEPHEN GRAHAM is Professor of Cities and Society at the Global Urban Research Unit in Newcastle University's School of Architecture, Planning and Landscape. He has a background in geography, urbanism, and the sociology of technology and his research addresses the politics of cities, focusing especially on issues of mobility, infrastructure, technology, security, surveillance, and political violence. Publications include *Telecommunications and the City* and *Splintering Urbanism* (both with Simon Marvin), *The Cybercities Reader* and *Cities, War and Terrorism* (Blackwell, 2004). His two most recent books are *Disrupted Cities: When Infrastructures Fail* (Routledge, 2009) and *Cities under Siege: The New Military Urbanism* (Verso, 2010).

MAREN HARNACK has studied architecture, urban design, and social sciences in Stuttgart, Delft and London. She taught at HafenCity University in Hamburg where she received her doctorate under Michael Koch and Martina Löw in 2010, and is now Professor of Urban Planning at Frankfurt University of Applied Sciences. She is a founding member of the urban design practice and consultancy urbanorbit and has been involved in various research projects funded by the German government and the Wüstenrot Foundation.

ANDREW HARRIS is Lecturer in Geography and Urban Studies at University College London. His research focuses on the role of art and artists in recent processes of urban restructuring, and on three-dimensional geographies of contemporary cities. He has published articles in various journals including *Urban Studies, The London Journal* and *Transactions of the Institute of British Geographers*. Working between London, Mumbai, and Buenos Aires, he uses comparative frameworks to highlight particularities both between and within cities, and to fashion more diverse and cosmopolitan agendas for urban research and policy-making.

SANDRA JASPER is completing her doctorate at the UCL Urban Laboratory. Her research interests focus on the body-city nexus and embodied encounters with space in the late-modern metropolis. Her PhD thesis, "Cyborg Imaginations: Nature, Technology and Urban Space in West Berlin (1948-1984)," draws from diverse fields, such as sound art, engineering, and architecture. Examples explored in the thesis are Berlin's hidden spaces that emerged from the city's division, the experiential aspects of acoustic and cinematic landscapes, and the use of technologies as socio-political tools in activist practices. She has taught on the MSc Urban Studies and convenes the annual international postgraduate research workshop *Stadtkolloquium*.

ROGER KEIL is Director of the City Institute and Professor in the Faculty of Environmental Studies at York University. He researches global suburbanism, cities and infectious disease, and regional governance. Among his recent publications are *The Global Cities Reader* (ed. with Neil Brenner; Routledge, 2006); *Networked Disease: Emerging Infections and the Global City* (ed. with S. Harris Ali; Wiley-Blackwell, 2008); *Changing Toronto: Governing the Neoliberal City* (with Julie-Anne Boudreau and Douglas Young; UTP 2009); *Leviathan Undone? The Political Economy of Scale* (ed. with Rianne Mahon, UBC Press 2009); and *In-between Infrastructure: Urban Connectivity in an Age of Vulnerability* (edited with Douglas Young and Patricia Burke Wood, Praxis (e)Press).

KAROLINA KENDALL-BUSH is currently completing a PhD in Film Studies in the Centre for Intercultural Studies at University College London. Her PhD thesis brings together historical, cinematic, and ethnographic research to explore how walking tours and cinema have navigated London since the end of the nineteenth century. She has a background in film studies, art history, and design and is a member of UCL's interdisciplinary research centres at the Urban Laboratory and the Film Studies Space.

KÖBBERLING & KALTWASSER
Folke Köbberling studied Fine Arts at Kunsthochschule Kassel/Germany and at the Emily Carr Institute of Art and Design in Vancouver. Martin Kaltwasser studied Fine Arts at the Academy of Fine Arts in Nuremberg, Germany before he studied the Technical University Berlin, where he made his Diploma in Architecture. Both were guest scholars at the Art Centre College of Design, Pasadena, in the Fine Art Graduate Program in 2009/2010. Recent awards

include the first prize in the Architects' Journal Small Projects Awards (the AJ Small Buildings Sustainability prize), a fellowship for a one-year residence in Los Angeles from the Senate of Berlin/Cultures affairs, and a grant from Kunstfonds Bonn to publish their book *Hold it!* (jovis, 2009).

MARTIN KOHLER is a photographer and urbanist. He studied landscape architecture and environmental planning at the University of Hannover and at the Southern Australia University, Adelaide. He has taught urban photography at HafenCity University, Hamburg, since 2003 and has founded and curated several art projects in public spaces such as the Hafensafari (2009). He has deployed photography as a research method in various projects including a series of "urban transects" in London, Istanbul, Seoul, the Ruhr district and elsewhere.

PATRICK LE GALÈS is CNRS Research Professor at the Centre d'études européennes of Sciences Po, Paris, and visiting professor at King's College, University of London. He has published widely on public policy, European cities, economic sociology, and political economy. His books include *Le Retour des villes européennes: Sociétés urbaines, mondialisation, gouvernement et gouvernance* (Presses de Sciences Po, 2010); *The New Labour Experiment: Change and Reform under Blair and Brown* (with Florence Faucher-King; Stanford University Press, 2010); and *European Cities: Social Conflicts and Governance* (Oxford University Press, 2002).

LUCREZIA LENNERT is a PhD candidate at the UCL Urban Laboratory. Her doctoral research is interested in the practices and experiences of collective self-organization in autonomous spaces in Berlin and explores the forms of resistance these anarchic spaces present in the context of the neo-liberal urbanism of post-unification Berlin. Her work is also interested in interrogating the political implications of Gilles Deleuze's philosophy from within these sites of resistance and seeks to understand concepts such as "immanent becoming" and "nomadic war machines" as tools for anti-capitalist thought and practice. She lives in Berlin where she is active in struggles for autonomous spaces.

NOAM LESHEM teaches at Royal Holloway, University of London, and completed his PhD at the London Consortium, University of London, where he was a Wingate Political Science Fellow 2006–2009. His research focuses on urban and social history in Israel and Palestine, geographies of social protest, and the political use of death spaces. Recent publications include: "Memory Activism: Reclaiming Spatial Histories in Israel," in *The Politics of Cultural Memory* (Cambridge Scholars Press, 2010); and "Towards a Spatial History of Israel," in *Memory Forgetfulness and the Construction of Space* (Van Leer Jerusalem Institute, 2011).

LEANDRO MINUCHIN is Lecturer in Architecture and Global Urbanism at Manchester Architecture Research Centre, University of Manchester. He has studied political theory, Latin American Studies, and urban geography in Argentina, Spain, and the UK. His current research focuses on the politics of construction and material imaginaries in Latin American cities. He has written about urban theory, materialisation and architectural thought, specialising in modern Buenos Aires.

ULRIKE MOHR is a Berlin-based artist whose work is concerned primarily with the meaning and characteristics of public space. Her work involves critical observations of signs, processes, measurements, and systems and includes interventions in relation to spontaneous nature (*Restgrün*, 2006; *Neue Nachbarn*, 2008), and processes of transformation such as charcoal making (*Welt-Kataster*, 2010). Solo shows include: Kunsthaus Kloster (2009); Cluster, Berlin (2008); and Kunstverein, Hildesheim (2007); along with numerous group exhibitions such as the 5th Berlin Biennale (2008) and the Momentum Biennale, Norway (2011). She has received support for her work from various sources including the Istanbul Foundation of the Berlin Senate and the Kunstfonds Foundation. www.ulrikemohr.de

LOUIS MORENO is completing a PhD at the UCL Urban Laboratory exploring the growth of financial services and its effect on changes to the urban form and architectural design of UK cities. He is also a visiting tutor in Visual Culture at Goldsmiths, University of London, and was a researcher at the Commission for Architecture and the Built Environment. With Andrew Harris, he was a co-organiser of the Creative City Limits project, an international research network reassessing the place of creativity in urban economic growth.

LAURA OLDFIELD FORD studied at the Slade School of Art and the Royal College of Art and has become well known for her politically active and poetic engagement with London as a site of social antagonism. Her solo exhibitions include: *Poster Sites,* Arnolfini, Bristol (2009) and *London 2013: Drifting Through the Ruins,* Hales Gallery, London (2009). Selected group exhibitions include: *Freedom Centre,* Hales Gallery, London (2008); *Fusion Now,* Rokeby Gallery, London (2007); *Spent,* Three Colts, London (2006); and *AAABAM Indexed,* ICA, London (2006).

GILES OMEZI is a PhD candidate at the UCL Urban Laboratory. He studied architecture at the University of East London and has worked for various London practices, notably Nicholas Grimshaw and recently Allies and Morrison. He now runs his own architecture and urban design studio in London with projects mainly in Nigeria. Currently, he is working with government policy review teams on urbanism and housing in Lagos and is a technical adviser on architecture and urbanism to the Abuja Technology Village. He also teaches architectural history and theory at the University of East London. His primary research interests are Nigerian contemporary urbanism and architecture.

JANE RENDELL is an architectural designer, historian, theorist, and writer, whose work explores interdisciplinary intersections between feminism, art, architecture, and psychoanalysis. Her authored books include *Site-Writing* (2010), *Art and Architecture* (2006), and *The Pursuit of Pleasure* (2002); and she is co-editor of *Pattern* (2007), *Critical Architecture* (2007), *Spatial Imagination* (2005), *The Unknown City* (The MIT Press, 2001), *Intersections* (2000), *Gender, Space, Architecture* (1999), and *Strangely Familiar* (1995). She is Professor of Architecture and Art, and Vice Dean of Research at the Bartlett, UCL. http://www.janerendell.co.uk/

JENNIFER ROBINSON is Professor of Human Geography at University College London and Honorary Visiting Professor in the African Centre for Cities at the University of Cape Town. Her book, *Ordinary Cities: Between Modernity and Development* (Routledge, 2006), established a post-colonial critique of urban studies, arguing the case for urban studies to draw on the diversity of urban experiences across the globe in developing more general accounts of cities. Her current work extends this analysis, focussing on regrounding comparative methods to support a more international urban studies, and developing an empirical comparative research project on the politics of city strategies.

REBECCA ROSS is interested in interactions between graphical and urban spaces from the perspectives of both civic and professional engagement. Her PhD, in progress, considers interactions between broad cultural enthusiasm for viewing the city from above and visual practices associated with the development of urban planning as a profession. She holds an MFA in Graphic Design from Yale and an MSc in Human Geography from UCL and is currently Senior Lecturer in Graphic Design at Central Saint Martins, London, as well as a PhD candidate in Urban History and Theory at the Graduate School of Design, Harvard University.

JOACHIM SCHLÖR received his PhD from Tübingen University and is currently Professor for Modern Jewish/non-Jewish Relations at the University of Southampton. His books include: *Das Ich der Stadt: Debatten über Judentum und Urbanität 1822–1938* (Vandenhoeck & Ruprecht, 2005); *Endlich im Gelobten Land? Deutsche Juden unterwegs in eine neue Heimat* (Aufbau, 2003); *Nights in the Big City: Berlin, Paris, London 1840–1930* (Reaktion, 1998); and *Tel Aviv: From Dream to City* (Reaktion, 1999).

CHRISTIAN SCHMID is a geographer and urban researcher. He is Professor of Sociology at the Faculty of Architecture at ETH Zurich and scientific director at the ETH Studio Basel / Contemporary City Institute. In 1991, he was a co-founder of the International Network for Urban Research and Action (INURA). He is the author of *Stadt, Raum und Gesellschaft: Henri Lefebvre und die Theorie der Produktion des Raumes* (Steiner 2005), which provides a detailed reconstruction of Henri Lefebvre's theory of the production of space. Together with the Swiss architects Roger Diener, Jacques Herzog, Marcel Meili, and Pierre de Meuron, he has co-authored *Switzerland—An Urban Portrait* (Birkhauser 2005), a novel analysis of urbanisation in contemporary Switzerland.

HYUN BANG SHIN is Lecturer in Urban Geography at the London School of Economics. His main research interests lie in critically analysing political and economic dynamics of contemporary urban development and its socio-spatial implications, with special emphasis on Asian cities. He is currently involved in URBACHINA, a four-year international research collaboration funded by the EU Seventh Framework Programme (FP7), and is one of the key organisers of the Urban Studies Seminar Series (2011–2012), *Towards an Emerging Geography of Gentrification in the Global South*, funded by the Urban Studies Foundation and the Urban Studies journal.

ABDOUMALIQ SIMONE is an urbanist with particular interest in emerging forms of social and economic intersection across diverse trajectories of change for cities in the global South. He is currently Professor of Sociology at Goldsmiths College, University of London, and Visiting Professor of Urban Studies at the African Centre for Cities, University of Cape Town. Publications include: *In Whose Image: Political Islam and Urban Practices in Sudan* (University of Chicago Press, 1994); *For the City Yet to Come: Urban Change in Four African Cities* (Duke University Press, 2004); and *City Life from Jakarta to Dakar: Movements at the Crossroads* (Routledge, 2009).

ERIK SWYNGEDOUW is Professor of Geography at Manchester University and was Professor of Geography at Oxford University until 2006. His research interests include political-ecology, urban governance, democracy and political power, water and water resources, the political-economy of capitalist societies, and the politics of globalisation. Recent books include: *Urbanising Globalisation* (co-edited; Oxford University Press, 2003), *Social Power and the Urbanization of Water—Flows of Power* (Oxford University Press 2004); and *In the Nature of Cities* (co-edited; Routledge, 2006).

MARK TEWDWR-JONES is Professor of Spatial Planning and Governance in the Bartlett School of Planning at University College London and Co-Chair of UCL Sustainable Cities Grand Challenge. Educated in planning, politics, and film, he is a recognised authority on urban planning, the politics of the city, and the use of land. He is the author or editor of twelve books, including: *The European dimension of British planning; The planning polity, Territory, identity and spatial planning;* and *Urban Reflections.* He is a Visiting Professor at University College Dublin, Adjunct Professor at the University of New South Wales, and an Academician of the Academy of Social Sciences.

C. CLAIRE THOMSON is Head of the Department of Scandinavian Studies at University College London. She edits the journal *Scandinavica,* and has published widely on Danish and Nordic film and literature, with an emphasis on intercultural, multi-sensory, and ecocritical approaches. Her publications include: *Northern Constellations: New Readings in Nordic Cinema* (ed.; Norvik Press, 2006); and *Thomas Vinterberg's Festen (The Celebration)* (University of Washington Press, forthcoming).

KAREN E. TILL is Lecturer in Human Geography at the National University of Ireland Maynooth and founding member of the Mapping Spectral Traces international network (http://www.mappingspectraltraces.org/). She has also taught at Royal Holloway, University of London; the University of Minnesota; and Virginia Tech. Her geoethnographic research and curatorial practice explores the interrelationships between place and personal and social memory in the context of contemporary cities marked by state-perpetrated violence. Her publications include: *The New Berlin* (2005); *Mapping Spectral Traces* (2010); *Textures of Place* (2001); and *Walls, Borders and Boundaries* (forthcoming), in addition to numerous book chapters and articles. Karen's book in progress, *Wounded Cities,* highlights place-based ethical, artistic, and activist approaches that contribute to more socially just cities.

MEIKE WOLF is a research fellow at the Institute of Cultural Anthropology and European Ethnology at the Goethe-University, Frankfurt/Main. Her current ethnographic research focuses on the globalisation of influenza and its impact on the regulation and constitution of urban environments. Other academic interests include the ageing process as a gendered experience, vaccination policies, the anthropology of prevention and the cultural construction of the human body. Previously, she has been a visiting professor at the Goethe-University and worked as a research fellow at the Institute for the History, Theory and Ethics of Medicine at the Johannes Gutenberg-University in Mainz.

BENEDIKTE ZITOUNI is an urban sociologist at the University of Brussels. She has studied at Oxford University, l'Ecole des Mines and Sciences Po in Paris, and is currently a Visiting Scholar at UC Berkeley, where she is developing a socio-ecological and perspectivist approach to urban studies. Her most recent publications are *Agglomérer. Une anatomie de l'extension bruxelloise (1828-1915)* (University of Brussels Press & ASP, Brussels, 2010, with a preface by Eric Corijn and postscript by Bruno Latour) and *Usus/usures, Etat des lieux / How things stand* (Brussels, CFWB Press, 2010, with Rotor and Ariane d'Hoop for the Venice Architecture Biennale).

© 2011 by jovis Verlag GmbH
Texts by kind permission of the author.
Pictures by kind permission of the photographers/
holders of the picture rights.

Cover images: From top left (clockwise):
Buenos Aires (2008); Lagos (2003); London (2008);
Lagos (2003); Berlin (2006); Copenhagen (2011);
Mumbai (2006); San Francisco (2007).
All photos by Matthew Gandy

Design and setting: Susanne Rösler, Berlin
Lithography: Bild1Druck, Berlin
Printing and binding: fgb freiburger graphische betriebe

Bibliographic information published by the
Deutsche Nationalbibliothek
The Deutsche Nationalbibliothek lists this publication in
the Deutsche Nationalbibliografie; detailed bibliographic
data are available on the Internet at
http://dnb.d-nb.de

jovis Verlag GmbH
Kurfürstenstrasse 15/16
10785 Berlin

www.jovis.de

ISBN 978-3-86859-118-7